Exploring the D
of Human Deve

Exploring the Dynamics of Human Development

of Human Development

An Integrative Approach

CATHERINE RAEFF

OXFORD
UNIVERSITY PRESS

OXFORD
UNIVERSITY PRESS

Oxford University Press is a department of the University of Oxford. It furthers
the University's objective of excellence in research, scholarship, and education
by publishing worldwide. Oxford is a registered trade mark of Oxford University
Press in the UK and certain other countries.

Published in the United States of America by Oxford University Press
198 Madison Avenue, New York, NY 10016, United States of America.

© Oxford University Press 2016

Library of Congress Cataloging-in-Publication Data
Names: Raeff, Catherine, 1964– editor.
Title: Exploring the dynamics of human development : an integrative approach / Catherine Raeff.
Description: 1 Edition. | New York : Oxford University Press, 2016. |
Includes bibliographical references and index.
Identifiers: LCCN 2016011888 (print) | LCCN 2016016063 (ebook) |
ISBN 9780199328413 (hardback) | ISBN 9780199328420 (ebook)
Subjects: LCSH: Child psychology. | Child development. | Thought and thinking. |
Cognitive psychology. | BISAC: PSYCHOLOGY / Developmental / Child. |
PSYCHOLOGY / Social Psychology. | PSYCHOLOGY / Cognitive Psychology.
Classification: LCC BF721 .R277 2016 (print) | LCC BF721 (ebook) | DDC 155—dc23
LC record available at https://lccn.loc.gov/2016011888

1 3 5 7 9 8 6 4 2

Printed by Sheridan Books, Inc., United States of America

In Memory of
Ina Č. Užgiris
and
Elizabeth and Serge Hughes

CONTENTS

ACKNOWLEDGMENTS

I am pleased to recognize and thank the people who, in one way or another, have sustained me while writing this book. Many of their voices echo throughout the pages of the book, though the flaws are mine alone. I firmly believe that one of the best decisions I ever made was to attend graduate school at Clark University where the foundations for my ideas about action and development were formally laid and guided. I spent five happy years there, enjoying and benefitting from classes and discussions with Ina Č. Užgiris, Bernard Kaplan, James V. Wertsch, Seymour Wapner, Nancy Budwig, and Michael Bamberg. My deepest respect and appreciation go to the late Ina Užgiris, whose words and work I still ponder and find endlessly illuminating. During that time, I had the good fortune to become friends and colleagues with Michael F. Mascolo, to whom I am grateful for invaluable feedback and insights, as well as for unwavering support, both personal and professional. Clark also connected me with Janette B. Benson, whom I thank for generous feedback and good-humored support. My parents, Marc and Lillian Raeff, shaped early and enduring foundations for my pursuits by nurturing love of learning, history, art, and language. I thank my sister, Anne Raeff, for her abiding interest and encouragement, and for lively discussions that help me to articulate my ideas. I continue to remember and appreciate the consistent presence of Betts and Serge Hughes. I am indebted to the following friends in innumerable ways. Many thanks go to the Scott family for more than three decades of warm welcomes and ardent support. I am grateful to Lorna H. Power for the enrichment of her perspective and good company on some fine days in New York. I cannot imagine life in Indiana, PA without Susan Zimny, Cari and Bill Meil, Aleksandra and Krys Kaniasty, Ron Donoughe, and Debra and Birch Frew of Stoke Hole Pottery where I have spent many hours of happy distraction.

Since the hot summer day in 2012 when I first met them, working with Oxford University Press senior editor, Sarah Harrington, and associate editor, Andrea Zekus, has been a pleasure. I thank them for their enthusiasm from the beginning, and for shepherding the book and me through the publication process. Thank you also to senior production editor, Emily Perry. Somehow I wrote this book while teaching four courses each semester. A course release during the spring 2014 semester and one during the spring of 2015 were supported at Indiana University of Pennsylvania by a Dean's Alternative Workload Initiative.

INTRODUCTION: SEARCHING FOR
THE FOREST AMONG THE TREES

From cells to societies, development is ubiquitous. Development is certainly ubiquitous among human beings, and as a reader of this book, you have certainly developed. But what about people develops? What happens during development? How does development happen? Answering these questions is not straightforward because human development is complex. Sometimes we are able to pinpoint great moments in our own and others' development, but sometimes we may be at a loss to understand anyone's development. Human development is universal, yet also culturally particular. It is experienced individually, yet shaped in part by other people. The central goal of this book is to offer a theoretical framework for thinking systematically about human action and development in a way that encompasses the ongoing dynamics of multiple and interrelated processes. As a brief preview, this theoretical approach makes the following basic claims. It first holds that much of what develops during human development are cultural ways of acting in relation to others. Second, this approach holds that the development of such action occurs in relation to cultural meanings and involves differentiation and integration within and across action constituents. Third, the theoretical approach holds that the development of action happens through interrelated individual, social, and cultural processes as individuals actively participate with others in cultural practices.

Developmental psychologists have been investigating varied aspects of development for generations, and over the years, developmental psychology has become a huge academic discipline. Although the size of the field befits the complexity of the topic, developmental psychology has become rather undisciplined. Whenever I look at the table of contents for a developmental journal, I invariably find myself suspended between contradictory feelings. On the one hand, I enjoy the anticipation of learning something new about development, but on the other hand, I dread feeling overwhelmed by a journal full of disconnected studies about development within isolated domains of human functioning. Domains of

functioning refer to aspects of behavior that develop, such as perceiving, thinking, feeling, moving physically, using language, setting goals, constructing values,
interacting with others, perspective taking, and self/identity. I keep wondering
how all of this disparate information fits together to form a systematic and integrative view of development. One simply cannot see the forest for the trees. The
trees are certainly important, but I believe that the field of developmental psychology needs a way of keeping the forest in view with an integrative theoretical framework for thinking systematically about basic developmental processes.
Basic developmental processes refer to the dynamics of what happens during
development and how development happens.

By focusing on basic developmental processes, a major concern here is with
identifying the forest among the trees. Of course, I readily recognize that the forest is made up of trees, and the trees are certainly not being ignored. However,
the trees derive their meaning by being part of a wider whole, namely the forest.
The forest-and-trees metaphor applies here in several ways. For example, when
psychologists focus on isolated domains of functioning, they are focusing on the
metaphorical trees, and it is easy to lose sight of the functioning or action of a
whole person. In this case, action by a whole person is the "forest" that is made up of
the varied domains of functioning occurring simultaneously. That is, when people act, they are moving physically, perceiving, thinking, feeling, using language,
interacting with others, discerning others' perspectives, believing and valuing,
setting goals, regulating themselves, and constructing conceptions of themselves,
all at the same time. In addition, based on the premises that all human beings
are separate individuals as well as connected to others, and that human action
reflects cultural meanings, human functioning is also taken to be constituted by
individual, social, and cultural processes. Thus, it is necessary to conceptualize
what people do in a way that encompasses the dynamics of multiple and simultaneously occurring processes.

The forest-and-trees metaphor can also be applied to research in developmental psychology, which typically involves investigating age-based changes,
or changes over time, for relatively isolated domains of functioning. Within this
context, developmental psychology has become a vast and fragmented catalog of
changes over time, and in this case, the disconnected findings about change over
time are the "trees." This work has certainly yielded much valuable information
and innumerable insights. However, it is not always clear that all changes over
time are necessarily developmental changes. In addition, when development is
presented as a catalog of new forms of behavior that occur at particular ages, one
is left wondering what happens in between the specified ages that enables the new
forms of behavior to develop. Thus, developmental psychology could now benefit
from a wider conceptualization of development, by identifying criteria for developmental change that would permit analyzing the ongoing developmental processes that enable new forms of behavior to emerge. A wider conceptualization of

what happens during development, beyond age- and time-based change, would be the forest within which local findings about development have meaning.

Another way in which the forest-and-trees metaphor is applicable here concerns the basic developmental process of how development happens. In developmental psychology today, there are innumerable studies of the causes of human development, from the brain, to relationships, to education, to socioeconomic status, to culture. In this case, the vast array of possible causes of development are the trees. The forest that needs to be found is a coherent theoretical approach and systematic way of thinking about how development happens that can encompass varied possible causes, as well as how they are interrelated.

This book is not meant to be a comprehensive catalog of research about what people do at different ages within isolated domains of functioning. Instead, the goal is to articulate a theoretical framework for thinking systematically and holistically about human functioning and development without getting bogged down in fragmented minutiae. Toward that end, the book is organized around what I refer to as three basic developmental questions, namely: What develops during development? What happens during development? How does development happen? The research that is discussed and used to address these questions is meant to provide examples of central theoretical points and to illustrate how to use the current theoretical approach to think systematically about basic developmental processes. I also raise varied issues regarding the complexities of action and development, and suggest how to start thinking systematically about them through the prism of the current theoretical framework. In addition, the current theoretical approach does not come out of nothing or out of the blue. It is partly a synthesis of seminal ideas and research findings that continue to be corroborated and elaborated by recent scholarship. Thus, I draw on both classic and contemporary theory and research to derive and illustrate major theoretical points.

It is also important to say at the outset that aspects of the current theoretical framework are unconventional and sometimes depart from dominant or traditional practices in psychology, including developmental psychology. As already suggested, I start from an integrative position regarding human functioning as a whole that leads away from breaking down what people do into independent parts. In addition, the current framework does not assume that development necessarily occurs with age, and instead provides ways of discerning *if* development occurs as people get older. Rather than characterizing human functioning and development primarily in terms of quantifiable variables, the current approach leads to making sense of human functioning and development in terms of ongoing and dynamic individual, social, and cultural processes, as well as the developmental processes of differentiation and integration. The current theoretical framework is also not method driven, meaning that I do not start with a particular method and then conceptualize issues, or ask empirical questions in ways that can be studied according to that method alone. Instead, this book is my attempt to think about development by first conceptualizing human functioning and development in a systematic and integrative way. This conceptualization can then be used to construct methods that are best suited for investigating its claims and implications empirically. By offering an alternative approach, I am not suggesting that conventional methodological practices be abandoned. Rather, the point is that different methods can be used and integrated flexibly, depending on the research questions posed and how they are conceptualized. Ultimately, thinking outside the box of conventional and traditional practices can lead to new insights into the complexities of human functioning and development.

In Chapter 1, I first expand on some of the issues just raised to explain my view that developmental psychology needs an integrative theoretical framework for thinking systematically about basic developmental processes. Then I present systems theory, which serves as the overarching theoretical foundation for the current conceptualization of action and development. The central claim of systems theory is that complex phenomena—such as human functioning—are made up of multiple and interrelated constituent processes (Ford & Lerner, 1992; Mascolo & Fischer, 2010, 2015; Meadows, 2008; Overton, 2006, 2010, 2013; Thelen & Smith, 1994/1996; van Geert, 2003, 2011; von Bertalanffy, 1969/1998; Witherington & Heying, 2013). To say that system constituents are interrelated means that they mutually affect and constitute each other, and that each constituent is inseparable from the others. While system constituents have their own distinct characteristics, they are also defined in terms of how they function in relation to each other to comprise a wider whole.

With these basic systems premises as a backdrop, Chapter 2 provides a systems conceptualization of the human functioning that develops during development in terms of multiple and interrelated processes. I argue here that, insofar as human beings are separate individuals who engage with each other in cultural practices, human functioning emerges out of interrelated individual, social, and cultural processes. Individual processes include what a person does as a separate being. For example, as separate individuals, people think for and about themselves, set some of their own goals, make some of their own choices, construe experience from a subjective perspective, define themselves, interact with others, believe and value, feel and express emotions, and regulate aspects of their own behavior. At the same time, such individual functioning is inseparable from, or occurs in relation to, social and cultural processes. With regard to social processes, a person may regulate him- or herself by waiting his or her turn to speak and listening to whomever is speaking at the moment. Or, a person might decide what to do in a situation by considering how his or her action might affect other people. A person might follow someone's lead, or order someone around, or succumb to someone's pressure. Throughout the world, a person's action in relation to others is also structured in culturally particular ways, or in ways that reflect cultural beliefs, values, and guidelines for acting. Examples of cultural action in relation to others abound, from eating a family meal, to working, to playing in the neighborhood, to going to school, to attending a sports event, to walking down a crowded city street, to attending a birthday celebration, to consoling a friend—the list could go on for pages. Taken together, we can say that much of what develops during human development are cultural ways of acting in relation to others, and that cultural ways of acting in relation to others emerge through or are caused by concurrent and interrelated individual, social, and cultural processes.

In addition, when a person acts in relation to others in cultural practices, such action involves interrelations among varied domains of functioning, such as perceiving, thinking, feeling, moving physically, using language, social interaction, and self-construction. These varied constituents of action can be interrelated in different ways to comprise different ways of acting in relation to others in cultural practices. For example, eating a family meal, going to a professional meeting of some kind, caring for younger siblings, and telling stories all involve individual, social, and cultural processes, as well as varied domains of functioning. However, these constituent processes may be organized in different ways to comprise different modes of action.

By starting with this conceptualization of action, we are starting with the forest, or the wider whole of human functioning that encompasses the dynamics of multiple and interrelated constituent processes. Thus, conceptualizing what develops in terms of cultural action in relation to others, or acting in relation to others in cultural practices, provides a way of overcoming some of the fragmentation that plagues much of contemporary psychology, including developmental psychology. More specifically, cultural action in relation to others refers to the wider whole of human functioning that encompasses individual, social, and cultural processes, as well as the varied domains of functioning that are typically analyzed separately. The constituents of action can be distinguished analytically, but the current systems approach also leads to thinking about how they function in relation to each other to comprise varied forms or modes of action.

Based on this conceptualization of what develops during development, Chapter 3 offers a conceptualization of what happens during development. When action is understood from a systems perspective, development involves changes in the ways that action constituents are structured and interrelated, resulting in new forms of action. However, people certainly undergo a lot of changes during their life spans, making it reasonable to question whether all of those changes constitute development (Kaplan, 1967, 1983a,b, 1986). If any change over time is considered to be development, and if development refers to any new form of action that emerges, then there is nothing particularly significant about the term *development*. Thus, it is necessary to identify more specific criteria for developmental change.

To address the issue of what happens during development, I turn to organismic-developmental theory, which was initially articulated by Heinz Werner in the

1940s and then elaborated throughout his career (Werner, 1940/1980; Werner & Kaplan, 1963/1984). Organismic-developmental theory starts from the systems premise that human functioning emerges through interactions among constituent processes. From an organismic-developmental perspective, the development of action involves the differentiation and integration of action constituents in relation to cultural meanings and expectations for development. Thus, it is not assumed that all new forms of action necessarily represent developmental changes. Instead, development refers to the emergence of new forms or modes of action that are more differentiated and integrated relative to previous modes of action. Defining development in terms of differentiation and integration focuses attention on the increasing differentiation and integration that occur within and across action constituents.

For example, research on caregiver–infant interaction in the United States indicates that during the first half of the first year, infants and their caregivers are mutually attentive and responsive to each other (Rochat, 2001/2004; Schaffer, 1984; Stern, 1977, 1985). It is commonplace to mark the onset of such action in terms of age, at about 2 to 3 months. However, from an organismic-developmental perspective, a way of acting does not simply start at a particular age. After all, nothing will come of nothing. Instead, the development of action is conceptualized as building on previous modes of action in ways that involve differentiation and integration within and across constituent processes. During early caregiver–infant interaction, infants use varied motor means to establish and maintain mutual attention, including, smiling, gaze shifting, head turning, and reaching. From birth on, these varied means undergo ongoing differentiation out of global and whole-body movements. They are also increasingly integrated with each other as babies use several means simultaneously to direct their attention to and from others. These means are further integrated with vocalizing to establish and maintain mutual attention. In turn, global vocalizing (e.g., reflex crying) undergoes differentiation into increasingly distinct sounds, which are integrated to produce full-fledged words, which are differentiated and integrated to express more complex meanings.

In addition to its utility for understanding what happens during development, my use of organismic-developmental theory is part of an effort to revive a rather neglected voice in the history of developmental psychology. Heinz Werner (1890–1964) was a contemporary of Jean Piaget (1896–1980) and Lev Vygotsky (1896–1934), and he addressed many of the same issues for which they are well known. Although Werner has largely been forgotten in the wake of Piaget's and Vygotsky's dominance in developmental psychology, more recent treatments show that Werner's claims resonate with contemporary concerns in this field (Raeff, 2011; Siegler & Chen, 2008; Valsiner, 2005). Werner sought to understand the functioning of organisms in their contexts, and he eschewed dividing human functioning into separate domains and isolated parts (Glick, 1983, 1992).

Instead, he began with "an organism in the process of acting" (Glick, 1983, p. 51), and he was concerned with discerning how organismic functioning is made up of interrelations among varied processes. He also posited that understanding any psychological process can be enhanced by analyzing it from a developmental perspective. As such, development is not an area of specialization within psychology, nor is it essentially age based. However, these basic premises ran counter to dominant trends in psychology during Werner's lifetime, and they still run counter to many conventional practices in psychology today. Then and now, psychologists favor slicing human functioning into separate domains. Then and now, developmentalists use age as a central organizing and analytic criterion. Then and now, little attention is paid to the development of psychological processes outside of the specialized field of developmental psychology. In addition, defining development in terms of increasing differentiation and integration presents difficulties for empirical research because these broad and rather abstract constructs can be played out in different, specific ways. This definition of development is also not formulated in a way that generates specific hypotheses or predictions about specific developmental sequences and thus stands in contrast to conventional experimental practices in psychology. What this definition of development does do is provide a conceptual basis for understanding and thinking systematically about development. As such, organismic-developmental theory can advance the field of developmental psychology because understanding and systematic analysis are central to scientific and intellectual undertakings.

Although dominant practices in psychology have muted other ways of conceptualizing and studying human functioning, calls for alternative approaches have been steady since the late 1800s when psychology split from philosophy to become an "official" scientific discipline whose legitimacy as a science was based on using natural science methods. In developmental psychology today, increasing interest in systems theory and integrative approaches suggests that the time is ripe for revisiting organismic-developmental theory (Sameroff, 2010; Siegler & Chen, 2008; Valsiner, 2005). Within an overall context of disciplinary fragmentation, some developmentalists have criticized the dominant separate domains paradigm, and calls for integrative analyses of development can be heard. For example, a volume on emotional and cognitive development begins with the claim that "a more integrated view that acknowledges the mutual influences of both sets of processes may be more fruitful when considering the complex developmental skills that clearly draw on both domains" (Calkins & Bell, 2010, p. 4). Some attempts at integrating domains of action address connections between two domains, such as social and emotional development (Brownell & Kopp, 2007), emotional and cognitive development (Calkins & Bell, 2010), or motor and language development (Iverson, 2010; Smith, 2010). Linking issues of social development and cognitive development comprise what is known as "social cognition," which has become a domain of developmental inquiry in and of itself. Taken together, the current systems approach to action and organismic-developmental theory provide a way to understand the development of action in terms of how varied constituent processes are organized and interrelated.

The goals of Chapter 4 are to illustrate and apply the current conceptualization of action and of what happens during development more concretely. In Chapter 4, I build on Chapters 2 and 3 by thinking about and exploring what happens during the development of action in relation to others during infancy and early childhood from the current approach to action and from the perspective of organismic-developmental theory. Chapter 4 argues that the development of action involves differentiation and integration within and across varied constituent processes. Thus, findings from research across the vast field of developmental psychology are synthesized to consider how varied domains of functioning contribute simultaneously to the development of action in relation to others. In addition, in order to analyze pathways of development for action during infancy and early childhood, research findings are translated into the discourse of differentiation and integration. In this chapter, I draw on research conducted in the United States, and I focus on the development of action in the context of caregiver–child interactions. From this research I posit a sequence of five developmental periods for the development of acting in relation to others during infancy and early childhood. In an effort to eschew cataloging static forms of action, I describe the five periods in terms of the ongoing dynamics of differentiation and integration. Chapter 4 also raises some issues regarding the development of action in relation to peers during early childhood.

Chapter 5 goes beyond the United States, as well as beyond infancy and early childhood, to illustrate how to think systematically about what happens during the development of action in different cultures with the conceptual tools of the theoretical approach presented in this book. Developmental research is spotty in different parts of the world, making it difficult to posit a sequence of developmental periods for action at any time during the life span in particular cultures. Thus, I draw on research from various cultures to consider varied cultural expectations for development throughout the life span, and I try to discern pathways of differentiation and integration in different cultures. Chapter 5 includes a consideration of the wide range of classic and contemporary research on development in cultures where there is little formal schooling and where life revolves around subsistence work. In addition, the development of sibling caregiving is taken up in Chapter 5. Research on the development of storytelling in Taiwan as well as among different socioeconomic groups within the United States is discussed, and some research on the development of action in Japan is considered. Chapter 5 concludes with a brief discussion of development in relation to cultural change.

Once the questions of what develops and what happens during development are addressed, it is possible to conceptualize the basic developmental process of how development happens in Chapters 6 and 7. Again, the conceptualization for this piece of the theoretical framework presented here proceeds from the systems premise of emergence through interactions among multiple constituent processes. Chapter 6 lays the groundwork for the conceptualization of how development happens, with a general consideration of how nature and nurture interact during development. Focusing on interactions between nature and nurture goes against what I see as some current tendencies to explain behavior and development primarily in terms of genetic and neurological processes. In no way do I deny the necessity and significance of genes and brains. However, people are more than genes and brains, and neither action nor development can be reduced to either one or to the independent functioning of both (Ehrlich, 2000; Griffiths & Tabery, 2013; Ho, 2013; Johnston & Lickliter, 2009; Overton, 2011, 2013). Thus, a goal of Chapter 6 is to briefly summarize some genetic and neurological research which shows that genetic and neurological processes are inseparable from environmental processes. We will see that genes are chemical combinations that produce proteins. As such, they are not viewed as the rock-bottom causes of action and development, because action and development require much more than chemical processes. In addition, we will consider how human action and development are not equivalent to or ultimately determined by neurological processes, because a person acts and develops with the aid of the brain, which is also developing because the person is acting.

The analysis then moves on to an overview of how nurture has been treated in developmental psychology. It quickly becomes apparent that it is impossible to keep up with all the findings about the innumerable experiential variables that have been implicated in how development happens. We are lost among the trees, in a thicket of findings about the myriad of possible causes of development. To find the forest among the trees, I turn to contemporary sociocultural theory, which posits that development happens as an individual participates with others in cultural practices (Bronfenbrenner, 1979; Cole, 1996; Rogoff, 2003; Vygotsky, 1978, 1986/1987; Wertsch, 1991).

In Chapter 7, I synthesize sociocultural theory and organismic-developmental theory by discussing how development-as-differentiation-and-integration happens through interrelated cultural, social, and individual processes as people participate with others in cultural practices (Raeff, 2011). This conceptualization holds that cultural processes shape development because development occurs in relation to cultural goals for development, and because people act in relation to others in culturally specific practices. In turn, development involves the differentiation and integration of culturally specific ways of structuring or organizing action in relation to others. With regard to social processes, development happens through interacting with others in ways that provide opportunities for differentiation and integration. Interacting in ways that involve making distinctions within and among action constituents has the potential to facilitate differentiation. Interacting in ways that involve constructing connections within and among action constituents has the potential to facilitate integration. With regard to individual processes, people themselves are taken to contribute to their own development by actively participating in cultural practices, by interpreting experience from a subjective perspective, and by setting some of their own developmental goals.

In Chapter 8, I link the major themes and issues of the previous chapters and use the book's theoretical framework to think systematically about some of developmental psychology's most vexing issues. Implications for thinking about what happens during development include thinking about the criteria for developmental change, developmental variability, generalizable and context-specific aspects of action and development, and how development is both continuous and discontinuous. With regard to how development happens, I consider some issues commonly discussed in developmental psychology today, namely patterns of childrearing and socialization. In addition, the chapter includes sections on the theoretical framework's implications for conducting research on what happens during development and how development happens. The book ends by going back to the forest of what develops during development to think about cultural action in relation to others as the wider whole of human functioning. As a way of conceptualizing the wider whole of human functioning, cultural action in relation to others represents an integrative construct that can be used in psychology more generally to address some of the complexities and dynamics of human functioning.

Exploring the Dynamics
of Human Development

1

Basic Developmental Processes and Basic Systems Premises

> Psychology has long operated as a fragmented discipline. Different researchers focus on different local problems using a variety of theoretical perspectives. . . . As a result, it is often difficult to recognize the person amidst the cacophony of findings spawned from disconnected disciplinary subfields. Persons, however, do not act as sets of isolated or disconnected modules. . . . Thus, there is a need for the formation of theoretical frameworks that allow us to study the nature and development of integrative structures . . . at the psychological level of the person as he or she operates within particular sociocultural contexts.
> —Michael F. Mascolo (2013, p. 186)

As people go about their lives in all corners of the world, development is a fact of life. Quite simply, everyone develops. Of course, there are cases of babies who are born with conditions that severely obstruct development from the outset, and a person can certainly face developmental challenges at any time during the life span. But circumstances have to be quite dire for someone not to develop at all. Development sometimes seems to be happening right in front of us, and we are just sure that a person is developing before our eyes. Parents of young children may tell you that a child seems to be doing something new and more complex almost every day. An adult may tell you about achieving some important goal, or about being able to function more effectively in some situation. Yet sometimes it can be very difficult to describe and pin down the ongoing processes that led to that new kind of functioning. A person might say that he or she practiced and worked at it, or perhaps got advice and help of some kind from someone, or that it just clicked one day. The process of what happens during development and the process of how development happens sometimes remain vague and elusive. Even though we all develop, it is not so simple after all. Even though development is familiar and universal, it is also incredibly complex, culturally specific, highly individualized, and often unpredictable. The central goal of this book is to offer a theoretical framework for thinking systematically about basic developmental processes and for bringing disparate findings about development into coherence. *Basic developmental processes include the dynamics of what happens during development and the dynamics of how development happens.*

Rather than attempting to summarize the disconnected and often conflicting findings from the never-ending supplies of data that comprise much of contemporary developmental psychology (and psychology overall), this book provides a theoretical framework for thinking systematically about basic developmental processes. In my view, it is important to be able to think systematically about developmental processes, and I am using the word "thinking" here in contrast to "knowing." If you are thinking about a phenomenon, you are not necessarily certain about how it will play out, and you are actively pondering its possibilities and ramifications. In contrast, claiming to know something implies that one's view of it is certain, and that there is a fixed or static body of knowledge that can be learned and known about it. However, human functioning is dynamic and varied, making certainty sometimes difficult to establish. I hope that as the book proceeds, it will become apparent to the reader that there is no single or fixed body of knowledge about human development to know and memorize. To be sure, in our common humanity, all human beings experience some of the same basic developmental processes, and this book certainly addresses aspects of that common experience. Yet at the same time, basic developmental processes are dynamic and can play out in different specific ways because the vicissitudes of individual and social and cultural circumstances shape varied developmental experiences across time and space. For example, expectations for male and female behavior have certainly changed over the course of history in many cultures around the world, making it difficult to know THE facts about gender and development that are applicable to all males and females for all time. Nevertheless, we can work to think systematically about and understand how basic developmental processes have and are played out for males and females in varied circumstances.

Even when people develop some similar ways of acting, their developmental experiences may still vary in some ways, making it impossible to know THE facts about development that are applicable to all people for all time. For example, the broad contours of Piaget's theory of cognitive development may be applicable around the world, but there is also much variability in cognitive development across individuals and cultures. (See Box 1.1 for an overview of Piaget's stages of cognitive development.) Thus, while I am certainly in favor of knowing about Piaget's theory of cognitive development, I also believe that it is important to be able to think systematically about how its claims may play out in different circumstances. Aspects of basic developmental processes may be similar, but they can also be particularized in different ways. Our task is to be able to think systematically about, or make sense of and understand, the processes occurring as people develop any particular ways of functioning, at any time, anywhere in the world.

Box 1.1 **Overview of Piaget's Stages of Cognitive Development**

STAGE I—SENSORIMOTOR STAGE

Infants construct knowledge through sensorimotor or physical activity that provides sensory feedback. This stage starts with reflex acts (e.g., sucking, grasping, looking, hearing) and ends with the beginning of symbolic thinking.

STAGE II—PREOPERATIONAL STAGE

Young children can manipulate symbols mentally, but their thinking is characterized by incomplete logic. During the course of this stage, children overcome various barriers to logical thinking, such as focusing on a single dimension of a situation, thinking about the world only from one's own point of view (egocentrism), focusing on momentary states rather than transformations between states, and having trouble understanding that some acts or events are reversible (e.g., up and down).

STAGE III—CONCRETE OPERATIONAL STAGE

Children can think logically about concrete information—that is, information accessible to direct perception or direct physical activity.

STAGE IV—FORMAL OPERATIONAL STAGE

Adolescents increasingly think logically about abstract information.

In other words, we need a systematic framework for exploring the dynamics of human development.

Thinking systematically about basic developmental processes involves addressing the following three interrelated basic developmental questions:

- What develops during development?
- What happens during development?
- How does development happen?

Insofar as we are concerned here with the development of human functioning, our theoretical enterprise begins with a conceptualization of what human functioning is about. Hence the first question of this framework: What develops during development? To answer this question, I will argue that cultural action in relation to others develops during development. Once the wider whole of human functioning that develops has been conceptualized, we can move on to addressing the basic developmental process and question of what happens during development.

To answer this question, I turn to organismic-developmental theory, which claims that development occurs in relation to cultural meanings, and involves differentiation and integration within and among action constituents. Finally, once we have ways of conceptualizing what happens during development, we can tackle the basic developmental question and process of how development happens. This book's theoretical approach holds that development happens through individual, social, and cultural processes as individuals participate with others in cultural practices.

Developmental psychology has certainly addressed these questions and has provided a great deal of useful information about them. At the same time, however, developmental psychology has become a rather vast and fragmented academic discipline, with innumerable studies filling innumerable professional journals and books about development. With regard to the issue of what develops during development, developmental psychology has become increasingly fragmented as researchers focus on relatively separate domains of functioning, such as perceiving, thinking, feeling, moving physically, using language, setting goals, interacting with others, perspective taking, and self/identity. In turn, developmentalists carve up each of these domains into further subdomains. For example, researchers who study social development address issues ranging from parent–child interactions to attachment, empathy, aggression, and peer status. It has become impossible to keep up with all of the approaches and findings in all of the domains and subdomains. One is left overwhelmed and wondering how to make sense of it all. Where is the forest among all of these trees? (See, for example, Figure 1.1.) Certainly, action and its development are complex, and it is important to know about the distinct processes that comprise varied action constituents or domains of functioning. At the same time, however, we also need ways to think about and explore how they occur in relation to each other and in the service of a wider whole, namely an actual person who is acting and developing.

Moreover, a person's functioning at any given time involves varied domains simultaneously. As people go about their lives at any time during the life span they do not perceive the world for a while, then think for a moment, feel some emotion at another moment, then use language for a while, interact a little later, and then go back to thinking or perhaps to feeling. Instead, these processes are ongoing and occur *at the same time* as people engage with each other in varied activities. For example, a child who is playing on the playground is seeing and hearing people and objects, moving physically, thinking about what to do during play, possibly feeling varied emotions while playing with others, using language to interact, and constructing him- or herself in relation to the other children. An adult who is at work is perceiving the world, thinking about how to carry out a project, possibly feeling varied emotions while working with others, using language to interact with colleagues, and constructing him- or herself in relation to colleagues. In these ways, the domains of functioning interact to comprise wider cultural forms of behaving or acting. In addition, in both of these examples, the person's action

Figure 1.1 It is hard to make sense of the picture on the left until one looks at the picture on the right and sees that the objects are trees within a wider forest in winter, illuminated by the sun. Just as these trees function and have meaning within this wider forest, this wider forest is made up of these trees. Painting courtesy of the artist, Ron Donoughe.

is shaped by individual, social, and cultural processes. Therefore, the question arises: How can all of the local findings about disparate bits and aspects of behavior be brought together to form an integrated understanding of human functioning and development? Even if developmentalists have a command of findings for different domains, we need a way of thinking about how they may be linked. To overcome the fragmentation of developmental psychology (and psychology in general), I believe that an integrative theoretical framework for thinking systematically about development best begins with conceptualizing the functioning that undergoes development as a whole, and in a way that encompasses varied processes and domains of functioning as well as their interrelations.

With regard to what happens during development, in much developmental research development is defined as age-related change, and studies are designed to discern what people can do at different ages. One may find out that 3-year-olds do X, 5-year-olds do Y, and 7-year-olds do Z. Or, one may find out that 25- to 30-year-olds do A, 35- to 40-year-olds do B, and 45- to 50-year-olds do C. In addition, X, Y, and Z, as well as A, B, and C, may be identified as stages or milestones. Although such research provides invaluable information about life span development, it is overwhelming to make sense of all the findings for different ages, within different domains of functioning. Vastness and fragmentation take over again. Moreover, one is left wondering: What happens in between the ages, stages, and milestones? If 3-year-olds do X, if 5-year-olds do Y, and if 7-year-olds do Z, what about 4- and 6-year-olds? What is the process of development that occurs along the way to make new forms of functioning possible? Grouping people by age permits statistical analyses of group differences according to age, but calculating statistical differences for the behavior of this and that age group leaves us with some open questions about basic developmental processes. For example, it does not tell us what happened to the behavior of the individuals within the different groups, nor does it tell us how the behavioral differences across age groups came about. Focusing on forms of action that characterize what people do at different ages obscures the processes through which the forms of action emerge. A person goes from behavior X at one age to behavior Y at another age rather miraculously or mysteriously. The time is now ripe to be more explicit about the developmental processes that occur between X and Y.

I am reminded of a phone interview I had years ago, during my last year in graduate school when I was applying for postdoctoral positions. A prominent developmentalist's first question was, "What age range are you interested in?" I was not prepared for this question and became increasingly tongue-tied. I really was not interested in a particular age group but rather with understanding what goes on during development, no matter what age. I was, and remain, concerned with the wider issues, or the forest, of basic developmental processes. Finding the forest within which all the local findings about what people do at different ages are located can provide a basis for thinking systematically about what happens during development.

Along similar lines, developmental research may be designed to discern when or at what age people do X, Y, or Z. However, when the empirical concern is with discerning the age at which some form of behavior starts or first appears, the processes through which it emerges and through which it may continue to develop are obscured. When I am asked age-of-onset questions, I usually respond by saying that understanding development is not about identifying the particular moment at which some form of action appears. Rather, understanding development is about discerning the systematic processes through which some form of action emerged and through which further new forms of action will emerge. In addition, I start to explain that the development of some new form of action depends on varied processes, such as the culture a person is living in, and on the activities a person engages in with others. People's eyes begin to glaze over, and I can tell that they regret having asked the question in the first place. They thought they were asking a simple question. Maybe I should simply recommend one of the many developmental psychology textbooks that provide age-based information about stages and milestones for varied domains of functioning. Indeed, many developmental analyses are organized around determining when some form of behavior first appears. However, nothing comes from nothing, and I again find myself wondering about the forest of basic developmental processes. What was the person doing before this new form of behavior emerged? What developmental processes occurred that enabled the person to move from one way of behaving to another?

Defining development in terms of age-based changes quickly turns development into a rather static catalog of stages and milestones and their ages of onset to memorize. However, people's developmental experiences have varied throughout history, suggesting that stages and milestones are not static over time. For example, on the American frontier in the 19th century, girls and boys, as well as women and men, spent their days very differently than children and adults today. Historical research shows that children "spent countless hours doing much of the essential work of western settlement" (West, 1989, p. 73). They planted and plowed, hunted and gathered, herded and fed animals, cooked and cleaned, ironed and scrubbed, churned butter and canned food. The activities and technology that shape the developmental experiences of American children and adults today would likely astonish their pioneer counterparts. Moreover, since the 1980s, researchers have focused increasingly on how people's developmental experiences vary across cultures. Within-culture differences also provide evidence against the idea that development entails a single set of universal stages or milestones.

Taken together, a theoretical framework is needed for exploring and thinking systematically about basic developmental processes. In this case, thinking systematically about development involves conceptualizing what happens during development, beyond age-based change. To maintain theoretical consistency, it is also necessary to link the conceptualization of what happens during development with the conceptualization of the first basic developmental question regarding what develops during development.

Much research in developmental psychology is directed toward discerning what causes development, or investigating the basic developmental process of how development happens. Again, we find ourselves lost among the trees, in a thicket of findings about a wide range of independent variables thought to influence development, ranging from genes to the brain; to child-rearing patterns, peer interactions, and attachment patterns; to socioeconomic status, marital status, and occupation; to media influences, to culture, to the amount of talk directed toward children, to stress. The list goes on and on. Thinking systematically about how development happens could be facilitated with a theoretical framework for organizing and synthesizing findings about varied possible causes of development. And, for the sake of theoretical consistency, conceptualizing how development happens needs to be linked systematically to conceptualizations of what develops, and of what happens during development.

Systems Theory

The conceptual framework articulated in this book provides ways to begin clarifying these issues and ultimately can lead developmental psychology in new theoretical and empirical directions. The book is organized around the three basic developmental questions, and systems theory provides an overarching theoretical starting point for our approach to thinking systematically about basic developmental processes. Using *systems theory* thus helps us to think *systematically* about human development.

In the 20th century, the biologist Ludwig von Bertalanffy (1901–1972) was among the first to elaborate contemporary systems principles and to consider their applicability to varied disciplines, including psychology. Despite the relatively recent elaboration of systems principles in developmental psychology, systems ideas are steeped in Western philosophical traditions, traced back to Aristotle (Kaplan, 1967; von Bertalanffy, 1969/1998, 1972). Systems ideas are also compatible with some Eastern philosophical traditions that emphasize integration and holism. von Bertalanffy initially articulated general system theory in reaction to the mechanistic paradigm that has dominated scientific discourse and practices for centuries and is derived from the metaphor of a machine to describe human functioning. This mechanistic paradigm focuses on reducing "complex phenomena into elementary parts and processes" (von Bertalanffy, 1972, p. 409), and it is certainly entrenched practice in psychology to slice human behavior into separate parts or domains of functioning. In turn, these parts of human behavior are often viewed in isolation from one another. There is also often an empirical focus on identifying the independent causes of these isolated aspects of behavior. While this approach is suitable for understanding machines, as well as aspects of some natural science phenomena, it is not necessarily always suitable for understanding the subjective and value-laden behavior of human beings.

Human beings are active agents who create and use cultural signs to construct beliefs and values, to set and pursue goals, to construct experience subjectively, and to negotiate meanings with others. People also reflect on themselves, envision alternative courses of action, feel varied emotions, and interact with each other in cultural contexts. Imagine you are in a neighborhood restaurant and you see a woman walking across the room, just as you see a pool ball rolling across a pool table. Both the woman and the pool ball are moving, but you would probably describe and explain their respective movements in very different ways. Regarding the pool ball, it is sufficient to talk about quantifiable variables such as force, vectors, and velocity. Regarding the person, you would probably not be satisfied with only that kind of information. You would want to know more about her as a person. You might wonder, why did she walk across the room at that moment, what did she want, what was she feeling, what was important to her, what did her grimace mean, why did she smile, what is her story?

Systems theory provides a widely applicable alternative to the mechanistic assumptions that continue to pervade much of psychology. Although there are differences among contemporary systems theorists, they share some fundamental premises about human behavior and development in addition to the ones just presented. The goal here is to provide an overview of the systems premises used in subsequent chapters that inform the current theoretical approach to thinking systematically about basic developmental processes. See Box 1.2 for an overview of the main points of systems theory.

Box 1.2 Overview of the Main Points of Systems Theory

MULTIPLE AND INTERRELATED CONSTITUENTS

Systems are made up of distinct constituents that are inseparable, interrelated, and mutually constitutive. The meaning and function of a system's constituents depend on the whole of which they are parts, and the functioning of the whole depends on the organization of the parts.

EMERGENCE

System functioning is dynamic and always emerging or coming into being through ongoing interrelations among constituent processes.

SOFT ASSEMBLY

Because system constituents can be interrelated in different ways, they can assemble into different patterns of functioning and thus are not "hardwired" or predesigned. Some assemblies, called *attractors*, may be more likely or stable than others in some contexts or at different times.

INTRAINDIVIDUAL VARIABILITY

An individual's functioning is characterized by variability in relation to different people, different cultural practices, different physical settings, and different conditions (e.g., stress, fatigue).

INTERINDIVIDUAL VARIABILITY

Variability in functioning occurs between individuals due to different interrelations among constituent processes.

CANALIZATION

Development may be guided in certain general directions rather than others. Yet development is not determined, because the dynamic processes through which system functioning and development emerge can be structured and interrelated in varied ways.

EQUIFINALITY

Different early conditions can be related to similar later outcomes, and similar outcomes can be achieved via different developmental pathways.

Multiple and Interrelated Constituent Processes

A *system* is some phenomenon that is made up of and emerges through multiple and interrelated parts or constituents. When constituents are interrelated, it means that they do not occur or function in isolation or independently of one another. Rather, they mutually affect, constitute, and sustain each other. Thus, changing one part of a system does not simply affect that one part of the system; it has implications for the other parts of the system and, ultimately, for the functioning of the system as a whole. The world is full of systems, from the physical environment, to the human body, to large-scale economies, to automobile production; to armies and governments; to families, school districts, and universities; to sports teams and tennis games; to orchestras. It is not a coincidence that some of these examples are commonly referred to with the word *system*, such as an economic system, a political system, an ecosystem, a school system, or the central nervous system.

It is also not a coincidence that many of these examples of systems involve human functioning in some way. Indeed, the current theoretical approach to human functioning and development starts from the position that human functioning can be viewed systemically as a phenomenon that is made up of and emerges through multiple and interrelated constituent processes (Ford & Lerner, 1992; Mascolo & Fischer, 2010, 2015; Overton, 2006, 2010, 2013; Thelen & Smith, 1994/1996; van Geert, 2003, 2011; von Bertalanffy, 1969/1998; Witherington & Heying, 2013). As pointed out earlier, human functioning consists of varied or multiple domains of functioning—from perceiving, to moving physically, to thinking, to feeling, to using language, to constructing goals and values, to perspective taking, to interacting with others, to constructing oneself. In addition, human functioning is simultaneously constituted by individual, social, and cultural processes. To say that these system constituents of human functioning are interrelated means that they mutually affect and sustain each other so that the functioning of each constituent is inseparable from the functioning of other constituents. While system constituents have their own distinct characteristics, they are also defined in terms of how they function in relation to each other to comprise a wider whole. As Overton explains: "Holistically, the whole is not an aggregate of discrete elements but an organized system of parts, each part being defined by its relations to other parts and to the whole" (Overton, 2013, p. 44). Therefore, the wider whole of human functioning cannot be reduced to any single constituent or even to a set of constituents operating independently (Basseches & Mascolo, 2010; Overton, 2006, 2010, 2013; Thelen & Smith, 2006; van Geert, 2011; van Geert & Fischer, 2009; Witherington, 2011). Rather, in a system, the distinct processes are interrelated, and "control over the construction of action and meaning is distributed throughout the coacting elements" of the system (Basseches & Mascolo, 2010, p. 43).

Within the theoretical context of systems theory, when several constituents are interrelated or interact, it means that they mutually affect and sustain each other. Qualitative processes (X and Y) that are taken to represent some constituents of human functioning mutually affect each other to comprise a wider whole (Z), as in

$$[X \longleftrightarrow Y] \longleftrightarrow Z$$

Moreover, Z, as the wider whole, also affects the functioning of the constituent processes X and Y. Bidirectional arrows are used here to represent mutual influence or reciprocal interactions among system constituents.

Varied terms can be used and have been used to articulate the premise that system parts or constituents are fundamentally interrelated. For example, system parts are described as interrelated, inseparable, interdependent, or interpenetrating. System parts co-act on, co-regulate, and co-determine each other. They interact, or mutually influence each other. There are bidirectional interactions among system constituents. There are reciprocal interactions among system parts. Throughout this book, I use these varied terms interchangeably. In addition, my use of the term "inseparable" does not mean there are no distinctions among system constituents. Rather, it means that system constituents mutually constitute and affect each other, but at the same time it is acknowledged that they consist of their own particular processes that can be distinguished analytically (Sawyer, 2002). Ultimately, understanding system constituents requires analyzing not only their distinct processes, but also how they operate in relation to each other.

Although the premise that system constituents are interrelated or inseparable is incredibly illuminating, it is also potentially paralyzing, because it is easy to start thinking about how everything is always connected to everything else. As Meadows (2008) points out, systems analysts "have a habit of producing diagrams that cover several pages with small print and many arrows connecting everything with everything" (p. 98). But then we get overwhelmed and lost in the trees. The claim that system constituents are interrelated is a basic starting premise, but it does not mean that everything is connected to everything else in the same way within a system. Some connections may be weaker or stronger than others. Some connections among system constituents may even be additive at times. Some connections may be direct, while others are indirect. For example, Bronfenbrenner's ecological systems perspective draws attention to both direct and indirect sources of action and development (Bronfenbrenner, 1979). He posits that developing individuals are directly affected by the contexts and interactions in which they actually participate, such as when a child interacts with parents at home or with peers at school. At the same time, a child's engagement in these contexts may also be shaped indirectly by the parents' experiences at work or by schoolmates' experiences at home. Moreover, systems connections are dynamic and can change during development. A challenge for systems theory and research is to discern the different ways in which constituents are interrelated to comprise different modes of systemic functioning, for different systems. The point I am trying to emphasize here is that systems are messy phenomena that cannot be characterized only or primarily in terms of linear, unidirectional, or additive effects. They cannot be reduced to or characterized in terms of the independent functioning of constituent parts.

It is also important to point out that the multiple and interrelated parts of a system may also be systems, and thus it is more precise to say that systems are made up of multiple and interrelated subsystems. Some systems include subsystems, sub-sub-systems, sub-sub-sub-systems, and so on. Each of the psychological processes listed earlier (perceiving, moving physically, thinking, feeling, valuing, using language, constructing goals, perspective taking, interacting with others, constructing oneself) can be viewed systemically. In addition, an individual's functioning also includes biological systems and subsystems, from the heart, to the liver, to the kidneys, to the brain. An individual may be a subsystem of varied systems, such as a family, a sports team, a church, temple, or mosque, or a local club or organization—all of which may be subsystems of neighborhoods and communities, which today are usually subsystems of states or provinces or regions, which are subsystems of countries, which are subsystems of global economic, political, and ecological systems. All of the systems and subsystems that make up human functioning may certainly be worthy of investigating and understanding. However, it is impossible to cover everything all at once. Thus, the goal of this book is to offer an overarching theoretical framework for thinking systematically about human action and development in ways that can encompass any subsystemic constituents.

Emergence

With regard to conceptualizing the causes of human behavior, systems theory posits the concept of *emergence* (Fogel, 2011; Gershkoff-Stowe & Thelen, 2004; Howe & Lewis, 2005; Lewis, 2000, 2011; Mascolo, 2013; Overton, 2006, 2010, 2013; Thelen & Smith, 2006; van Geert & Fischer, 2009; Witherington, 2007, 2011; Witherington & Heying, 2013). It is argued that behavior emerges out of interrelations among "ongoing processes intrinsic to the system" (Lewis, 2000, p. 38). Claiming that human functioning emerges through interrelations among intrinsic constituent processes means that one does not have to invoke external, antecedent, or independent factors to explain what people do. In addition, the concept of emergence stands in explicit contrast to any conceptualization of behavior and development as predesigned or predestined by, for example, genetics or how the brain is "hardwired." Rather, what a person does emerges, or is always coming into being, through the ongoing dynamics of constituent processes. In keeping with the premise that the constituents are interrelated, they are viewed as "coequal partners" with "none holding privileged causal status in the real-time construction of the action pattern" (Witherington & Heying, 2013, p. 167). As such, there are no single or rock-bottom causes of behavior and development, such as the brain or genes or parents or the media. Another term that systems theorists use to refer to the emergence of behavior through interrelations among constituents is *self-organization*, whereby human behavior is taken to occur through interactions among the constituent processes of behavior itself.

Sometimes, one part of a system may seem dominant, and we may easily start viewing it as the main source, or even as an independent source of the system's overall functioning. The dominance of one constituent process may seem particularly apparent when a person's functioning goes awry in some way. For example, some conditions, such as Down syndrome, are known to be caused by a specific genetic abnormality. Brain damage often causes behavioral problems. Even within a range of "normal" behavior, people sometimes search for one main cause of why a person does what he or she does, as in "It's genetic," or "He read a lot as a child." From a systems perspective, we are led to thinking about how the structuring of one part of the system affects the other parts, weakly or strongly, directly or indirectly, and which *together* still comprise the whole functioning of the system.

Stability and Variability

Insofar as the constituents of human behavior can be interrelated in varied ways, they can assemble into different modes or forms or patterns of behavior. As such, human behavior is "'softly assembled' rather than hardwired or programmed" (Thelen & Smith, 2006, p. 274). Systems theorists posit that some assemblies may be more likely and stable than others at certain times during development or in particular contexts. Relatively stable forms of behavior in particular contexts are referred to as *attractors* (Fogel, 2011; Howe & Lewis, 2005; Thelen & Smith, 2006; van Geert & Steenbeek, 2005). It is argued that "the system 'settles into' or 'prefers' only a few modes of behavior. . . . [T]his behavioral mode is an attractor state, because the system—under certain conditions—has an affinity for that state" (Thelen & Smith, 2006, p. 272).

While stability is a characteristic of system functioning, emphasizing the variability of human behavior and development is another hallmark of systems theory (Fischer & Bidell, 2006; Fischer, Yan, & Stewart, 2003; Fogel, 2011; Howe & Lewis, 2005; Mascolo & Fischer, 2010, 2015; Spencer, Clearfield, Corbetta, Ulrich, Buchanan, & Schöner, 2006; Thelen & Smith, 2006; van Geert, 2011; van Geert & Fischer, 2009; van Geert & Steenbeek, 2005; Yan & Fischer, 2002, 2007). Insofar as system constituents can be assembled or interrelated in different ways, varied modes of action can potentially emerge at any given time. Thus, not only are there differences between people in the organization of their functioning, but any one individual's functioning can vary in relation to different people, in different cultural practices, and in different physical settings. In addition, a person's functioning can vary in relation to processes such as stress or fatigue. From a systems perspective, interindividual and intraindividual variability are considered to be "pervasive rather than abnormal or exceptional. The complexity of activity varies widely and systematically from moment to moment within and across contexts" (Yan & Fischer, 2002, p. 144). Accordingly, a systems approach leads to explicitly conceptualizing and investigating patterns of interindividual variability and intraindividual variability.

Let us illustrate these rather abstract systems premises with a concrete example. Reaching, grasping, and throwing are constituents of countless wider systems of action, and they can be executed in relation to each other (and to other constituents) in different ways for different purposes. Reaching for a ball, grasping it, and throwing it when playing baseball are parts of one wider cultural action system, whereas reaching for a ball, grasping it, and throwing it at someone in anger are parts of quite another. Thus, the meaning, structuring, and function of the constituents depend on their interrelations and on the wider cultural action system of which they are momentarily parts. Moreover, system functioning—in this case, human action in the forms of playing baseball and expressing anger— is emerging through interrelations among the constituent parts. Neither way of acting can be reduced to any single constituent. There can be stability in the way a person throws a baseball during a baseball game or throws an object to express anger. Yet these modes of action are also characterized by intraindividual variability insofar as a person throws balls somewhat differently during and across particular games of baseball, or during and across particular events that arouse the person's ire. Interindividual variability is also involved, as these modes of action can be carried out in somewhat different ways by different people. In addition to interrelations among reaching, grasping, and throwing, throwing a ball when playing baseball and throwing a ball at someone in anger emerge through interrelated individual, social, and cultural processes. That is, one can identify a particular individual who is throwing an object for his or her own reasons and in his or her own ways. Social processes are involved, as a person may end up throwing different objects in different ways in relation to different people. Baseball is a cultural practice because it reflects wider cultural beliefs and values, and expressing anger can be structured in varied culturally particular ways.

Besides throwing objects, people act in relation to others in a variety of cultural practices throughout the life span, from engaging with caregivers during infancy, to riding in a car on a family road trip, to eating dinner at home and in restaurants and at other people's houses, to participating in varied school activities, to gathering at the mall on weekends, to going to parties, to working, to dating, to making financial decisions, to engaging as caregivers with infants. In some cultures, children act in relation to others when they take care of younger siblings and when they contribute to a community's economic subsistence. All of these practices involve modes of action that emerge through interrelations among individual, social, and cultural processes, and may be assembled in varied ways depending on the vicissitudes of particular circumstances.

Moreover, these varied forms of action in relation to others involve perceiving, thinking, feeling, moving physically, believing and valuing, using language, setting and pursuing goals, interacting with others, and constructing self-conceptions. In other words, cultural action in relation to others is a system that involves individual, social, and cultural processes as well as multiple domains of functioning that occur simultaneously and in relation to each other. For example, research on caregiver–infant interaction in the United States indicates that during the first half of the first year, infants and their caregivers are mutually attentive and responsive to each other. However, acting in this way is not a purely social phenomenon, within the isolated domain of social interaction. It also involves cognition or thinking, as an infant uses varied means to achieve different ends, such as engaging with others and disengaging from others. It involves emotion or feeling, as the infant seems to enjoy engaging with others, or expresses dissatisfaction in some way with what is happening. Such action involves self and other awareness as the infant shows awareness of the other's attention to him- or herself. It also involves physical self-direction as the infant exerts some control over how he or she moves physically to engage with the caregiver. Such action has developed over the course of the first 2 months of life and will continue to develop thereafter. Thus, when babies interact with their caregivers, they are engaging in cultural ways of acting in relation to others, and their action emerges through multiple and interrelated constituents that undergo development.

Development

From a systems perspective, development is viewed as a specific kind of emergence through interrelations among constituent processes, namely the emergence of new forms of behavior. Insofar as development emerges, the same systems premises just explained for behavior in general may be applied to development. For example, both stability and variability are taken to characterize development. That is, at the same time that development involves consolidating and stabilizing new ways of acting, variability remains characteristic of human functioning insofar as a person may engage in more and less developed modes of action in different situations (Mascolo & Fischer, 2010, 2015; van Geert & Fischer, 2009; Yan & Fischer, 2002, 2007).

In addition, as an emergent process, development is taken to occur through or be caused by interrelations among system constituents, and not through some kind of predesign (e.g., a genetic blueprint or the brain's "hardwiring") or through the intervention of factors viewed as independent of the system. Also, the development of new forms of functioning is not reducible to any single constituent or to the independent functioning of several constituents. Sometimes one constituent or another may seem to dominate as a cause of a person's development. However, from a consistent systems perspective, there are no single rock-bottom causes of development. Therefore,

> we cannot say that this one element causes a developmental change because the influence of this element is only within the particular constellation of all the other contributing elements at a particular time. It is not a static or permanent arrangement. (Gershkoff-Stowe & Thelen, 2004, p. 17)

Insofar as different configurations of constituent interrelations are possible, it is possible for varied new forms of behavior to emerge during development. Therefore, development is viewed as a probabilistic process that cannot be predicted exactly (Gottlieb, 2007; Griffiths & Tabery, 2013; Lewis, 2011; Valsiner, 1997; Witherington, 2007).

While development cannot be predicted exactly, it is also not taken to occur randomly. Drawing on roots in biology, systems theory holds that development is canalized, meaning that species-specific genetic processes guide biological development in particular directions rather than others. Gottlieb posits that experience can also be a source of canalization during development, whereby there is a "narrowing of responsiveness as a consequence of experience" (Gottlieb, 2001, p. 4). However, canalization does not fully determine any individual's ongoing development because narrowing is not equivalent to limiting development in one particular way. In addition, systems theory posits that development is characterized by variability between people. One way of conceptualizing developmental variability can be found in the biological systems principle of equifinality, which holds that different early conditions can lead to similar developmental outcomes, and that organisms with similar early conditions can follow different routes to similar outcomes (Gottlieb, 2001; von Bertalanffy, 1969/1998). With regard to psychological development in humans, equifinality means that the development of similar modes of action can be achieved despite different early conditions and along different developmental pathways (Fischer, 1980; Ford & Lerner, 1992; Valsiner, 1997). The opposite scenario is also possible: People with similar early conditions may develop different ways of acting. Indeed, even identical twins act differently and are not exactly the same.

Summary

To recapitulate, systems theory starts from the premise of interrelations among multiple constituent processes. From a systems perspective, what people do is viewed as emerging out of interrelations among constituent processes and therefore cannot be understood solely in terms of single, independent, or linear effects. What people do is further understood as dynamic and subject to ongoing emergence. As such, human functioning is understood in terms of both stability and variability across contexts and circumstances. These basic systems premises are also applicable to development, which involves the emergence of new forms of behavior. Taken together, these systems premises provide an overarching theoretical orientation for answering the basic developmental questions and for conceptualizing basic developmental processes. We now turn to thinking more specifically and systematically about what develops during development.

2

What Develops during Development?

> It is necessary to study not only parts and processes in isolation, but also to solve the decisive problems found in the organization and order unifying them, resulting from dynamic interaction of parts, and making the behavior of parts different when in isolation or within the whole.
>
> —Ludwig von Bertalanffy (1969/1998, p. 31)

Basic developmental processes refer to the dynamics of what happens during development and the dynamics of how development happens. To be able to think about and explore these processes systematically and more specifically, it is first necessary to step back and conceptualize the human functioning that is undergoing development. Thus, this chapter addresses the basic developmental question of what develops during development, and more specifically in our case, what develops during human development. This question may seem odd insofar as it is clearly people who develop during human development. People develop throughout the life span, but what about people develops? Their action or behavior develops. Their ways of functioning develop. But what about their functioning develops? What does it mean to function? What is action?

As pointed out in Chapter 1, contemporary psychologists typically split human functioning into different domains or constituents of behavior that develop. In developmental psychology, different developmentalists consider the development of varied domains of behavior, including but not limited to moving physically, perceiving, thinking, interacting with others, feeling, self/identity construction, perspective taking, pursuing goals, and using language. Thus, we can say that people's behavior within these varied domains develops. Certainly, people's cognition or thinking develops, as do their social abilities and ways of conceptualizing themselves, as do their emotions and language. However, we want to avoid treating domains of functioning separately because they do not occur separately when people act. Rather, a person's functioning involves varied domains simultaneously. As people go about their lives in all corners of the world, they do not think at one moment, feel some emotion at another moment, perceive the world for a bit, then use language for a while, interact a little later, and then go back to thinking or perhaps to feeling. Instead, these processes are ongoing and occur *at the same time*, as people engage with others in varied activities. The field of psychology has contributed much to our knowledge of human functioning and development within these varied domains, characterized by distinct processes that are certainly important to investigate. However, by viewing domains of functioning in relative isolation, psychology starts with the trees, and thus we know less about how the varied domains are connected to comprise the functioning of a *whole person*. Accordingly, it is useful to start with the forest within which the varied domains of functioning are played out and have meaning. To find the forest, we turn here to systems theory and its central premise that human functioning is made up of and emerges through interactions or interrelations among multiple constituent processes. This chapter focuses on explicating how human action emerges through interrelations among individual, social, and cultural processes and consists of interrelations among varied domains of functioning.

Individual, Social, and Cultural Processes

The present theoretical approach to human functioning as a whole is based on the premises that human beings are separate individuals as well as connected to others and that human functioning is always cultural. As such, I assume that human functioning consists of individual, social, and cultural processes, and from a systems perspective, individual, social, and cultural processes represent multiple and interrelated constituents of human functioning. A central point here is that people are not wholly separate individuals. Rather, we function separately, and we simultaneously function in relation to others. People are thus individuals who act in relation to others. In addition, action in relation to others always occurs in the context of culturally organized activities that reflect cultural meanings. Taken together, we are individuals who act in relation to others in cultural practices.

Examples of cultural action in relation to others abound. During childhood, children act in relation to others in varied cultural practices, at home and at school. People act in relation to others when they are sitting together in a car, on the way to one place and activity or another, or when walking on a crowded city street. They act in relation to others in a grocery store, or in an open-air market. Around the world, adults act in relation to others in different work settings. People act in relation to others when eating with others at home or in a restaurant. In some cultures, children act in relation to others as they take care of younger siblings, spend the day in mixed-age peer groups, and contribute to community subsistence. Around the world, when caregivers command children to "Behave!," issues of acting in relation to others may be at stake. For example, in some cultures, children may be fighting in the back seat of the car, and the command "Behave!" is a call to stop fighting and to act differently in relation to each other. The command may also be a call for the children to act in relation to others who are in the car, such as the driver who is distracted by the fighting. When caregivers command children, they, too, are acting in relation to others. People may also act in relation to others when they are alone. For example, a person sitting alone on a remote mountain top might be thinking about how to handle an interpersonal situation, mulling over what the other person said, and imagining what to say to that person if and when they see each other again. Or the person may be trying to decide whether or not to accept a lucrative job offer, by considering possible consequences for varied other people in his or her life.

We can thus posit that as people act within cultural practices, much of what develops during development is the cultural action of individuals in relation to others. Another way of putting this claim is to say that an individual's cultural modes, forms, or ways of acting in relation to others develop. These terms for expressing the wider whole of human functioning all explicitly refer to individual, social, and cultural processes. However, these expressions are rather long and unwieldy. Therefore, "action in relation to others" or "acting in relation to others" and simply "action" or "acting" will also be used as shorthand terms. Once again, people are separate individuals who act in relation to others in cultural practices, and thus their action emerges out of interrelated individual, social, and cultural processes. As illustrated in Figure 2.1, from a systems perspective, individual, social, and cultural processes are understood as distinct, yet also as always occurring simultaneously and, importantly, in relation to each other. We first conceptualize individual, social, and cultural processes as analytically distinct, and then we consider how they are utterly interrelated causal constituents of human action.

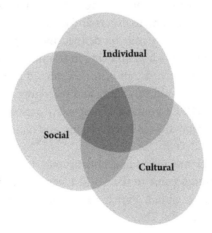

Figure 2.1 A systems view of cultural action in relation to others. Human action emerges through distinct and interrelated individual, social, and cultural processes. Each process contributes 100% to human action. None is prior or primary. They do not occur in a particular order; they co-occur and mutually affect each other.

Before proceeding further, I am compelled to point out that I typically refer to individual, social, and cultural processes in that order. However, in no way do I mean to suggest that individual processes are primary, social processes are secondary, and cultural processes are least significant of all. I could just as well write social, cultural, and individual processes; or cultural, individual, and social processes; or cultural, social, and individual processes, and so on. As system constituents, these processes are taken to occur simultaneously and in relation to each other, and thus they do not occur in any particular order at all. In Figure 2.1 they are represented as overlapping circles. Language, however, is linear, and it is simply impossible to refer to these processes without putting one first, another second, and another third.

Individual Processes

Claiming that human action is partly constituted by individual processes means that people function as separate and distinct individuals, and that individuals construct experience and meaning from a unique subjective perspective. As a person develops modes of acting, those modes of acting become constituents of individual processes because they are carried out in individualized ways and characterize an individual's ways of acting. Human beings also think about themselves—in the past, present, and future—as separate people and in relation to others. Viewing human functioning in terms of individual processes additionally means that a person's action is taken to be partly generated or caused by that individual. In other words, individuals are active agents who choose and decide, who want and hope, who set and pursue goals that reflect values and standards, and who can direct or regulate aspects of their own action. As agents, individuals act in terms of how they interpret and give meaning to events and situations (Bronfenbrenner, 1979; Mascolo, 2013). *Human agency* may be defined more specifically as "the deliberative, reflective activity of a human being in framing, choosing, and executing his or her actions in a way that is not fully determined by factors and conditions other than his or her own understanding and reasoning" (Martin, Sugarman, & Thompson, 2003, p. 82). Of course, such agentive action develops, as neonates clearly do not make major choices and decisions, and their self-regulating abilities are rather limited.

Nevertheless, there are individual constituents to action from the outset, because all human beings come to the world as separate individuals whose functioning is partly self-generated. Perhaps most obviously, newborns can move physically, and move they do! They

> blink their eyes and turn them to track sounds and moving objects. They rotate their heads from side to side, protrude their tongues, open and close their mouths, and purse their lips. They arch their backs, turn their

torsos, flail their arms, kick their legs, open and close their hands, and wiggle their fingers and toes. (Adolph & Berger, 2005, p. 233)

Infants also

kick their legs in alternation, repeatedly whack one foot against the floor, or flex and then extend both legs simultaneously. They bang their arms and hands against surfaces, flap their arms up and down, bend and straighten their elbows, and rotate their hands in circles. (Adolph & Berger, 2005, p. 233)

Piaget (1953) points out that such sensorimotor activity allows infants to begin subjectively construing the world from the outset because it provides sensory stimulation that the infant can experience and construct individually. In addition, sensorimotor activity provides a basis for development to occur because it enables "the infant to engage with the world not in a rigid manner, but in a dynamic way, that is open to modification through the continual interplay of assimilation and accommodation" (Užgiris, 1996, p. 20) or through use, feedback, and adjustment.

Social Processes

At the same time, individuals act in relation to each other, and thus individual processes are inextricably intertwined with social processes. Indeed, interacting with others is necessary for infants to survive physically, and it is necessary for human development to occur. At any time during the life span, a person's action depends in part on the person or people with whom he or she is interacting. For example, if one observes an individual with one person, the individual may come across as rather shy and reticent. However, multiple observations of this person with varied other people in varied situations may reveal someone who can also be quite outgoing and sociable. In addition, when people interact, there is ongoing mutual adjustment among them. For example, you may have rehearsed what you are going to say to someone, but then while you are actually speaking to that person, you are also reacting to what the other person is doing simultaneously (perhaps raising eyebrows and interrupting). And you end up making statements you never could have imagined making because the other person's action is partly constitutive of your action, and your action is partly constitutive of the other person's action.

A person's action may involve social processes even when he or she is alone. For example, classic analyses of a young child's (named Emily) pre-sleep monologues show that she talked to herself about various people and social situations in her life

(Nelson, 1989). Moreover, in her monologues, she used aspects of the conversations she had with her father just before he left her on her own to go to sleep. At the same time, these monologues cannot be reduced to social processes, because they are also the unique products of Emily's active and subjective constructing. Throughout the life span, people may ponder what others do when those others are not immediately present, and they interpret what others do from their own and others' perspectives.

Varied and venerable traditions have long emphasized social aspects of self or identity construction as people position themselves in relation to others and construct conceptions of themselves in relation to others (e.g., Bamberg, 2011, 2012; Bowlby, 1969/1982, 1973; Bruner, 2002; Cooley, 1902; James, 1890/1983; Mead, 1934/1962). Within the philosophical tradition of American Pragmatism, George Herbert Mead (1934/1962) posited that people become conscious of and understand themselves by taking the attitudes of others toward themselves. Along similar lines, Charles Horton Cooley (1902) posited a "reflected or looking-glass self" (p. 152), whereby a person constructs him- or herself in relation to others by going through the following three-step process: "the imagination of our appearance to the other person; the imagination of his judgment of that appearance, and some sort of self-feeling, such as pride or mortification" (p. 152). According to William James (1890/1983), people define themselves in terms of varied characteristics, including their social roles and relationships with others. Building on these perspectives, contemporary dialogical approaches draw attention to how thinking, feeling, and self-construction involve engaging in private or imaginary dialogues with varied others (Hermans, 2003; Watkins, 2000/2005).

Cultural Processes

People are also always acting within cultural practices, and thus action emerges through cultural processes as well. Culture is a notoriously vexing concept to define, and definitions of culture certainly abound. As Jahoda (2012) points out, culture is a construct that encompasses "a vastly complex set of phenomena" (p. 300), and trying to define and make sense of the varied phenomena that comprise culture all at once is futile. Insofar as it is impossible to define culture definitively, at best one can explain how one is using the term and identify what particular dimensions of culture are being addressed.

I have long found it useful to approach culture through an emphasis on action and meaning. According to Miller and Goodnow (1995), as people engage in cultural practices together, their action is "invested with normative expectations and with meanings or significances that go beyond the immediate goals of the action" (Miller & Goodnow, 1995, p. 7). That is, action within cultural practices is symbolic, and it reflects commonly held as well as contested meanings that may be expressed implicitly and explicitly (Gjerde, 2004). Cultural meanings refer to historically based beliefs, values, ways of constructing experience, and guidelines for behavior. Culture also includes the symbolic means and technologies through which culturally meaningful action is carried out (Bruner, 1983, 1990; Rogoff, 2003; Valsiner, 1997, 2011; Werner & Kaplan, 1963/1984; Wertsch, 1998). In particular, language is the central symbolic means that human beings use to act. Culture further includes economic and political processes, as well as the ways in which issues of power and authority are played out in cultural practices.

As with individual and social processes, human functioning is cultural from the outset because newborns' experiences are guided by others who are acting in relation to them in culturally particular and meaningful ways. For example, in some cultures it is not unusual to see people encouraging babies and young children to flap one of their hands up and down. Some caregivers may even physically guide the child's hand up and down. This hand moving is part of a culturally meaningful practice whereby a caregiver is telling the child to wave and say goodbye to someone who is departing the scene. Children may be prompted to wave goodbye when they themselves are taking leave of others. Waving goodbye may also be accompanied by saying how nice it was to see the person, thanking him or her for a lovely time, telling the departing person to come again soon, and/or telling the departing person to get home safely. In these ways, flapping one's hand up and down, in conjunction with parting words, is meaningful action that reflects cultural values and guidelines for acting in relation to others. As such, taking leave in this way is not simply a matter of executing the physical mechanics of hand waving or of saying particular words. It also involves what can be called the "manner of action" (Užgiris, 1996, p. 28), which refers to explicit, as well as often implicit and elusive, cultural values and standards about how to act in relation to others.

Let us consider again the example of shyness, to illustrate how cultural processes partly constitute human functioning. To understand a person's shyness in relation to others, it is necessary to consider the cultural meaning of acting shyly in that person's culture. Some research shows that acting shyly in China is understood differently than it is in Western settings, thus indicating that shyness may reflect different values in different cultures (e.g., Xu & Farver, 2009). In Western cultures, shyness is associated with peer rejection, but this association does not necessarily hold in China where shyness has long been associated with "accomplishment, mastery, and maturity" (Chen & Wang, 2010, p. 436). Thus, acting shyly is inseparable from the cultural processes through which it is given different meanings in different parts of the world. It is interesting to note that some research suggests that the meaning of shyness in China may be changing as China's economy becomes increasingly capitalistic. That is, between 1990 and 2002, shyness continued to be associated with peer acceptance, but it was also increasingly associated with peer rejection (Chen, Cen, Li, & He, 2005; Chen, Chung, & Hsiao, 2009). Change is fundamental to cultural processes, and it remains to be seen how the meaning of shyness and any other ways of acting in any cultural context are played out in relation to varied dynamic cultural processes, including economic and political changes.

Other examples of culturally different interpretations of the ostensibly "same" forms of behavior can be considered. In Western cultures, eye contact is an important part of social interaction, but in varied cultures around the world people do not look each other in the eye when they interact. Among Navajo Indians, gaze aversion is taken to be a sign of respect for individual autonomy. According to Chisholm (1996), "for the Navajo, to look directly into another's eyes can be construed as an attempt to impose one's self, or will, on that person—to control that person" (p. 179). For the Gusii of Kenya, averting one's gaze is part of the Gusii "code of restraint" and reflects the belief that "excessive sociability [is] dangerous for a person of any age" (LeVine et al., 1994/1998, p. 47). Within this context, Gusii mothers avoid eye contact with babies, but American mothers interpret such action as being unresponsive (LeVine, 2004). When Gusii mothers watched a videotape of an American mother, they retorted that not holding a baby at all times is neglectful, including leaving a "crying child lying on the changing table momentarily while [turning] to pick up a clean diaper" (LeVine, 2004, p. 155).

Interrelated Individual, Social, and Cultural Processes

Individual, social, and cultural processes have just been discussed as analytically distinct constituents of human action. (See Box 2.1 for an overview of individual, social, and cultural processes.) However, from a systems perspective, human action is taken to be made up of multiple constituent processes that operate in relation to each other. Thus, even though individual, social, and cultural processes can be understood as distinct systemic processes with their own systemic subconstituents, they are also understood as utterly interrelated constituents of action. To say that individual, social, and cultural processes are interrelated means that each process affects the other, making them mutually constitutive. Moreover, no single process is prior to the others, and no single process has primacy over the others. Thus, human action cannot be reduced to nor explained in terms of individual, social, or cultural processes alone. Rather, human action is taken to emerge through simultaneously occurring and interrelated individual, social, and cultural processes.

Parent–infant attachment provides an example of action that emerges out of interrelated individual, social, and cultural processes for both children and their adult caregivers. In developmental psychology, attachment refers to the

> affectional tie that one person or animal forms between himself and another specific one—a tie that binds them together in space and endures over time. The behavioral hallmark of attachment is seeking to gain and to maintain a certain degree of proximity to the object of attachment. (Ainsworth & Bell, 1970, p. 50)

Box 2.1 **Overview of Individual, Social, and Cultural Processes**

Individual Processes—Aspects of functioning that involve being a separate individual

- Construing experience from a subjective perspective
- Individualized ways of acting
- Agency

Social Processes—Aspects of functioning that involve connections among people

- Direct social interaction
- Continuous mutual adjustment
- Orienting to others when alone
- Constructing oneself and experience in relation to others

Cultural Processes—Aspects of functioning that reflect common and contested meanings and wider societal processes

- Common and contested beliefs, values, and guidelines for action
- Structuring of action within cultural practices
- Symbolic means and technologies
- Economic and political processes
- Structuring of power and authority

Individual and social processes are interrelated in establishing and maintaining an attachment relationship as a child acts in ways that elicit the attention and proximity of others and as a caregiver acts in ways that are responsive to a particular child. From a systems perspective, attachment does not emerge only through the individual child's attempts at eliciting attention or through the child's individual ways of handling distress in the absence of caregivers. Nor does it only involve the caregiver's ways of responding to the child. Rather, what each person does contributes to what the other does. At the same time, however, attachment is not solely a social phenomenon, because a child's particular ways of seeking proximity contribute to the attachment relationship, as do a caregiver's particular ways of responding. Research also points to how parents' ideas about attachment issues and their ways of responding to children vary culturally (Harwood, Miller, & Irizarry, 1995; LeVine, 2004). In cultural circumstances where infant mortality is high, mothers may eschew establishing an attachment relationship with their babies (Scheper-Hughes, 1985). Taken together, what each attachment partner does emerges out of interrelated individual, social, and cultural processes to co-constitute their ways of acting in relation to each other.

Many other forms of action that are often attributed to individuals occur at the nexus of individual, social, and cultural processes. For example, one may hear statements about someone's parenting skills, or that so-and-so is a certain type of parent. Similar statements may be used to characterize teaching and teachers. However, neither teaching nor parenting is located wholly in individual parents or teachers. Insofar as parents are the parents of particular children, and teachers teach particular students, parenting and teaching are also inherently social processes. Moreover, there are culturally particular ways of understanding and enacting what it means to be a parent and teacher. Thus, a parent's action and a teacher's action emerge out of interactions among individual, social, and cultural processes. In addition, from a systems perspective, although parents and teachers may act in some consistent or stable ways, their action is taken to be softly assembled and thus may vary across contexts and in relation to different children and students.

Let us consider driving as a different kind of example of action that emerges out of inseparable individual, social, and cultural processes. At first glance, it is easy to think of driving largely as a physical skill located primarily in the individual. We may speak of so-and-so who is a good driver or a bad driver. However, driving also involves social and cultural processes. With regard to social processes, drivers share the road, and individual drivers have to continuously adjust what they are doing in relation to what other drivers are doing. With regard to cultural processes, driving involves using varied symbolic means and technologies to regulate action (e.g., blinkers, lights of different colors, road signs) as well as following varied rules of the road. In addition, being able to drive reflects cultural values, such as self-reliance or providing for one's family. A person's driving may settle into relatively stable attractors, but driving still always remains softly assembled. Thus, in addition to interindividual variability, there is also intraindividual variability as a person's driving emerges in different specific circumstances.

Saying that action emerges through or is caused by individual, social, and cultural processes highlights the point that individual, social, and cultural processes are not being viewed as independent variables that have separate effects on behavior. In other words, action does not occur independently of these processes. These processes are intrinsic to the action system, and thus action emerges or comes into being through these simultaneously occurring and interrelated processes. Viewing individual, social, and cultural processes as essential and interrelated constituents of human action further means that they are not being viewed as independent variables whose effects can be quantitatively partitioned from each other. From a systems perspective, understanding action as a system is not so much a matter of partitioning the constituents and quantifying their independent or additive contributions, because individual, social, and cultural processes are taken to contribute 100% or to be "completely involved" (Lerner, 1986, p. 84). Moreover, these constituent processes are taken to operate in relation to each other or interdependently (Vreeke, 2000). Thus, understanding action involves exploring the qualitatively distinct contributions of co-equal individual, social, and cultural processes, as well as the dynamic ways in which they are interrelated. As the cases of attachment, acting as a parent or teacher, and driving show, any form of action emerges out of or is causally constituted by ongoing reciprocal interactions among completely involved individual, social, and cultural processes. The conceptualization presented here leads to discerning how these processes are structured and interrelated to comprise wider modes of action.

Context

Conceptualizing individual, social, and cultural processes as interrelated causal constituents of action also has implications for our understanding of context and the links between context and action. According to a systems framework, context (which includes social and cultural processes) is viewed as a co-constituent of an individual's action or as intrinsic to the action system. As such, "the interplay between person and context is very intricate; it is a continuous dynamic loop" (van Geert & Fischer, 2009, p. 321), with person and context always mutually constituting each other. Insofar as contexts include social and cultural processes, and insofar as the people who act in contexts are distinct individuals, we come back to the premise that action emerges through interrelated individual, social, and cultural processes. Thus, we are led to thinking about and investigating how individual, social, and cultural processes are structured and interrelated to comprise a person's action in any context or situation. For example, perhaps you are interested in studying people's action in terms of a particular context dimension, such as whether they live in a nuclear family, a multigenerational household, or a single-parent household. Or maybe a researcher is interested in discerning how development differs for children who live in contexts that differ with respect to books and toys. The systems approach discussed here leads to thinking about and investigating the cultural meaning of books and toys, and it leads to investigating what people do together with toys and books. This approach leads to investigating the cultural meaning of differently structured households as well as to the ways in which people in differently structured households act in relation to each other. In these ways, books and toys, as well as household structure, are not being treated as variables that are antecedent to or independent of people's action, but rather as dimensions of the interrelated individual, social, and cultural processes that constitute how people act in relation to each other.

When context and behavior are understood independently rather than in relation to each other, there is a tendency to reify context. In particular, the word *context* takes on the connotation of a place or of a physical location that one enters and exits. Certainly, all human functioning takes place in some physical space and does not occur separately from it. But the same forms of action do not always occur in the same physical spaces. In some cultural circumstances, people live and develop in one-room dwellings. Does that mean that the context of their action and development is always the same? Not necessarily. In addition to the physical location, it is useful to conceptualize contexts in terms of the cultural practices and forms of action that constitute them. Thus, even in a one-room dwelling, people may engage in varied practices and modes of action during the course of a day, such as washing up in the morning, preparing meals for the family, eating meals with others, taking care of children, caring for older family members, and reading, playing, singing, or arguing. Defining contexts in terms of what people do takes us back to the point that people act and that action emerges through interrelated individual, social, and cultural processes. As such, contexts are understood as action circumstances in which what people do emerges through interrelated individual, social, and cultural processes. In addition, when individual, social, and cultural processes are organized in different ways, different ways of acting in different contexts can emerge. It is also important to point out that as people act in varied contexts, those contexts can be interrelated. Furthermore, contexts in which a person does not participate directly may also affect his or her action and development through someone with whom the person interacts directly (Bronfenbrenner, 1979). For example, an adult may be indirectly affected by his or her spouse's work context.

Another way of thinking about these issues is to consider that contexts are constituted in part by people through their action. Just as all action occurs in some context, the contexts in which people act and develop come into existence or emerge through human action. Take a classroom setting, for example. Students and teachers know how to act in a classroom, and at first glance it can seem as if the classroom context is controlling or determining or causing what they do. However, the classroom context does not exist independently of the students and teachers who constitute and construct it by acting. Indeed, the physical space could be used for varied purposes and a classroom can also be created outside of a room in a specifically designated school building. Of course, teachers and students act in certain ways because they know they are in a classroom setting, which is structured in culturally typical ways. Nevertheless, the practices that make a classroom setting what it is still need to be established and maintained through people's action. And such action comes into being through individual, social, and cultural processes. And such action also develops.

Furthermore, when contexts are viewed independently of action one is easily led to a relatively static conception of context that does not account for the dynamics of development. For example, a restaurant typically consists of tables and chairs, eating utensils, food, customers, servers, and cooks. At a restaurant, people act to constitute that context by perusing menus, ordering food, eating food, and talking to each other. While there is variability among particular restaurants and people's action in restaurants is softly assembled, there seem to be certain immutable aspects of action that make up restaurants and not some other action circumstance. However, this view of contexts does not take development into account. The action that comprises particular contexts, such as restaurants, develops, and therefore the restaurant context changes for a person as he or she develops with regard to the forms of action that comprise going to a restaurant. More generally, all action contexts—from homes to schools, to playgrounds and farms, to markets and offices, to restaurants and bars, to vacations at the beach— are experienced dynamically by developing people. Thus, it is problematic to characterize contexts in terms of static variables or factors that operate independently of human action and its developmental organization (Bronfenbrenner, 1979; Bronfenbrenner & Morris, 2006; Užgiris, 1977; Witherington & Heying, 2013).

Taken together, these points about context indicate that understanding of context issues can be facilitated by viewing contexts as the totality of action circumstances. From this viewpoint, contexts include the physical location and physical space in which action occurs. Additionally, contexts include the cultural practices in which different modes of action are played out, through particular ways of structuring individual, social, and cultural processes. The term *practice* "is an extremely polysemous concept; it seems to inhabit a common semantic space with such concepts as activity, context, situation, and event" (Cole, 1995, p. 105). For current purposes, I view cultural practices as relatively demarcated and as the sites where modes of action are organized or structured in relatively particular and consistent ways. For example, eating a family dinner is a cultural practice that can be relatively set off from other practices, it occurs repeatedly, and acting in relation to others while eating dinner can occur in relatively consistent ways from day to day. I use the term "relatively" here intentionally because cultural practices, and the modes of action that comprise them, vary with regard to being demarcated, repeated, particular, and consistent in general, as well as during development more specifically.

Individualism and Collectivism

In this section I would like to raise one more context-related issue. Discussing behavior and development within cultural contexts, or in relation to cultural processes, inevitably leads to issues of individualism and collectivism, which have dominated cultural analyses of behavior and development for decades. This book is not intended to be a review of the vast amount of research on individualism and collectivism. For current purposes, it suffices to summarize several points which I take as given within the conceptualization of action and development presented here.

At least since Hofstede (1980/2001) suggested that cultures can be classified in terms of individualism and collectivism, these constructs have largely been treated dichotomously as mutually exclusive and opposing dimensions of culture, behavior, and development. From a dichotomous perspective, cultures are classified as either individualistic or collectivistic, or as relatively individualistic or collectivistic. People in individualistic cultures allegedly value independence and develop independent ways of acting, whereas people in collectivistic cultures allegedly value interdependence and develop interdependent ways of acting. Independence generally encompasses aspects of functioning that involve being a separate individual, such as self-direction, self-expression, pursuing individual goals, and defining oneself separately from others. Interdependence generally encompasses aspects of functioning that involve connections to others, including cooperating with others toward attaining common goals, being considerate of others, and defining oneself in terms of interpersonal relationships and social roles.

Rather than viewing independence and interdependence dichotomously, however, I take the position that human action entails both independence and interdependence, because all human beings are simultaneously separate from and connected to others. Therefore, people all over the world are *both* independent and interdependent. This position in no way denies that there are cultural differences in action or in the structuring of independent and interdependent aspects of action. On the contrary. However, rather than claiming that action in this or that culture is more or less individualistic/independent or collectivistic/interdependent, cultural differences are taken to lie in how independence and interdependence are understood and organized (Raeff, 2006a). Indeed, many have argued that dichotomous conceptions of independence and interdependence obscure cultural complexities and ignore research that points to the fundamental importance of *both* independence and interdependence around the world (e.g., Killen & Wainryb, 2000; Oyserman, Coon, & Kemmelmeier, 2002; Raeff, 2006a,b,c, 2010a; Tamis-LeMonda et al., 2008; Turiel, 1983/1985; Turiel & Wainryb, 2000; Waterman, 1981).

For example, in many cultures around the world, families participate in co-sleeping arrangements, whereas Americans typically prefer separate sleeping arrangements for adults and children. From a dichotomous perspective, co-sleeping is viewed in terms of how it fosters interdependence or relating to others, in the form of close family ties. In contrast, separate sleeping arrangements are taken to emphasize independent self-regulation and being separate from others. However, research in a Mexican Mayan community shows that when children are around 5 years old, they can choose "when, how long, and with whom to sleep" (Gaskins, 1999, p. 40). In this way, children are making their own, or individual, choices about a social situation and are therefore acting *both* independently and interdependently. For American families, separate sleeping arrangements are organized partly in terms of the adult family members' needs and schedules (Richman, Miller, & Solomon, 1988; Shweder, Jensen, & Goldstein, 1995), which suggests that independent sleeping is inseparable from the interdependence of being considerate of others' preferences.

Or consider the following example of how both independence and interdependence may be played out in different cultures:

> Americans expect a boy to learn to clean his room, while the Gusii expect a boy to learn how to build his new house. In that respect, the Gusii youth becomes more self-sufficient. But the traditional Gusii son was expected to consult both parents in the choice of a wife and to bring her home to his mother for help in setting up their household, while the American youth is expected to make his own marital choice and set up an independent household. In this domain, the American is more autonomous. (LeVine, 1990, p. 472)

It is also important to note here that the American youth is making an individual choice about a social relationship, pointing to interrelations between independence and interdependence. Taken together, research from around the world shows that both independence and interdependence are valued in varied cultures, but they may be understood and structured differently within and across different cultures, as well as during development.

Biological Processes

Of course, biological constituents also make up human action and development. One might immediately think of the roles that genes and the brain play in behavior and development. Some issues regarding genetic and neurological contributions to how development happens will be taken up in Chapter 6. At this juncture it suffices to make two basic points about genetic and neurological processes.

First, from a systems perspective, genetic and neurological processes are treated the same as any other systemic constituent of human functioning. That is, they are considered to consist of their own multiple and interrelated constituents, and they interact with the other processes that make up human action. These processes are not isolated from other processes and do not operate either as antecedent or independent causes of action and development. As such, genetic and neurological processes are viewed as intrinsic to the system of human functioning, and they are not privileged as the ultimate foundations or determinants or causes of human action and development (Fogel, 1993; Griffiths & Tabery, 2013; Johnston & Lickliter, 2009; Meaney, 2010; Overton, 2013; Oyama, 2000; Thelen &

Smith, 2006). A systems perspective thus "democratizes" genetic and neurological constituents of action and development (Fogel, 1993, p. 49).

Moreover, other biological processes and bodily organs are necessary for human functioning, and therefore Gergen (2010) questions whether and how "to demarcate the brain from the remainder of the bodily activity of which it is a part" (p. 804). He argues further:

> It is also apparent that the neural system is scarcely independent of the pulmonary system; each depends on the other for its functioning. And, too, neither of these could function effectively without the digestive system, skeletal structure, and so on. Remove any part of the system and "behavior" is essentially negated. (p. 804)

Thus, one could also easily attribute behavior to the lungs or to the stomach. The point here is that both genetic and neurological processes are certainly necessary for human action, but they are not sufficient, and therefore other individual as well as social and cultural processes are required in order for human action to emerge. In other words, just as people are constituted by or made up of blood and guts, so too are they constituted by or made up of social and cultural processes. Just as a person cannot function without a brain or without blood coursing through his or her veins, a person cannot function without a system of cultural meanings with which to construct experience, orient him- or herself in the world, or participate in any form of recognizably human action. When it comes to development, a newborn with an intact brain and a particular genetic profile will not develop ways of acting in relation to others without social interaction in a cultural setting.

The second point to make here is that, as parts of a system, biological processes are constituted in part by human action, just as human action is constituted in part by biological processes. Thus, not only do genes and the brain shape human action, but human action (with its individual, social, and cultural constituents) shapes genetic and neurological processes (Gottlieb, 2007; Johnson, 2005; Johnston & Lickliter, 2009; Krimsky, 2013; Meaney, 2010; Wahlsten, 2013; Wexler, 2006). Moreover, with regard to neurological processes, the brain is an organ that develops and is thus not an immovable mover of action (Johnson, 2005). The brain develops in mutual relation to the development of action, meaning that the brain and action mutually constitute each other, as inseparable constituents of a single system. In other words, the brain may enable us to act and develop as we do, but acting as we do, enables the brain to develop.

The claim that there are ongoing interactions between the brain and action is also in keeping with findings about human evolution. For example, it is argued that the brain and functioning within relatively large and complex social groups co-evolved (e.g., Ehrlich, 2000; Gazzaniga, 2011). Thus, it is not simply the case that a larger brain enabled people to engage in increasingly complex social relationships. It is also the case that engaging in increasingly complex social activities contributed to the evolution of the human brain. Taken together, biological processes are forever linked in ongoing interactions with action and have neither priority nor primacy over any of the other processes through which action emerges (Miller & Kinsbourne, 2012). They are all 100% necessary.

Multiple and Interrelated Action Constituents

Thus far, the conceptualization presented here holds that human action emerges out of interrelated individual, social, and cultural processes. In addition, as people act in relation to others in cultural practices, they think for and about themselves, and they make some of their own choices. They feel and express their own emotions. They set and pursue goals. They construct meaning from a subjective perspective, and they try to understand others' perspectives. They believe, value, and desire. Individuals also interact with varied others, and they establish and maintain various kinds of relationships. We have thus come back to psychology's domains of functioning which refer to aspects of behavior that develop.

Although psychologists, including developmental psychologists, tend to treat these domains separately, they are utterly intertwined as people act in relation to others in cultural practices. For different modes of action, different domains may seem more or less salient, but only at first glance. For example, when a child is making an effort to share toys with another child who is upset, perspective taking seems salient. The salience of one or another domain can deceptively lead us back to analyzing domains of functioning in isolation. However, analyzing the domains separately gets us lost in the trees, and we must work to keep the forest in view. By defining what develops in terms of action in relation to others, we are starting with a wider whole that encompasses the usually separate domains of psychological analysis. In the case of sharing a toy to console a friend, cognition is involved as a child might consider different ways to comfort his or her friend. Emotion is involved as the child is aware of the friend's distress and perhaps also starts to feel upset that the friend is upset. Language is involved as the child asks the friend what is wrong and offers words of solace. The two friends are interacting, perhaps by talking in turns and listening to each other. The same can be said of an adult who is acting to help a friend in need. Starting with a wider whole means that we do not have to figure out how to put a person back together after analyzing separate aspects of action in isolation from one another. Instead, we are led to thinking about how action involves varied domains simultaneously. Toward that end, a systems approach again provides a useful theoretical framework for further conceptualizing what develops during development.

Specialized Skills and Knowledge

Before further conceptualizing action, I want to recognize that human functioning also involves what can be viewed as specialized skills and knowledge, such as reading, writing, and arithmetic; hitting balls with different kinds of objects, driving, shaping clay, and running; cooking and hunting; performing surgery, designing apps, and trading stocks; playing musical instruments and composing symphonies—the list can go on and on. Many of these skills further involve specialized physical abilities, which also develop. For example, making bowls out of clay clearly involves the manual skills of manipulating clay and feeling what is happening to the clay. In addition, expert potters and ceramicists enact all kinds of specialized knowledge, including knowledge about the ingredients in different kinds of clay, the chemistry of glazes, and the chemistry and physics of kilns. They can think about what might happen to clay in different circumstances.

School practices revolve around specialized cognitive skills and academic knowledge, and success in formal school settings depends largely on a student's cognitive achievements. Analyzing the development of cognitive skills is in keeping with mainstream psychology's habit of separating domains of functioning, not to mention the long-standing dualistic tradition in Western culture of separating mind and body. Moreover, formal schooling emphasizes decontextualized cognitive abilities, or abilities that are not specific to particular contexts, but are generalizable across contexts. For example, if a student can write a coherent essay in an English class, he or she may be expected to write a coherent essay in a history class. (As it turns out, writing coherent essays in different classes is not a given; we will return to this issue later.) In addition, much of what is learned in school involves preparing students for future activities, especially in work settings where the decontextualized cognitive abilities will be used. However, it is not always immediately apparent to students why they are learning varied skills or how they will apply the cognitive skills learned in school to their adult work activities. In these ways, cognition takes on a life of its own, and it becomes rather easy to treat cognition as a separate domain of functioning.

In cultures where there is little or no formal schooling, children also develop varied specialized skills and knowledge, but they typically do so as they participate with others in practices that support family and community subsistence (Lancy, 2008/2010; Rogoff, 2003). Children as young as 3 or 4 years old may be found gathering wood, sweeping, and running errands. As children show increasing competence, they are held responsible for increasingly complex tasks. In addition, the skills that children are learning are not decontextualized, and children can see their immediate relevance. The skills develop as children engage in the very practices for which those skills will be used throughout their lives.

When both children and adults contribute to their communities in these ways, their specialized skills and knowledge are not independent of their cultural action as individuals in relation to others. As Lave and Wenger (1991/2008) argue, the development of specialized skills whose immediate relevance is obvious is inseparable from becoming a member of a "community of practice" and all the social connections that it entails. It also involves constructing oneself in relation to others and in terms of sociocultural roles. In addition, a community of practice includes "who is involved; what they do; what everyday life is like; how masters talk, walk, work, and generally conduct their lives; how people who are not part of the community of practice interact with it; what other learners are doing" (p. 95). As such, skilled activity and specialized knowledge within a community of practice can be understood as constituents of cultural action in relation to others.

For example, weaving among the Kpelle of Liberia enables a girl to " 'look nice' " and to "match the appearance of women" (Lancy, 1996, p. 154). Weaving may also involve interacting with other weavers, as well as interacting with people when selling one's products. In their classic cross-cultural analysis, Whiting and Edwards (1988) point out that their research assistants in Kenya "remembered from their childhood that to be assigned a chore was to be part of the family, to be important in the mother's eyes. To be overlooked when work was handed out was interpreted as disapproval" (p. 185). Along similar lines, in a Yucatec Mayan village in Mexico, "children like to work. It allows them to feel proud of their competence and includes them in the ongoing social life of the household" (Gaskins, Haight, & Lancy, 2007, p. 192). In Bemni, a Himalayan mountain village, children go at least to primary school and also contribute to sometimes grueling subsistence work. Children there "perceived household and agricultural work to be more meaningful than was schoolwork. . . . The poor standard of government schooling in and around Bemni dampened students' interest in formal education" (Dyson, 2014, p. 59). The work enabled them to engage with peers, gain status in their families and community, and to exercise control over some of their activities.

These examples indicate that when a child is developing specialized skills, he or she is doing so within the wider whole of developing ways of acting in relation to others by contributing to the family's well-being and by participating in the community's practices (Paradise & Rogoff, 2009; Rogoff, 2003). In addition, using and developing specialized skills and knowledge are inseparable from other domains of functioning, as "a learner pushes cognitively, socially, emotionally, and physically . . . to the very limits of mastery and beyond," making for an "alignment of social, cognitive, emotional, and physical" processes (Paradise & Rogoff, 2009, p. 131). In the previous section of this chapter, driving was discussed as an example of action that goes beyond the physical skills of driving to encompass individual, social, and cultural processes. As a mode of action, driving can also be analyzed in terms of varied domains of functioning, including perceiving, thinking, feeling, using symbols, self-presentation, and perspective taking.

Returning to the issue of students' performance in school, we can go overboard in emphasizing cognitive issues because even in formal school settings, the development of specialized academic knowledge and the development of cognitive skills are fully part of acting in relation to others. Indeed, school is not only about academic lessons. It is also about acting in relation to others as students engage with peers and teachers, as well as with their parents about school-related issues. Analyses of group learning sessions in an American kindergarten indicate that much time can be spent in getting children to consider others' perspectives and to follow turn-taking customs (Raeff, 2006b). In addition, research shows that children's school performance is linked to other domains of functioning besides cognition, including self-conceptualization, emotion, and peer interaction (Herrenkohl & Mertl, 2010; Wentzel, 2009). Preschool observations in Japan point to the importance of learning how to get along with others and to work in groups (Peak, 1991/1993; Tobin, Wu, & Davidson, 1989), as well as to the importance of ensuring that all individuals contribute energetically to common activities (Lewis, 1995/1999; White, 1987). Beyond school and beyond childhood, the decontextualized or generalized modes of thinking that are valued among schooled people are also inseparable from other domains of functioning as people act in relation to others in varied cultural practices. For example, in work settings, adults act in relation to others, and their thinking occurs in tandem with self-conceptualization, feeling, and social interaction.

Along similar lines, a study of computer learning among older Korean adults showed that more than cognition and specialized computer skills are involved, as the study participants acted in relation to others in varied ways (Kim & Merriam, 2010). That is, the process of computer learning occurred in a social setting with teachers and other students. Thus, learning to use a computer involved interacting with others, as well as constructing an identity as a member of the class and as a computer user. In addition, some of the study participants reported that learning to use a computer enabled them to connect with their families in new ways, through email and by knowing more about what is of interest to their children and grandchildren.

Taken together, such studies show that when people develop specialized skills and knowledge, it can be viewed as part of developing ways of acting in relation to others, and these modes of action involve varied domains of functioning. Although this book does not focus on specialized skills and knowledge, they are taken to be constituents of action in relation to others that develop. As such, the theoretical framework presented here for thinking about action and development is fully applicable to them as well.

Constituents and More Constituents

From the outset of this chapter, the point that human functioning consists of individual, social, and cultural processes has been emphasized, and it informs the derivation of cultural action in relation to others as the wider systemic whole of functioning that develops during development. An individual's cultural action in relation to others is also conceptualized in terms of multiple and interrelated constituent domains, including but not limited to perceiving, thinking, moving physically, intending, valuing, interacting with others, perspective taking, feeling, using language, and self-construction. Thus, we can now say that individual, social, and cultural factors are constituents of action and that the varied domains just listed are also constituents of action. In addition, these constituent domains are action based and refer to what people do. For example, cognition can be defined through verbs that refer to what people do, such as thinking, knowing, understanding, remembering, and paying attention. Self/identity includes symbolically constructing ways of understanding one's experience and positioning oneself in relation to others. Taken together, there are varied constituents of action, and those constituents also refer to ways of acting, which together make up action in relation to others. There is much potential for confusion here.

To prevent confusion, allow me to repeat some of the basic claims of the larger conceptualization that have been presented thus far and then explain how varied terms will be used throughout the book. This conceptualization holds that it is individuals who act in relation to others in culturally particular ways. Such action is conceptualized as a system, and a system by definition consists of multiple and interrelated constituent and subconstituent processes. But if we refer to all system constituents in the same way we invite confusion, and thus we must make some analytic distinctions among constituent processes. Within any system, there can be different kinds of constituents that serve different functions, and I cannot fathom identifying and explicating the many constituents of action. In order to articulate a theoretical framework for thinking systematically about basic developmental processes, my focus here is on two kinds of constituents.

Insofar as action emerges through or is partly caused by interrelated individual, social, and cultural processes, individual, social, and cultural processes are being treated as "causal constituents" of action. As such, they will be referred to as "causal constituents," or as the individual, social, and cultural processes through which action emerges. I use the terms *individual processes, social processes,* and *cultural processes* to refer to these processes as causal constituents of action and, as we will eventually see, of development as well. Action is also taken to consist of processes within varied and interrelated domains of functioning, including but not limited to moving physically, perceiving, thinking, feeling, intending, valuing, interacting with others, using language, perspective taking, and self/identity construction. These interrelated domains of functioning are what action is made up of, and they represent aspects of action that develop.

A person's ways of moving physically, perceiving, thinking, feeling, inter-acting, intending, valuing, using language, and constructing self-conceptions develop, and thus their development contributes to the wider development of a person's ways of acting in relation to others. Accordingly, the domains of func-tioning can be thought of as "developmental constituents" of action. I considered always referring to them as such, but "developmental constituents of action" or "action constituents that develop" seem rather unwieldy as terms to be used repeatedly in our discussion. As the book proceeds, I will mostly refer to these developmental constituents of action as "constituents of action" or as "action constituents." Unfortunately, there are no ideal terms, and some terms work bet-ter than others within different expository contexts. Thus, I will also sometimes use the terms "domains of functioning" or "domains of action," and sometimes "action domains" and "constituent domains."

These terms are not ideal because one could argue that any system constitu-ent plays some kind of causal role within the system insofar as the constituent contributes to the system's functioning. What I am calling action constituents can contribute causally to modes of action because they contribute to the organ-ization of action. There is thus some overlap between what I refer to as "causal constituents of action" and "action constituents" because both are constitutive of action, albeit in different ways. There is also overlap between causal constituents and action constituents because modes of action, which are made up of action constituents, provide a basis from which an individual acts at any time. As such, action constituents are also constituents of individual processes, which are being conceptualized and referred to as causal constituents of action. Once again, sys-tems are complex and messy, and it can be difficult to pin down a system's varied constituents and their dynamic interrelations. The causal roles that different sys-tem constituents play further depend on how one defines causality, which can be, and has certainly been, defined in varied ways. However, it is not necessary to take up the long history of conceptions of causality at this point.

For current purposes, it is important to remember that causality within a sys-tems perspective refers to how a system's functioning emerges through interre-lations among "ongoing processes intrinsic to the system" (Lewis, 2000, p. 38). The systems conceptualization presented here holds that a person does what he or she does partly because of past experience, but also because of the ways in which individual, social, and cultural processes are structured and interrelated while the person is acting. In other words, individual, social, and cultural processes are ongoing processes that enable us to do what we do and give meaning to what we do. If we want to know why so-and-so did something or what so-and-so's action means, we would discern how individual, social, and cultural processes are struc-tured and interrelated. A description of what the person did or is doing—of the person's action—would involve invoking varied action constituents, such as moving physically, perceiving, thinking, feeling, interacting, intending, valuing, using language, and constructing self-conceptions. Thus, the main distinction between the two kinds of constituents that are the focus of this book is that individual, social, and cultural processes are being used to conceptualize why a person acts in one way or another and what his or her action means, whereas action constituents or constituents of action are being used to conceptualize the domains of functioning that comprise what a person does when he or she acts in relation to others. In addition, action constituents are the constituents whose development is currently being conceptualized. We can now proceed with considering action constituents or constituents of action more specifically from a systems perspective.

Action Constituents

To say that acting in relation to others consists of multiple action constituents is another way of saying that varied action constituents are involved simultaneously any time a person is acting. From a systems perspective, action constituents are further viewed both as distinct and as fundamentally interrelated when a person acts. Thus, the meaning and the function of the action constituents depend on their interrelations and on the wider whole of which they are momentarily parts (Overton, 2010, 2013; Witherington, 2011; Witherington & Heying, 2013). Once again, we come to the key systems premises that the whole cannot be reduced to its constituents, and that the constituents of action do not function independently to produce action. Rather, it is the interrelations among the constituents that comprise the whole, and thus the constituents of action may be structured and interrelated in different ways to comprise different modes of action. Accordingly, "analysis of parts must occur in the context of the parts' functioning in the whole" (Overton, 2013, p. 44).

For example, a person may be thinking about what another person is saying, feeling badly about the other's comments, and considering how best to respond to save face. At another time, a person may be thinking about a friend's feelings and considering how best to respond in order to help that person feel better. In these two examples, an individual is acting in relation to others, and that action involves varied action constituents, including thinking, feeling, valuing, using language, self-awareness, and perspective taking. However, the action constituents are structured and interrelated in different ways to comprise different modes of action—namely, saving face in one case and consoling a friend in another. Thus, the meaning and organization of the action constituents can only be understood as they occur in relation to each other and as constituents of different wholes, or modes of action.

Let us consider another example from the domain of physical movement, within which reaching and grasping are subconstituents. As people act, reaching and grasping are subconstituents of countless forms of action and are executed in relation to each other and other action constituents in different ways for different purposes in different action contexts. For instance, throwing a ball involves reaching and grasping, among other constituent processes. However, as discussed in Chapter 1, reaching for a ball, grasping it, and throwing it when playing baseball are constituents of one wider action system, whereas reaching for a ball, grasping it, and throwing it at someone in anger are constituents of quite another. These examples show how different modes of acting in relation to others involve some of the same action constituents and subconstituents. Yet the organization or structuring of the action constituents differs in relation to the wider action system of which they are momentarily parts.

Conceptualizing action constituents from a systems perspective does not mean that there are no distinctions among constituents to be made. On the contrary: system constituents are taken to be made up of distinct subconstituent processes, and it is readily apparent that domains of action partake of distinct and interrelated subconstituents. For example, cognition or thinking involves multiple and interrelated subconstituent processes. An adolescent may be thinking about his or her college application personal statement, which involves varied interrelated cognitive processes, such as remembering, categorizing ideas into topics and subtopics, and presenting ideas in an organized way. The personal statement may involve comparing and contrasting multiple perspectives on an issue and making judgments about those perspectives in terms of particular criteria. The same goes for an adult writing a personal statement for a job application. To use another example, classic research on Girl Scout cookie sales (Rogoff, Baker-Sennett, Lacasa, & Goldsmith, 1995) shows how cognition in the service of selling Girl Scout cookies involves varied interrelated subconstituents carried out with an "elaborate system of color-coded forms" (p. 49) that have been modified over several generations of Girl Scouts. With regard to cognitive subconstituents, "the layout of the order form is designed to facilitate calculation of amounts of money, presentation of information to customers, and the keeping track of deliveries" (p. 49). In addition, the whole enterprise, from beginning to end, involves planning.

Yet at the same time that action constituents are distinct, they are not only distinct—they are distinct AND inseparable. A systems approach to any particular constituent involves considering how it is inseparable from the other constituents that comprise ways of acting in relation to others. Clearly, writing a personal statement involves language, as does selling Girl Scout cookies. Writing a personal statement for a college or job application involves perspective taking as well, because the statement is being written for others to read. Applying to college or for a job can be an emotional roller coaster ride, ranging from paralyzing self-doubt to energizing euphoria. Writing a personal statement is also a way of defining oneself and presenting oneself to others in a particular light. Selling Girl Scout cookies involves interacting with varied people, including peers, Scout leaders, parents, and customers. Thus, the cognition of selling cookies is inseparable from the social domain of functioning. Rogoff et al. (1995) point out that selling Girl Scout cookies further involves identity issues as girls integrate the sociocultural role of cookie seller into how they think about themselves in different ways. Taken together, girls selling Girl Scout cookies are acting in relation to others, and applying to colleges involves acting in relation to others, as does applying for a job. In all of these cases, the multiple domains of functioning or the multiple constituents of action are inseparably interrelated.

To recapitulate, according to the current theoretical approach, cultural action in relation to others develops during development. Such action emerges through interrelated individual, social, and cultural processes, and such action is also made up of interrelated action constituents or domains of functioning (e.g., moving physically, perceiving, valuing, intending, thinking, perspective taking, feeling, interacting, self/identity). As summarized in Box 2.2, there are varied advantages and implications of this conceptualization of action. Conceptualizing what develops during development in terms of acting in relation to others provides an integrative construct, or unit of analysis, for developmental psychology (indeed, for psychology in general) that makes it possible to think systematically about human functioning as a whole, as well as about basic developmental processes more specifically. That is, one can think about how some studies of action or development within a particular domain of functioning may be linked to findings about action and development within other domains. One can also think about the implications of findings from varied domains for

---

Box 2.2 **Advantages and Implications of Conceptualizing Human Functioning in Terms of Cultural Action in Relation to Others**

- Provides an integrative construct that permits viewing the "trees" of fragmented findings about behavior from the wider "forest" of what people do in relation to others in cultural practices
- Provides a basis for thinking about how action emerges through individual, social, and cultural processes
- Provides a basis for relating findings about one action constituent to findings about other constituents
- Provides a basis for thinking about how action constituents are interrelated to comprise wider modes of action
- Provides a basis for relating findings about development within distinct action constituents to the development of other constituents and to the development of wider modes of action

the wider development of action in relation to others. As such, conceptualizing what develops in terms of cultural action in relation to others offers ways to overcome some of the fragmentation that characterizes so much of psychology as well as developmental psychology, because acting in relation to others is a construct that encompasses varied action constituents that are typically analyzed separately. Action certainly consists of varied distinct constituents which themselves can be analyzed developmentally. Thus, local findings about the development of different domains of functioning are important. However, the systems approach presented here leads to thinking about how the domains function in relation to each other to comprise wider modes of action. It also leads to thinking about the development of action in terms of development within and across the domains. This conceptualization of action further provides a theoretical basis for thinking about action and development in terms of individual, social, and cultural processes. In these ways, action in relation to others provides a view of the trees from the wider perspective of the forest.

The conceptualization of action presented here is compatible with those systems theorists who emphasize conceptualizing and investigating some variant of a person–environment system (e.g., Mascolo, 2013; van Geert & Fischer, 2009; Wapner, 2000). For example, van Geert and Fischer (2009) assert that behavior and development refer to "a person–context assembly throughout the life span" (p. 327). Within a person–context assembly, the person and his or her typical contexts are viewed as inseparable and mutually constitutive. Along similar lines, using the person–environment system as the wider whole highlights the inseparability of the person and environmental processes, whereby "the elements of the person–environment system are inseparable as causal processes in the production of action and experience" (Mascolo, 2013, p. 190). I agree with these conceptualizations, but by talking about cultural action in relation to others, I am trying to emphasize what people do, which entails the claims that what people do emerges out of interrelated individual, social, and cultural processes and is also made up of interrelated action constituents.

In addition to overcoming some of the fragmentation of current developmental psychology, a systems conceptualization of cultural action in relation to others provides a theoretical framework for addressing aspects of behavior and development that people may view as important but that are not readily addressed by conceptualizing the constituents of action separately. For example, in varied cultures there may be expectations that people develop to become productive members of society, good people, successful, self-reliant, happy, autonomous, free, connected to others, and/or responsible. In some cultures, some adults strive to be happy, or successful, or free, or at peace. These goals of development are not easily understood in terms of any one of psychology's separate domains alone, or in terms of a few domains combined additively. Instead, they can be understood in terms of varied domains of functioning operating in relation to each other, as well as in terms of interrelated individual, social, and cultural processes, to comprise cultural modes of acting in relation to others.

When individual, social, and cultural processes are organized in different ways, and when action constituents are organized in different ways, different modes of action can emerge. For example, different modes of action in relation to others include cooperating to achieve a common goal, arguing and fighting, saving face, consoling a friend, teaching, leading, and following. We thus encounter another list of examples of cultural action in relation to others that could get rather long. These modes of action can be particularized in different ways depending on the dynamic vicissitudes of individual, social, and cultural processes, and they also involve different ways of organizing action constituents. Moreover, these and other modes of acting in relation to others *develop*, and so we are ready to think about what happens during the development of action.

Before moving on to conceptualizing what happens during the development of an individual's action in relation to others, some final comments about terminology are in order. In this discussion of what develops, I have talked about the development of acting or action, and I have argued that much of what develops during development is action. At times, I have also used the term "functioning" to refer to what people do and I have also talked about "behavior." Unfortunately, the term "behavior" comes with all kinds of theoretical baggage in psychology. Notably, within the behaviorist framework, "behavior" implies a relatively passive respondent who behaves in reaction to antecedent and independent sources of reinforcement. Because I am seeking a term that encompasses individual, social, and cultural processes all at once, I will use "action in relation to others," "acting in relation to others," "cultural action/acting in relation to others," or simply "action/acting" to refer to what a person does in relation to others in cultural practices. I will use the term "behavior" when talking about scholarship that does not necessarily encompass action as conceptualized here. My use of these terms is in keeping with and builds on those who argue that action is the appropriate unit of analysis for psychology, because the term "action" reflects the position that individual agency and cultural meanings are partly constitutive of what people do (Mistry, 2013). In particular, Bruner argues that "cultural psychology, almost by definition, will not be preoccupied with 'behavior' but with 'action,' its intentionally based counterpart, and more specifically, with *situated action*—action situated in a cultural setting, and in the mutually interacting intentional states of the participants" (Bruner, 1990, p. 19). I have also drawn from the work of James Wertsch, who argues for "mediated action, or 'agent-acting-with-mediational-means'" as the unit of analysis for psychological inquiry (Wertsch, 1998, p. 24) because it encompasses active agency, as well as the cultural means or tools that mediate what people do. He explains further that action is not located in individuals alone, but in the interaction between individuals and cultural tools. Thus, if we ask who did such and such, the response would be "I and the cultural tool I employed did" (Wertsch, 1998, p. 29).

The present systems conceptualization of action focuses our attention on what a person is doing in a particular situation and leads to analyzing the organization, meaning, and function of what a person is doing. It is not so much that cultural practices require certain amounts of action, but rather certain forms or modes of acting. Thus, we are concerned with how individual, social, and cultural processes are structured and interrelated, and with how varied action constituents are structured and interrelated. Focusing on modes of action as defined here also has implications for thinking about basic developmental processes. That is, we are led to thinking about what happens during development by considering changes in the organization of action constituents. We thus now turn to addressing the basic developmental question of what happens during development.

3

What Happens during Development?

The developmental mode of analysis is the only method that can
truly explain the structures and functions of maturing and mature
organisms.

—Gilbert Gottlieb (2007, p. 1)

Now that a theoretical approach to what develops during development has been
articulated, we can conceptualize developmental change and address the basic
developmental question of what happens during development. This chapter
begins with an overview of contemporary developmental psychology's practice
of defining development in terms of age-related change and change over time.
The forest-and-trees issue surfaces again, as the trees, represented by the myriad of findings about age- and time-based change, obscure the wider forest of
basic developmental processes. A discussion of some issues and questions that
arise when studying the trees at the expense of the forest is followed by a presentation of organismic-developmental theory's alternative approach. According
to organismic-developmental theory, development is defined in terms of *certain
kinds of changes*, namely changes that involve differentiation and integration, as
well as progress toward cultural goals of development. To illustrate organismic-
developmental theory more concretely, we will apply it to Piaget's analyses of the
development of understanding object permanence during infancy. Organismic-
developmental theory will also be used to think systematically about a wide range
of research on life span self/identity development.

Developmental Psychology Today

Addressing the question of what happens during development depends on how
one defines development. Indeed, to define development is to make claims about
what happens during development. The term *development* can be and has been
defined in varied ways. For example, if someone says, "Well let's see how he develops," development could include any changes that might happen to a person over

a period of time. If someone says, "This is the way she has developed up until now," development includes the history of what has happened to this person over a period of time. If someone says, "He will develop that ability when he is about 10 years old," development refers to age-related change. If someone, says, "Hopefully, she will develop in that way soon," development involves changing toward a valued goal. As the following quotations from a few contemporary developmental psychology textbooks indicate, it is currently commonplace to define development in terms of age-related change and change over time.

> The science of human development seeks to understand how and why people—all kinds of people, everywhere, of every age—change over time. (Berger, 2012, p. 4)

> [C]hild development [is] an area of study devoted to understanding constancy and change from conception through adolescence. Child development is part of a larger, interdisciplinary field known as developmental science, which includes all changes we experience throughout the life span. (Berk, 2013, p. 4)

> [Developmental science is] the study of age-related changes in behavior, thinking, emotions, and social relationships. (Bee & Boyd, 2010, p. 2)

> [D]evelopmental psychology [is] the field of study that deals with the behavior, thoughts, and emotions of individuals as they go through various parts of the life span. . . . We are interested in the changes that take place within individuals as they progress from emerging adulthood (when adolescence is ending) to the end of life. (Bjorklund, 2015, p. 4)

These quotations imply that the answer to the question of what happens during development is that change happens during development. According to this definition, almost any change in behavior that occurs over time or with age can be considered developmental change, and thus it is not surprising that innumerable studies fill professional journals and books about development. It can be utterly overwhelming to think about how to deal with all the data. How can one ever keep track of all the changes that take place? Is there a way to organize the data? Are development and change equivalent? Is there a way to think systematically about what happens during development? Is there a forest amidst the trees?

One common way to make sense of all the changes that occur over time is to categorize people by age and life-phase. Thus, much of developmental psychology is a catalog of behavior at different ages and during different life-phases. We may find out that 3-year-olds do X, 5-year-olds do Y, and 7-year-olds do Z. Such age-based achievements are often presented as stages. That is, during stage 1, 3-year-olds do X, during stage 2, 5-year-olds do Y, and during stage 3, 7-year-olds do Z. Life-phases refer to larger age-based groups of people whose behavior can be characterized in some similar ways. Infants do A or are in stage 1, children do B or are in stage 2, adolescents do C or are in stage 3, emerging adults do D or are in stage 4, and adults do E or are in stage 5. These life-phases are often subdivided further into early, middle, and late subphases. It is also common to define age-based changes and achievements as well as stages in terms of milestones. When 3-year-olds do X, they have reached a milestone, and then we wait for the appearance of the Y milestone at around age 5, and so on. During early adulthood, people in varied cultures around the world reach the milestone of getting a first job, and then we wait for them to advance professionally during the middle adulthood years.

Classifying changing forms of behavior in terms of stages and milestones that are reached at certain ages can be useful, especially in the context of cultural practices in which people are grouped by age. For example, children are classified and grouped by age in formal school settings, making it important to know about the forms of behavior that are typical for children of varied ages. Age-based norms are useful for classifying some forms of adult functioning as well. Age-based norms for behavior are also useful for classifying developmental problems and for identifying people whose development may go awry. However, grouping people by age is not necessarily a common practice around the world (Rogoff, 2003). Moreover, varied vexing issues arise when development is defined in terms of age- or time-based changes and stages, as well as when development is understood in terms of the milestones metaphor.

Some Vexing Issues

Ages and Stages

As just pointed out above, defining development in terms of age-based change or in terms of change over time leads to describing what people typically do at different ages. One can then discern if there are statistical differences in behavior between age groups. However, I am left wondering what happens in between the ages. If 3-year-olds do X, if 5-year-olds do Y, and if 7-year-olds do Z, what about the 4- and 6-year-olds? What happened to the children's functioning in between X, Y, and Z? What developmental processes occurred along the way? If 25-year-olds do A, if 30-year-olds do B, and if 35-year-olds do C, what happens between 25 and 30, and between 30 and 35? Using age ranges that have no gaps, such as 25–30 years, 30–35 years, and 35–40 years, does not solve the problem. We still need to know about the developmental processes that are occurring within and between the age ranges. A theoretical framework is needed for thinking about the basic developmental processes that are occurring as new forms of action emerge.

Age-based analyses of development are also often directed toward capturing the ages at which varied new forms of behavior appear, or capturing the ages at which a stage of behavior starts and ends. However, such analyses obscure the processes through which the new forms of behavior developed and through which they will continue to develop. What I am suggesting here is that age does not have to be the central criterion for making sense of development. Age can be viewed as a rough correlate of development within particular cultures, but knowing a person's age does not necessarily tell us about the developmental processes that are occurring.

Just as we asked about what happens in between age ranges, we can also ask, what happens in between the stages? What developmental processes occurred along the way as the new forms of functioning, represented by stages, emerged? The very notion of developmental stages has long been a source of debate in developmental psychology. For example, although Piaget is known for his stage theory of cognitive development, stages were not his main concern. His concern with developmental processes is evident in the following statement:

> Why does everyone speak of stages? One tries to construct stages because this is an indispensable instrument for the analysis of formative processes. Genetic psychology attempts to envisage the construction of mental functions, and stages are a necessary instrument for the analysis of these formative processes. But I must vigorously insist on the fact that stages do not constitute an aim in their own right. (Piaget, 1955, p. 817)

In other words, stages typically describe a sequence of new forms of behavior, but they do not necessarily describe the developmental processes that occur as one form of behavior develops out of a previous form and provides a basis for the development of a subsequent form. Thus, we end up with a static catalog of types of behavior, without much insight into what happened in between the stages. According to Fogel (1993), stages serve as "cultural metaphors" for describing behavioral changes "that are normative or expectable at particular ages" (pp. 86–87). He points out: "Stages are, in a word, metaphors for development and not models of the developmental process" (p. 87).

In addition, as people get older, they may undergo all sorts of changes, and it is reasonable to question whether all changes that occur over time are developmental changes. Of course, development involves some kind of change over time. However, if any change over time is considered to be development, then there is nothing particularly significant about the concept of development. When development is lumped together with all kinds of changes, it is unclear why some change is considered to be development, other than that it occurred at a later time. Moreover, if development is any kind of change, then a person whose functioning is deteriorating would be considered to be developing. However, the term *development* usually implies some kind of progress in functioning, and thus it is not applicable to functioning that is deteriorating. Indeed, it would seem rather odd to claim, "My friend is really developing a lot right now. She forgets more and more every day." One might wonder if the person is joking. These points suggest that specific criteria for developmental change need to be identified because development cannot "be read off from the mere facts of change over time, either in the actual social order or in the individual member of a social order" (Kaplan, 1994, p. 5).

To be sure, developmentalists do often qualify statements about age- or time-based change by pointing out that development entails systematic change or orderly change. However, such statements beg the question: Systematic or orderly in what way? Varied criteria could be used to identify systematic or orderly changes in action throughout the life span. A definition of development that explicitly distinguishes development from change, or that specifies how development involves a particular kind of change, could help to clarify the ways in which development is systematic or orderly. Along similar lines, some developmental analyses suggest that behavior becomes increasingly complex over time or with age. However, in order to analyze increasing complexity, there must be some criteria for deciding what counts as more and less complex. A definition of development that specifies some criteria for developmental change could provide a conceptual basis for discerning increasing behavioral complexity.

Intraindividual and Interindividual Variability

Another vexing issue arises in relation to the systems premise that intraindividual variability is a hallmark of human functioning. For example, at any age, a person's action often varies widely across action circumstances, making it difficult to say that the person is in one particular stage of development. People typically function better when engaging in practices that are familiar to them, and people's action may also vary in relation to their physical and emotional conditions. Some children may be well known for melting down at certain times of the day, and as adults, we know how hard it is to perform optimally all the time, especially when we are tired or stressed. In addition, Vygotsky (1978) distinguished between a zone of actual development and a zone of proximal development, to make the point that a person's functioning can vary depending on whether he or she is doing a task independently or with assistance. With assistance in the zone of proximal development, people can typically solve more complex problems than they can typically solve independently in the zone of actual development. At any time during the life span, a person's functioning may be supported in varied ways by others, and others may also sometimes pose hindrances to a person's functioning. Due in part to such intraindividual variability in functioning, it becomes difficult to describe development in terms of a fixed series of linear stages and to claim that a person is in one of those stages at a given time or for a given period of time. In a nutshell, Fischer posits that the organization of functioning fluctuates, and thus people function within a "developmental range," between functional and optimal levels, rather than at a single developmental stage (Fischer & Bidell, 2006; Mascolo & Fischer, 2010, 2015; van Geert & Fischer, 2009; Yan & Fischer, 2002, 2007).

In addition, interindividual variability characterizes development, meaning not only that different people may develop different patterns of acting but also that people may develop similar patterns of acting in individualized ways, or along individualized developmental pathways. For example, Thelen's and Smith's (1994/1996) research shows that the development of reaching may involve varied individual pathways. They describe how one boy's reaching began with vigorous arm flapping, while another child began by moving her arms less energetically. In keeping with the systems principle of equifinality, these different starting points then led the two children along different developmental sequences toward mature reaching. Valsiner (1997) describes how three children experienced different developmental pathways on the way to being able to eat with culturally appropriate utensils. The children's development differed along several dimensions, including initial seating arrangements (high chair or being held by the mother), the extent to which they were allowed to manipulate food and utensils on their own, and the specific utensils that were used along the way (e.g., metal spoon, plastic spoon, fork). Yan and Fischer (2002, 2007) describe how different adults traversed different developmental pathways for learning a statistics program. During adulthood, individuals may reach similar work positions in different ways and at different ages, or they may establish and maintain a long-term committed relationship in different ways and at different ages. Even if varied developmental achievements do sometimes occur at roughly the same ages for many people, cataloging the achievements by age risks obscuring all kinds of potentially interesting and useful information about individual developmental experiences.

Milestones

A *milestone* is literally a stone on a road that marks each mile from a particular starting point. As a metaphor of development, reaching milestones implies that development is set in stone, or rigid, with clear achievements along a single universal route. Although some individual and cultural variability may be acknowledged, people are expected to reach milestones within a certain time frame or age range. The milestones metaphor further implies that people continue doggedly from one milestone marker to the next, without stopping somewhere in between markers, and without going back to previous milestones. However, given that a person's functioning fluctuates, it sometimes appears that a developmental milestone has been reached, only to disappear some minutes, hours, or days later.

Thus, it is argued that "there are no legitimate developmental milestones, stones fixed in the developmental roadway in one position. Instead, there are developmental buoys, moving within a range of locations affected dynamically by various supports and currents" (Fischer, & Bidell, 2006, p. 348).

The milestones metaphor also implies that development entails a series of places to stop along the way. That is, at milestone 1, a person does X, and then goes on to milestone 2 to engage in Y, and then proceeds to milestone 3 to engage in Z. Developmental psychology has mostly focused on those stops (Adolph & Robinson, 2008). While the stops are certainly important and interesting, the journey in between the stops is critical to the traveling experience. Focusing on the stops has led to viewing development in rather static all-or-none terms— either someone has reached the milestone by a certain age or he or she has not. Once again, this approach diverts attention away from the processes that occur during development.

Although the milestones metaphor of development is problematic, I find it difficult to settle on an alternative because no single metaphor can capture all of the complexities of development. Thus far in this book, I have referred to "pathways" a few times, and pathways is my metaphor of choice for the time being. Despite its limitations, I use pathways as a metaphor for development because it gets at some key aspects of development that are being discussed in this chapter and throughout the book. That is, one can potentially traverse different pathways, in different directions, toward different destinations, just as one can develop in different ways to achieve different developmental goals. In keeping with the systems principle of equifinality, it is also possible for different people to reach the same destination by taking different pathways, just as it is possible to reach similar developmental goals in different ways. A person can also go back and forth along pathways, just as one can go back and forth between more and less developed modes of action depending on the vicissitudes of individual, social, and cultural processes. In addition, pathways can be constructed jointly by people as they go, indicating that development is neither predetermined nor the solitary construction of isolated individuals. Pathways are initially roughly hewn and then can become well-trodden, just as developing modes of action become relatively stable through engaging in action itself. Even if a person tends to stick to one pathway or set of pathways, sometimes the person may veer off the usual route to take another one. Similarly, a person may act in relatively stable ways, and his or her development may be canalized along some routes rather than others, but variability is also endemic to human action and development. The pathways metaphor is compatible with the forest-and-trees idiom I have used to present the current theoretical framework because there are networks of pathways in forests around the world. As such, pathways are organized in relation to a wider whole, just as action constituents that develop are organized in relation to the wider whole of cultural action in relation to others. In addition, there can be major pathways, with connecting paths along the way, just as modes of action are made up of multiple constituent and subconstituent processes that are interrelated in varied ways.

Age and Time as Causes of Development

Another issue that arises when defining development in terms of age-based stages and milestones concerns the basic developmental process of how development happens. The term *change over time* implies that the passage of time is the main cause of change. The term *age-related change* implies that age is the main cause of change, or that development happens simply because a person gets older. However, as already suggested, not all changes that occur over time or with age are necessarily developmental changes. In addition, developmental psychology is replete with research showing that human development is caused by a wide range of complex processes, including genes, the brain, social interaction, education, socioeconomic status, and culture. Thus, developmentalists clearly recognize that development does not occur simply due to the passage of time or to getting older. We will address the basic developmental process of how development happens more specifically in Chapters 6 and 7. First it is necessary to explicate what happens during development beyond age- or time-based change. Then conceptions of what happens during development can be synthesized with conceptions of how development happens.

Organismic-Developmental Theory

A conceptualization of development that provides theoretical tools for thinking about development in terms of ongoing and dynamic processes that may or may not occur as a person gets older and/or as time passes can be found in organismic-developmental theory, which was articulated by Heinz Werner, an Austrian who lived from 1890 to 1964. Werner completed his doctoral studies at the University of Vienna in 1914, and he accepted a position at the University of Munich in 1915. He then held several positions in Germany until 1933, when, amidst the tumult of Hitler's rise to power, he immigrated to the United States. Werner worked at several American institutions, including Clark University, from 1947 to 1960, and was a prolific scholar. The presentation of organismic-developmental theory here is not meant to be an exhaustive summary of Werner's scholarship. Rather, the goal is to discuss some central theoretical claims that can be used for thinking systematically about what happens during the development of action.

As Kaplan (1967) explains, the "organismic" in organismic-developmental theory "has sometimes been used as a synonym for 'holistic', sometimes as an equivalent of 'systemic'" (p. 75). Thus, this approach to development is in keeping with the fundamental systems premises that inform the current theoretical approach to thinking about action and basic developmental processes. More specifically, organismic-developmental theory's "holistic assumption is opposed to any view that would treat an element (for example, a movement, a momentary experience) as if it possessed a fixed structure and meaning, irrespective of the whole or context of which it is a part" (Werner & Kaplan, 1963/1984, p. 4). Organismic-developmental theory is also compatible with the view that action consists of multiple and interrelated constituents. For example, Werner and Kaplan point out that perception is not an isolated domain of functioning but occurs in conjunction with other domains. They write: "On the level of perceptual apprehension of events, one does not always look on with affective or evaluative indifference; inherent in much of our perception is our feeling about the happenings in which we participate" (Werner & Kaplan, 1963/1984, p. 405).

Insofar as action is understood in terms of the organization of multiple and interrelated action constituents, development minimally involves changes in the structuring of action constituents as well as in the interrelations among action constituents. However, as pointed out earlier, it is problematic to equate development and change, and thus organismic-developmental theory holds that the term *development* be reserved for certain kinds of changes.

Development and Cultural Meanings

Given the prevalence of the view that development refers to change over time or age-related change, let us expand on this move to distinguish between development and change. In particular, before delving into organismic-developmental theory's criteria for developmental change, let us first consider a common connotation of the word *development*.

It is readily acknowledged that development minimally involves changes that occur over time. However, all of human functioning takes place over time. Even uttering, writing, or reading a single sentence takes place over time. People may experience all kinds of changes as time passes, and it is reasonable to ask whether all of those changes count as development. If development and change are the same, why do we need the term *development* at all? With regard to child development, Kaplan points out that "we want our children to develop, and we don't mean merely that we want them to change" (Kaplan, Josephs, & Bhatia, 2005, p. 145). The same can be said of adult development. Consider changes over time that are characterized as regression and deterioration. Is a person developing if his or her functioning is somehow regressing or deteriorating? As indicated earlier, it would seem odd if someone considered a person's failing memory to be developmental change. Regression and deterioration imply that the occurring changes are distinct from developmental change. Furthermore, we do not want people to regress or deteriorate, but we do want them to develop. Regression and deterioration imply that a person is moving away from some goal or some standard of action, whereas the term *development* connotes progress in relation to some expectations, or movement toward a desired goal. For example, referring to countries as "developing nations" implies that those nations are improving in some way, such as economically. In other words, "the process of development, in contradistinction to the process of mere change, is a movement towards perfection, as variously as that idea may be construed" (Kaplan, 1983b, p. 57).

Thus, one key to understanding developmental change is to recognize that the word *development* connotes some kind of improvement or progress in functioning in relation to some standard. During early development, the adults in children's lives—from parents to teachers to psychologists—keep track of children's development, but not in a vacuum. The assessment tools used by professionals to assess children's development revolve around varied cultural standards and expectations. Adult development can also be assessed in relation to cultural standards and expectations. In therapeutic settings, people's functioning is assessed in relation to cultural standards and expectations, as one can only discern if a person's functioning has gone awry in some way if there is some standard for assessment. It is also argued that in one way or another, "all successful psychotherapy functions by promoting developmental changes in patterns of acting, thinking, and feeling in order to meet adaptive challenges" (Basseches & Mascolo, 2010, p. 23). Adaptation always occurs in relation to a particular environment or context, which for human beings involves cultural meanings, including cultural standards and cultural expectations for ways of acting. It is also important to point out that counselors and therapists are not the only ones whose work is informed by and reflects developmental expectations and standards. Theory and research in developmental psychology reflect cultural meanings, as well as the (often implicit) values and assumptions of individual developmentalists (e.g., Burman, 1994; Kaplan, 1983b, 1986). Even in cultures where using standardized tests or other psychological assessments is not the norm, a person's development is still meaningful in relation to some cultural standards. More generally, discussing developmental standards and expectations is certainly not the exclusive purview of professional counselors and psychologists, as people construct developmental standards and expectations as they go about their lives in all corners of the world.

Cultural meanings regarding development, including standards for action, as well as expectations or goals for development are complex and dynamic and can be understood in terms of varied dimensions. Some developmental expectations may be relatively explicit, while some may be "dimly held or vaguely apprehended" (Kaplan, 1983b, p. 59). Some developmental expectations may be relatively general, and others relatively specific. In part because some cultural expectations for development are relatively general, development sometimes occurs in ways that people could not have predicted or even imagined in advance. For example, even though there may be some general cultural developmental expectations, such as having a job or getting married, people sometimes end up in jobs or relationships they did not foresee. Identity development also occurs in relation to cultural identity options, even though the content and sequence of a particular person's identity development cannot typically be specified in advance. In addition, general developmental goals can be particularized in different specific ways. Although some aspects of what happens during development cannot be specified in advance, development is not completely arbitrary, in part because it is played out with reference to some cultural meanings and developmental expectations. From a systems perspective, cultural meanings and developmental expectations can be understood as attractors. As attractors, cultural meanings and expectations may shape some of the broad contours of individual development, while simultaneously allowing for variability in people's individual developmental experiences.

A can of worms is being opened up here because standards of improvement, ideas about progress, and conceptions of developmental goals vary widely within and across cultures (Valsiner, 2011). In a nutshell, they are highly contested phenomena, and people's developmental experiences vary around the world, in part because of different ideas about goals of development within and across cultures. Within the current theoretical framework, I assume that all people are separate individuals and also connected to others in one way or another. Thus, everyone acts in relation to others, and such action develops. However, what it means to be a developed individual in relation to others or to engage in developed modes of action is also culturally contingent. For example, for adults in some cultures a goal of development is to choose one's own life partner, whereas in other cultures the goal is to enter into an arranged marriage. There are also different cultural conceptions of the life span, and thus one finds different cultural goals of development for people considered to be in different life-phases. For example, "unlike in Western societies, in traditional India, during the last phase of life, many Brahmin men leave the family in search of spiritual fulfillment" (Mascolo & Fischer, 2010, p. 170). With regard to child development, the proliferation of research since the 1980s on parents' beliefs, values, and goals is consistent with the position that development is tied to cultural meanings and conceptions of development. A vast amount of research shows that parents in different cultures construct varied ideas about children's development, reflecting cultural beliefs, values, and guidelines for behavior (e.g., Goodnow & Collins, 1990; Harkness & Super, 1996; Harkness et al., 2011; LeVine, Miller, & West, 1988; Ochs & Shohet, 2006; Raeff, 2000, 2003; Raghavan, Harkness, & Super, 2010; Sigel, 1985; Sigel, McGillicuddy-DeLisi, & Goodnow, 1992).

Considering developmental expectations and standards is further complicated in that conceptions of developmental goals reflect cultural values and assumptions, which are linked to issues of power and authority in varied ways. Within specific action circumstances, different goals may be privileged by different people who may wield power in different ways within those circumstances. Within cultures, some expectations and standards that are associated with power, authority, and a dominant majority may be resisted and even defied by those in subordinate or minority positions (Turiel, 2003, 2008; Turiel & Perkins, 2004; Turiel & Wainryb, 2000; Wertsch, 1998). Developmental expectations and standards are thus contested constructions that are subject to debate, negotiation, conflict, and sometimes violent strife.

In part because developmental expectations and standards are contested, they are subject to ongoing construction and reconstruction, and therefore, cultural conceptions of development change historically. For example, in some cultures, the practice of arranged marriages is on the decline. During the years of writing this book, defining what counts as a marriage in the United States underwent rather intense discussion and reconstruction. An obvious example of changing cultural goals of development can be found in gender-role expectations. Conceptions of male and female development have changed dramatically in the last century in varied parts of the world as women pursue education and jobs and as men are increasingly involved in child care.

Conceptualizing development in relation to cultural meanings is also a can of worms because the claim that development is linked to goals and expectations has unfortunately sometimes been misunderstood as meaning that development is a given in the nature of things, or that development follows an innate sequence toward some predetermined universal endpoint. However, the claims made thus far about cultural aspects of developmental expectations indicate otherwise. Insofar as developmental expectations and standards are taken to be human cultural constructions that are dynamic and contested, they are not being conceptualized as universal or as innately predetermined. If development were viewed as predetermined, it would make no sense to claim that development occurs in relation to changing cultural expectations, because we do not know in advance how cultural meanings will change or what new developmental expectations will be constructed.

In addition, development is not taken to be universally predetermined because conceptions of development are also subject to individual processes, as people construct ideas about development from their subjective or individual perspectives. And in some cultures it is a cultural goal of development to set, pursue, and achieve one's own goals. As people construct or set goals for their own development, one person's fulfillment may be another person's misery. Individual goals may be compatible with cultural conceptions of development, and they may also sometimes reflect resistance to, or even defiance of, cultural conceptions. Furthermore, a person's goals for his or her own development are inseparable from social processes, as the goals are constructed in relation to others.

Taken together, development is not being conceptualized here as predetermined, because developmental goals are considered to emerge through often unpredictable interactions among individual, social, and cultural processes. Moreover, insofar as goals emerge through individual, social, and cultural processes, new goals can always be constructed, and if constructing new goals is an emergent process, goals of development cannot be predetermined or known in advance. The claim that new goals can be constructed also means that developmental goals are not being conceptualized here as endpoints of development. Endpoints connote finality and imply that there are no possibilities for further development to occur. In contrast, the theoretical approach presented here holds that achieving a developmental goal is not equivalent to the end of development. Further goals can be constructed, and development can continue to occur in relation to other goals and meanings.

The claim that development is relative to varied and contested cultural meanings may be vexing to many, because it means that thinking about what happens during development involves thinking about complicated, controversial, and intractable cultural issues with sociological, economic, ethical, and political dimensions. Rather than throwing our hands up in frustration, we can first recognize that this predicament facilitates understanding some of the ways in which culture shapes development. Moreover, the frustration can also be overcome by viewing this predicament as liberating because it means that human development is fraught with possibilities. The same point applies when we recognize that development occurs in relation to individual goals. Insofar as development happens in relation to cultural and individual goals, we can strive for varied goals, partly of our own making, for ourselves and for people in our care. At the same time, the claim that developmental goals are neither predetermined nor absolute does not mean that anything goes because people are constructing goals that reflect values and standards. The complexities of and differing perspectives on values and standards will not go away, but they can be acknowledged, identified, and discussed as people construct and reconstruct goals of development.

Identifying goals of development is also critical for empirical analyses of what happens during development and provides a way of injecting some systematicity into thinking about and analyzing basic developmental processes. Witherington and Heying (2013) explain that positing developmental goals provides "meaningful contexts in which to embed the understanding of a phenomenon at any given time" (p. 171). Without some idea of a developmental goal, one cannot begin to identify developmentally relevant changes in action (Mascolo, 2013; Overton, 2006, 2010). As such, goals of development provide a way of identifying the wider organizational whole in which action at a particular time of analysis is embedded. For example, say you are trying to analyze the development of sharing. Without some idea of what it means to share and what counts as appropriate sharing, it would be hard to know where to begin analyzing relevant changes in sharing. Once developmental goals or standards have been identified, it becomes possible to analyze the developmental changes that occur as people progress toward them. With regard to sharing, some research suggests that the development of sharing is played out differently in relation to different cultural expectations during early childhood (Mosier & Rogoff, 2003). For middle-class European-American families, sharing between young children includes taking turns with a toy for equal amounts of time. For children in a Guatemalan Mayan community, sharing is more likely to involve figuring out how to play with a toy together. These expectations for sharing provide a basis for identifying the action constituents that undergo development. That is, if a goal of development is for young children to share with others by taking turns or by playing together, then action constituents must be organized in ways that make a particular mode of sharing possible. In turn, the development of sharing can be analyzed in terms of the changing organization of action constituents, which enable new modes of sharing to emerge. According to organismic-developmental theory, development is defined more specifically in terms of certain kinds of changes in the constituents of action. The specific changes that comprise development were articulated by Werner, in collaboration with Bernard Kaplan, in terms of the orthogenetic principle, to which we now turn.

The Orthogenetic Principle

The orthogenetic principle of organismic-developmental theory provides criteria for identifying developmental change by conceptualizing development in terms of particular changes in the organization of action. According to the orthogenetic principle, *developmental change* refers to changes that involve moving "from a state of relative globality and undifferentiatedness towards states of increasing differentiation and hierarchic integration" (Werner & Kaplan, 1963/1984, p. 7). To differentiate means to make distinctions among phenomena and to integrate means to coordinate phenomena. With regard to action in general, *differentiation* refers to the distinctions that can be made within and among action constituents, as well as to the refinement of action constituent functioning. In general, *integration* refers to the ways in which action constituents and subconstituents are connected.

Defining development in terms of differentiation and integration focuses attention on pathways of differentiation and integration within and across action constituents. For example, as already pointed out, grasping is a motor subconstituent of many complex forms of human action. Werner observes that initially grasping is characterized by a lack of differentiation and integration among constituents as "legs, hands, mouth, and feet are all used in the movements of grasping" (1940/1980, p. 200). Analyses of grasping within the context of eating suggest that a child's use of fingers to get food into the mouth is differentiated out of a more global manual and oral exploration of food (Valsiner, 1997). In other words, young children seem to enjoy "playing" with their food. From the perspective of organismic-developmental theory, when it looks like children are "playing" with their food, they are approaching the food in a global or undifferentiated way. They may also lunge toward the food with their whole upper bodies, and they may repeatedly plunge their whole hands into a bowl of food. They may succeed in grasping a morsel, only to let it drop out of their hands and watch intently as it falls to the floor or stare at their empty hands. Some research shows that seated 6-month-olds begin reaching toward food in front of them by rotating the shoulder to lift the hand, suggesting that lifting the hand is not differentiated from global arm movement (Sacrey, Karl, & Whishaw, 2012). They also do not open and extend their fingers or shape them in preparation for grasping as adults do. Young infants' ways of reaching for food are further described as "jerky" (Sacrey, Karl, & Whishaw, 2012, p. 548), which suggests a lack of integration among the subconstituents of reaching. Differentiation among action constituents can also include refining or improving action constituents and subconstituents, which in turn allows them to be integrated into new forms of action (e.g., Fischer, 1980). For example, as finger movements are increasingly refined and integrated, children can pick up and hold onto pieces of food of varying sizes and textures. Eating with utensils, from forks, to spoons, to chopsticks is made possible by further finger movement refinement and integration and may occur at any time during the life span.

The study of symbol formation, especially language development, is central to Werner's theory and research (Werner & Kaplan, 1963/1984), and language development involves differentiation and integration in varied ways. With regard to speaking, undifferentiated crying is differentiated into distinct forms of crying that may indicate different conditions, such as hunger or pain. Vowel and consonant sounds are differentiated and integrated as babbling and then as full-fledged words, which are initially used to convey global meanings. As a child's understanding of the meanings of words is increasingly differentiated, he or she also integrates words to construct more complex meanings. Language use develops well beyond early childhood as word meanings continue to be differentiated and as words are integrated to form new meanings while acting in relation to others.

In the quoted definition of the orthogenetic principle, development involves differentiation and *hierarchic* integration. Hierarchic integration means that previous forms of action do not simply disappear with development. Rather, they are reorganized as subsystemic constituents of new forms of action. As such, we encounter another kind of system constituent, namely a mode of action that serves as a subconstituent process of another mode of action. For example, grasping is a motor domain subconstituent that is integrated with other constituents to comprise varied forms of action, such as eating, or throwing a ball when playing baseball or throwing a ball at someone in anger. In keeping with contemporary systems theory, "any given form is both a whole in itself—a system in its own right—and a part of another whole—a component comprising another system" (Witherington, 2007, p. 149).

As a kind of corollary to the orthogenetic principle, organismic-developmental theory posits further that development can be understood in terms of several continuous and interrelated dimensions, including diffuse/global—articulated, labile—stable, and rigid—flexible. Action that is relatively undifferentiated and unintegrated is characterized by diffusion/globality, lability, and rigidity. Action that is relatively differentiated and integrated is characterized by articulation, stability, and flexibility. Many of the examples of differentiation and integration discussed earlier are also examples of movement along the diffuse/global–articulated dimension. For instance, differentiated or articulated grasping develops out of globally moving one's whole body toward an object, and articulate language develops out of global or diffuse vocalizing. Lability along the labile–stable dimension refers to a fragile or fluctuating organization of functioning, in contrast to stability, which involves consolidating ways of acting. As development occurs along this dimension, it is not necessarily a matter of moving from not being able to act in some way to being able to do so. It is more a matter of stabilizing the way in which a form of action is carried out as the constituents of action are differentiated and integrated. Within the organismic-developmental framework, stability is not equivalent to rigidity, because there is also movement along the rigid–flexible dimension, whereby increasingly differentiated action constituents and subconstituents can be assembled or integrated in varied ways to act in specific circumstances. In other words, "multiple means become available for the achievement of a particular goal, and multiple goals can be served by a single means" (Glick & Zigler, 2005, p. 326). Human language use is a prime example of flexible functioning, as the same words are integrated in different ways to construct different meanings, and similar meanings can be constructed through the integration of different words.

Intraindividual Variability and the Genetic Principle of Spirality

Organismic-developmental theory also posits the genetic principle of spirality, whereby sometimes less differentiated and integrated forms of action than a person is capable of characterize a person's functioning. The spiral metaphor connotes dynamic movement, meaning that any particular way of acting can be organized in more or less developed ways at different times. The top of the spiral represents more developed modes of functioning relative to the bottom of the spiral, and sometimes action is organized at the top of the spiral, sometimes at the bottom, and sometimes in between. As Werner and Kaplan put it, for varied reasons, and in varied ways, "experience is organized simultaneously at various psychogenetic levels" (Werner & Kaplan, 1956/1978, p. 95). This claim is in keeping with contemporary systems theory's conceptualization of intraindividual variability, which points to different forms and sources of intraindividual variability or spirality. For example, as discussed earlier, variability in functioning can be related to a person's physical or emotional condition. Indeed, children (and some adults) are notorious for falling apart or melting down when they are tired or hungry. Even without a complete melt-down, stress is certainly related to less than optimal functioning at any time during the life span. People's action can also vary across contexts, and thus it is not so surprising that a student who can write a good paper in an English class may not be able to do so in another class. At times, there can even be variability in a person's functioning in the same context. Indeed, we all have off days. As a dynamic system of dynamic processes, human action is a moving target (to use another metaphor). Thus, developmental variability or spirality is as essential to human functioning as are consistency and stability.

There can also be variability or spirality in functioning during the overall course of developing new modes of action. Systems research shows that the development of new modes of action is nonlinear, meaning in part that deterioration in functioning can accompany progress toward some desired goal (Fischer & Bidell, 2006; Mascolo & Fischer, 2015; Thelen & Smith, 1994/1996; van Geert & van Dijk, 2002; Yan & Fischer, 2002, 2007). Organismic-developmental theory also explicitly recognizes that development does not necessarily proceed linearly. In connection with the genetic principle of spirality Werner and Kaplan point out that there can be "a partial return to more primitive modes of functioning before progressing towards full-fledged higher operations" (Werner & Kaplan, 1963/ 1984, p. 8). It is not unusual for some deterioration to occur prior to development because the current mode of functioning has to be "partially dissolved" before the constituents can be differentiated and integrated into a new mode of functioning (Kaplan et al., 2005, p. 139). This conceptualization of spirality means that periods of developmental change can be interspersed with periods of nondevelopmental change. Although development is being conceptualized in terms of certain kinds of changes, organismic-developmental theory fully recognizes that other forms of change occur and that differentiation and integration are not inevitable. Defining development in terms of differentiation and integration specifies the types of changes that count as developmental change, and it provides a way to distinguish developmental change from nondevelopmental change. Once such distinctions are made, it becomes possible to identify when different kinds of changes occur, as well as to discern links between developmental and nondevelopmental change processes.

To briefly summarize some key points, within a systems framework, the development of action involves changes in the structuring of action constituents, as well as changes in their interrelations. However, it is problematic to equate development with any change that may occur over time or as a person gets older. Thus, we turn to organismic-developmental theory, in which development is defined in terms of the differentiation and integration of action constituents in relation to cultural goals, expectations, standards, and meanings more generally. As a corollary to the orthogenetic principle, development further involves movement along the continuous dimensions. In addition, organismic-developmental theory posits the genetic principle of spirality, which means that people may function in more and less developed ways, depending on the exigencies of particular circumstances.

It is important to point out that differentiation and integration were not picked out of a hat willy-nilly as criteria for developmental change, and there are several ways in which they are not arbitrary criteria for defining development. First, differentiation and integration are logically entailed within a systems approach. By definition, a system is made up of interrelated parts, and interrelatedness includes integration. And, if there are parts that can be integrated, the parts must be distinct or differentiated in some ways.

Second, I start from the position that being a distinct individual and being connected to others are fundamental to human experience and that individuality and connectedness are understood and played out in culturally particular ways. Thus, even though the details of what it means to act as an individual in relation to others may differ around the world, people are, by definition, simultaneously distinct or differentiated individuals, as well as connected to or integrated with others. Already at birth, all human beings are separate or differentiated individuals, and they certainly cannot survive, much less develop, unless they are connected to or integrated with others in some way. As such, differentiation and integration are logically entailed in our current conceptualization of action in relation to others.

The third way in which differentiation and integration are not arbitrary criteria for defining development is that differentiation and integration are fundamental life processes and thus hold up to empirical scrutiny. Indeed, "everywhere in life, there are tendencies toward fragmentation, partition, separation, division, multiplicity: The Many. Everywhere in life there are countervailing tendencies toward wholeness, constancy, synthesis, identity, unity: The One" (Kaplan, 1967, p. 84). For example, every human being starts out as a single-cell zygote, which undergoes rapid division or differentiation into more cells, forming a blastocyst, which differentiates into three layers, which differentiate into body parts and organs, which become integrated. Brain functioning is typically characterized in terms of structural and functional differentiation as well as neural connections or integration. As fundamental life processes, differentiation and integration can be understood as potentially universally applicable, yet they also refer to processes that can be instantiated in culturally particular ways. At the same time that differentiation and integration are viewed as fundamental life processes, they are not being viewed as inevitable or predetermined. They may occur, and they may occur frequently, but they do not always occur. A task for developmentalists is to discern if and under what conditions differentiation and integration occur and do not occur.

Finally, one can find the terms *differentiation* and *integration* and various synonyms, such as "refined" and "articulated" for differentiation and "coordination" and "connected" for integration, sprinkled about in developmental scholarship. In addition, statements about behavior becoming increasingly complex, organized, and/or coherent during development can be found in research reports. In one way or another, each of these terms (complex, organized, coherent) takes us to differentiation and integration. According to *Webster's New Collegiate Dictionary*, something complex is "a whole made up of complicated or interrelated parts," or something "in which the constituents are more intimately associated than a simple mixture." To organize means to "integrate; to arrange elements into a whole of interdependent parts." And cohere means "to consist of parts that cohere; to become united in principles, relationships, or interest." The use of these terms suggests that issues of differentiation and integration are highly compatible with a wide range of developmental research. By explicitly defining development in terms of differentiation and integration, the approach presented here brings implicit assumptions out of the shadows and into the foreground.

Organismic-Developmental Theory and Science

Before illustrating organismic-developmental theory more concretely, let us consider some issues regarding the theory's status as a scientific theory. I delve into this issue because a reason that organismic-developmental theory has largely been abandoned by developmentalists is that it is sometimes at odds with commonly held views about what scientific theories are supposed to do and it challenges some conventional research practices in psychology and developmental psychology (Glick, 1992; Siegler & Chen, 2008). Whether one considers organismic-developmental theory to be a bona fide scientific theory depends on how one defines a theory, as well as on how one defines science. Within the context of conventional scientific practices in psychology, there are two key criteria for a theory: 1) that it generate hypotheses that can be falsified or refuted with counter evidence and 2) that it enable researchers to predict behavior.

A key to understanding organismic-developmental theory is that it was designed to offer a non-age-based definition of development. Another key to understanding organismic-developmental theory is that Werner and Kaplan did not assume that development-as-differentiation-and-integration necessarily occurs as people get older or as time passes. On the contrary, Kaplan explained that by distinguishing "the meaning of development from the actualities of life" the orthogenetic principle "freed us from the specious supposition that changes with age were necessarily or intrinsically developmental" (Kaplan, 1983a, p. 195). Because one cannot assume that development occurs over time or with age, this definition of development was designed to provide a way of discerning IF people develop over time, or "whether development is present in a given data set" (Lerner, 2011, p. 37). The orthogenetic principle can be used to identify goals of development in terms of distinct and integrated constituents, to discern if individuals undergo differentiation and integration in relation to those goals, and to discern if different people undergo different sequences of differentiation and integration. As such, defining development in terms of differentiation and integration "was unabashedly recognized as an heuristic concept, serving to order phenomena from the most diverse domains" (Kaplan, 1983a, p. 195). Specific analyses of sequences of differentiation and integration then depend on the particular phenomenon under scrutiny (Glick, 1983). With this definition of development, organismic-developmental theory can be understood as constituting a perspective, or a way of looking at phenomena (Kaplan, 1983a; Lerner, 2011). That is, one can look at some phenomenon from a developmental perspective to discern if and in what ways it has undergone differentiation and integration in relation to some goals. However, by offering a preconceived or postulated heuristic construct, organismic-developmental theory's status as a scientific theory is unclear (Glick, 1983).

Organismic-developmental theory's status in relation to the falsifiability principle is ambiguous, because as "an heuristic concept" the orthogenetic principle is not stated in a way that is readily falsifiable. Nevertheless, one way to falsify or refute defining development in terms of differentiation and integration would be through instances of people achieving cultural goals of development without undergoing differentiation and integration. Identifying instances of changes that do not involve progress toward cultural goals or expectations would not count as evidence against this definition of development, nor would identifying instances of changes that do not involve differentiation and integration. Indeed, as pointed out earlier, Werner and Kaplan fully recognized that differentiation and integration are not inevitable during ontogenesis and that other kinds of changes occur. Rather than falsifying the definition, examples of changes that do not involve differentiation and integration would be viewed as nondevelopmental change, and they actually point to the importance of being able to distinguish among different types of change. Using an analogy, consider the definition of a square as a closed object with four sides of equal length and four equal angles. Although there are many other shapes in the world, those other shapes do not refute the definition of a square; they are simply not squares according to that definition. The existence of different kinds of shapes in the world points to the importance of being able to distinguish among them. Varied definitions of varied psychological phenomena have been offered, from intelligence to happiness, to love, to identity, and there can be considerable debate about how to define these phenomena. One can accept or reject a definition for varied reasons, as some definitions may be more problematic or limited than others and different definitions may be more or less useful for varied purposes. Thus, falsifiability is not the only criterion for assessing the utility and advantages of a definition of development (or of any psychological phenomenon).

It is possible that in some cultures or for some people, some goals of development may not involve increasing differentiation and integration of action constituents. For example, it might be considered highly developed to view oneself as wholly indistinguishable from some other creature or being. In this case, development might proceed from viewing oneself as differentiated from others to not differentiating oneself from a particular other being. Such cases would call into question the universal applicability of defining development in terms of goals that involve increasing differentiation and integration of constituent processes. Nevertheless, the definition of development can still be useful for exploring and making sense of development in a wide range of circumstances. As we will see in subsequent sections of this book, organismic-developmental theory enables us to think systematically about development in varied cultures in ways that preserve their cultural specificity, while simultaneously illuminating some common human developmental processes.

Defining development in terms of differentiation and integration has many advantages (see Box 3.1 for a summary of these advantages). One advantage is that it enables us to think about what happens during development from the vantage point of the forest without getting overwhelmed by the myriad of changes that may occur to people as they get older. By defining development in relation to cultural meanings, organismic-developmental theory orients us toward cultural dimensions of development. Defining development in terms of differentiation and integration enables us to distinguish among different types of change, which in turn provides a basis for discerning how different kinds of change may be linked. As constructs, the processes of differentiation and integration are widely applicable to varied phenomena yet can simultaneously be flexibly tailored to the particulars of those varied phenomena. For example, the orthogenetic principle can be applied to varied constituents and modes of action, as well as across cultures. It can be applied beyond individuals to couples, groups, and organizations; to economies and countries; and beyond humans to plants, trees, and animals. One can always analyze any changing phenomenon to discern if differentiation

---

Box 3.1 **Advantages of Organismic-Developmental Theory's Definition of Development: Differentiation and Integration in Relation to Cultural Meanings**

- Provides systematic criteria for understanding and analyzing developmental change
- Provides a systematic conceptual basis for distinguishing among different kinds of change (e.g., development, regression, deterioration)
- Provides a systematic way of analyzing development as a process that occurs in between ages, stages, and milestones
- Disentangles development and age
- Links development to cultural processes
- Applicable across individuals, action contexts, and cultures
- Applicable to any phenomenon that may develop, such as individuals, groups, institutions, economies, countries, ecosystems, and animals

and integration are occurring or have occurred. Conceptualizing development in terms of differentiation and integration also provides a way of thinking systematically about and analyzing the ongoing processes of development that occur in between ages and in between the emergence of new forms of action. The definition further enables us to disentangle development from age altogether.

With regard to the prediction criterion, organismic-developmental theory's status is also not straightforward. The orthogenetic principle is not formulated or articulated in a way that offers predictions about particular developmental sequences for any particular domains of functioning. Werner himself pointed out that the orthogenetic principle is not meant to be predictive (e.g., Werner, 1957). Not offering specific predictions about development is actually in keeping with organismic-developmental theory's systems origins. From a systems perspective, development is characterized as a process of "probabilistic epigenesis," meaning that development cannot be predicted exactly, because system processes can be assembled in varied ways that are often unknowable in advance (Ford & Lerner, 1992; Gottlieb, 1991, 2007; Gottlieb, Wahlsten, & Lickliter, 1998). Nevertheless, the advantages of defining development in terms of differentiation and integration are not negated by the lack of specific predictions.

Even though organismic-developmental theory was not designed to predict development, it can be and has been used to predict some developmental sequences. For example, Siegler and Chen (2008) argued that the differentiation and integration constructs help to specify the goals of development required for varied cognitive abilities. They then used the constructs to predict possible sequences for the order in which children use different rules to solve an unfamiliar physics problem involving water displacement. In addition, the genetic principle of spirality leads to predicting that deterioration in functioning occurs before developmental changes occur, and some systems research supports this claim (Fischer & Bidell, 2006; Mascolo & Fischer, 2015; Thelen & Smith, 1994/ 1996; van Geert & van Dijk, 2002; Yan & Fischer, 2002, 2007).

Even though predicting behavior is a valued practice in mainstream psychology, which is steeped in "the" scientific method of the natural sciences, predicting does not have to be treated as absolutely essential to all psychological inquiry (Ohlsson, 2010). Rather than thinking of science only in terms of "the" scientific method, there are varied ways of doing science and of studying human beings scientifically (e.g., Billig, 2013; Shotter, 1975; Toomela & Valsiner, 2010). Science can be defined partly in terms of making claims based on systematic or reasoned evidence. Insofar as organismic-developmental theory provides a framework for systematic empirical analysis of development, it can be considered scientific. Defining development in terms of differentiation and integration provides a systematic basis for analyzing development, because the definition is derived from a systematic conceptualization of human functioning as a whole that is made of up multiple and interrelated parts. In conjunction with the current theoretical approach to action, it also provides consistent constructs for systematically figuring out the particular changes to analyze when analyzing development. That is, we are first led to analyzing modes of action in terms of action constituents, and then to analyzing differentiation and integration within and across those constituents.

In addition, what can be thought of as a scientific attitude involves questioning truth claims based on tradition or convention or because they are handed down by authorities. By defining development in terms of particular kinds of change, organismic-developmental theory provides a systematic conceptual basis for questioning the conventional definition of development in terms of change over time or age-related change. With regard to the goals of scientific psychology, we can also question whether prediction is always necessary for scientific pursuits. As Bruner (1990) puts it,

> if we take the object of psychology (as of any intellectual enterprise) to be the achievement of understanding, why is it necessary under all conditions for us to understand in advance of the phenomena to be observed—which is all that prediction is? (p. xiii)

It is thus critical not to conflate predicting with either explaining or understanding, which can be viewed as central goals for psychology as an intellectual and scientific enterprise. We do not have to be able to predict future events in order to understand and/or explain current or past ones. Rather, understanding and explaining involve accounting for what happened and why it happened, or for what is happening and why it is happening. The current theoretical framework enables us to understand and think about the development of action by accounting systematically for what happens during development in terms of differentiation and integration between and among action constituents. And, as we will soon see, this theoretical framework also provides a systematic basis for explaining and understanding how such development-as-differentiation-and-integration occurs.

Starting to Apply Organismic-Developmental Theory

To illustrate organismic-developmental theory more concretely, we now consider some specific examples of how differentiation and integration can be played out. We first look at Piaget's classic analyses of the development of understanding object permanence during infancy from an organismic-developmental perspective. We will then also use organismic-developmental theory to think systematically about a wide range of research on self or identity development during childhood, adolescence, and adulthood.

A Classic Example: Object Permanence

There is much debate about how to characterize the development of understanding object permanence, with some research suggesting that such understanding is already evident in 3-month-olds (e.g., Baillargeon, 2004). However, these findings are subject to alternative interpretations and do not necessarily indicate that young infants have achieved the goal of full-fledged object permanence as defined by Piaget (Haith & Benson, 1998; Kagan, 2008a; Lourenco & Machado, 1996). Piaget himself was concerned with the process of development that occurs in relation to the goal of understanding that objects exist independently of one's own action and in terms of spatial, temporal, and causal relations. The classic tests of object permanence are to observe what a child does when an object is taken away and hidden—first just in one place, then over several visible displacements, and finally over several visible and invisible displacements. If the child searches for the object in the last location, it is assumed that he or she understands that the object still exists, or is permanent, even though it is not accessible to the child's direct sensorimotor activity. Such searching also indicates some awareness of physical causality and how objects relate to each other in space, independently of the child's own sensorimotor activity.

The point here is to consider how understanding object permanence involves undergoing the ongoing processes of differentiation and integration toward achieving a stipulated goal. Piaget did not conceive of object permanence as a concept that an infant does not understand and then does fully understand at a particular age. As he put it, the object is "constructed little by little" (Piaget, 1954/1986, p. 2). More specifically, Piaget identified a six-stage sequence of transformations in the development of understanding object permanence that parallels his conceptions of infant cognitive development more generally.

It is interesting to note that Piaget (1954/1986) himself recognized the utility of understanding development in terms of differentiation and integration. He wrote:

> These global transformations of the objects of perception, and of the very intelligence which makes them, gradually denote the existence of a sort of law of evolution which can be phrased as follows: assimilation and accommodation proceed from a state of chaotic undifferentiation to a state of differentiation with correlative coordination. (p. 397)

In his analyses of the development of constructing objects, Piaget emphasizes increasing differentiation between objects and one's own sensorimotor activity. At the same time, this development also involves differentiating among locations, understanding objects in relation to each other, and integrating differentiated means to search for an object. Insofar as the focus of the upcoming analysis is on cognition in relative isolation from other constituents of action, I will use the terms *activity* and *act*, rather than *action*, to refer to what infants do with objects. A summary overview of Piaget's analyses of object permanence is given in Box 3.2.

Box 3.2 **Overview of Piaget's Analyses of the Development of Object Permanence**

STAGES I AND II—NO SPECIAL BEHAVIOR RELATED TO VANISHED OBJECTS

- Sensorimotor manipulation of objects when they are encountered
- Recognizing familiar objects because they set in motion previously used sensorimotor acts
- Baby is globally aware that objects are permanent by repeating sensorimotor acts just used with an object and/or staring at the location of an object's disappearance
- Integration of sensorimotor acts

STAGE III—BEGINNING OF PERMANENCE EXTENDING MOVEMENTS OF ACCOMMODATION

- Continued use of previous stage's patterns
- Initial differentiation between sensorimotor activity and objects as baby searches visually for an object where he or she expects it to appear within the immediate visual field
- Differentiated manual searching for objects within arm's length

STAGE IV—ACTIVE SEARCH FOR VANISHED OBJECT BUT WITHOUT TAKING ACCOUNT OF SEQUENCE OF VISIBLE DISPLACEMENTS

- Differentiation between activity and objects as baby searches for a hidden object that is displaced once
- Differentiating and integrating varied means to search for a hidden object, such as looking, reaching, grasping, and lifting a cloth

STAGE V—CHILD TAKES ACCOUNT OF SEQUENTIAL DISPLACEMENTS OF OBJECT

- Further differentiation between sensorimotor activity and objects as children search for objects in the last location of a sequence of visible displacements

---

STAGE VI—REPRESENTATION OF INVISIBLE DISPLACEMENTS

- Full differentiation between sensorimotor activity and objects as children search for objects that have undergone some invisible displacements
- Integration by understanding objects in relation to each other

---

According to Piaget, during the first two stages, there is "no special behavior related to vanished objects" (1954/1986, p. 3), as infants react to objects that are immediately accessible to sensorimotor activity by looking at, listening to, and feeling objects when they are encountered. Repeated sensorimotor activity on objects leads to recognizing them as familiar, because they set in motion "the sensorimotor schema which was previously constructed for [their] use" (p. 5). This kind of recognition is "not dissociated from the action itself and put in a context of spatial and causal relations independent of the immediate activity" (p. 5). In other words, objects are not known separately from or are not differentiated from sensorimotor activity. Therefore, a child can only "know" an object through sensorimotor acts, such as touching, grasping, seeing, hearing, or sucking. During the course of these first two stages, the infant is globally aware of "the periodic disappearance of objects" (p. 99) by repeating the sensorimotor acts that he or she had just carried out in relation to an object (e.g., grasping, sucking) when it disappeared. Or a baby might stare at the location where an object was last seen with what Piaget took to be an expectant look. However, because there is no differentiation between objects and the baby's own sensorimotor activity, the baby "merely preserves the attitude of the earlier perception and if nothing reappears, he soon gives up" (p. 10). In addition, during the course of these stages, ongoing integration is occurring between sensorimotor acts or schemes, such as between seeing and hearing, when "the child tries to look at the objects he hears" (p. 6).

During the course of the third stage, "beginning of permanence extending the movements of accommodation," a child continues to engage in the patterns just established during the first two stages. In addition, these patterns are extended as a child starts to expect "future positions of the object and consequently endows it with a certain permanence" (p. 13). Overall, Piaget describes the third stage as one in which

> the present behavior patterns merely extend those of the second stage but reveal essential progress: the child no longer seeks the object only where he has recently seen it but hunts for it in a new place. He anticipates the perception of successive positions of the moving object and in a sense makes allowance for its displacements. (p. 18)

As such, some very basic initial differentiation between objects and one's own sensorimotor activity is occurring, but it remains quite limited in relation to the ultimate goal.

More specifically, rather than only staring at the location where an object was just seen, a child is figuring out where an object will end up when he or she sees it fall and thus searches visually for it around the location where the child expects it to appear. For example, Piaget observes that when his son, Laurent, drops an object himself, "he searches for it next to him with his eyes" (p. 14). Subsequently, Laurent moves on to visually searching "on the floor for everything I drop above him, if he has in the least perceived the beginning of the movement of falling" (pp. 14–15). However, when he drops something outside of the immediate visual area, Laurent returns to the reactions of the previous stage. For example, Piaget describes his son's reaction when he "loses a cigarette box which he has just grasped and swung to and fro" (p. 23) and the object ends up "outside the visual field" (p. 23):

> [Laurent] brings his hand before his eyes and looks at it for a long time with an expression of surprise, disappointment, something like an impression of its disappearance. But far from considering the loss as irremediable, he begins again to swing his hand, although it is empty; after this he looks at it once more! For anyone who has seen this act and the child's expression it is impossible not to interpret such behavior as an attempt to make the object come back. Such an observation . . . places in full light the true nature of the object peculiar to this stage: a mere extension of the action. (p. 23)

In this case, Laurent returns to repeating the sensorimotor activity that was just used with the object, namely swinging his hand to and fro. Laurent seems to expect that such activity will make the object appear, because object and sensorimotor activity are fused or undifferentiated. This example also points to the genetic principle of spirality, or intraindividual variability, insofar as Laurent can search visually for objects that fall within the immediate visual vicinity, but he returns to earlier patterns when visual searching does not immediately yield the object.

As the third stage proceeds, children increasingly engage in manual searching for fallen objects, but manual searching is initially independent of visual searching. In other words, visual searching and manual searching are highly differentiated and they await integration. As was the case for visual searching, children search manually for objects only around the location where they expect an object to be and when that location is within arm's length. For example, when Laurent drops the cigarette box another time, "he is satisfied to stretch out his arm in order to find it again, or else he stops searching altogether" (p. 23).

Differentiation between object and sensorimotor activity continues, and during the fourth stage, there is "active search for the vanished object but without taking account of the sequence of visible displacements" (p. 48). Children now actively search for hidden objects without recourse to the acts just performed in relation to them, and thus there is more marked differentiation between objects and their own activity. In addition, children's searching involves integrating visual and manual searching. They are also differentiating among and integrating varied means to search for an object, as in the case of lifting a cloth under which someone has just placed an object, reaching for the object, and retrieving it. However, even as the child notices multiple displacements, "the object remains dependent on its context and not isolated in the capacity of a moving body endowed with permanence" (p. 72). Thus, children will successfully search for an object that has been displaced once, but not over several displacements, because they rigidly link the object with one particular location. From an organismic-developmental perspective, the development of understanding objects can thus also be understood along the rigid-flexible continuum.

Subsequently, during the fifth stage, "the child learns to take account of the sequential displacements perceived in the visual field" (p. 73), and children increasingly search for objects in the last location of a sequence of visible displacements. This kind of searching reflects the increasing differentiation of objects from particular locations. Full differentiation between sensorimotor activity and objects occurs during the course of the final stage, as "the child becomes capable of constructing objects when the displacements are not all visible" (p. 87). Ultimately, a child

> henceforth imagines the whole of the object's itinerary, including the series of invisible displacements. Thus it can be said that the object is definitively constituted; its permanence no longer depends at all on the action itself but obeys a totality of spatial and kinematic laws which are independent of the self. (p. 92)

Objects are now understood as stable and fully differentiated from one's own activity. In addition, flexible means can be used to find objects in different locations.

This brief summary of Piaget's analyses indicates that new ways of apprehending objects involve ongoing differentiation and integration during infancy. Within the context of organismic-developmental theory, trying to pinpoint the earliest manifestation of object permanence, or trying to pinpoint the age at which object permanence is achieved, misses the point that the development of any form and constituent of action involves ongoing differentiation and integration. Early but partial manifestations of object permanence understanding do indeed occur, but Piaget treats them as part of a cumulative developmental process toward an identified goal. Using the differentiation and integration constructs as criteria for developmental change provides a way to systematically analyze the ongoing developmental processes that occur on the long way to full-fledged understanding of object permanence. It is interesting that Piaget often states that children seem to be in between stages, that there is not a single point at which they move from one stage to another, and that boundaries between stages are not always clear-cut. Rather than treating such variability as problematic measurement error, and rather than trying to categorize children's activity in terms of one stage at a time, Piaget's analyses of development emphasize the ongoing and dynamic processes that occur in between phases or stages.

In addition to providing tools for thinking systematically about what happens in between stages and phases of development, organismic-developmental theory can be used to synthesize and think systematically about aspects of action that have been the topics of a wide range of disparate studies in developmental psychology. We now turn to some of the wide-ranging and often disparate research on self or identity development.

Bringing Disparate Data into Coherence: Self/Identity Development

The self is one of psychology's most vexing topics. It has been and continues to be defined in varied ways, from varied perspectives. In addition, there is an abundance of theory and research on identity that often overlaps with an abundance of self scholarship. It all fills volumes, with studies of self and identity development comprising many of those volumes. The point here is not to delve into a comprehensive consideration of how the self and identity have been conceptualized and investigated but rather to apply the orthogenetic principle and use it as a way to enter into the morass of research on self and identity development. For current purposes, I will use the terms *self* and *identity* interchangeably. I start from the position that people engage in self-constructing activities, including thinking about and symbolically constructing their lives, experiences, and perspectives, as they go about their days acting in relation to others (Raeff, 2010b). Rather than considering a single stage or phase theory of self-construction, we can use the orthogenetic principle to synthesize findings from varied studies (with mostly American participants) that involve asking people to describe themselves or to provide a verbal account of their lives. A summary overview of self/identity development in terms of differentiation and integration can be found in Box 3.3.

When asked to describe themselves, young children typically do so in terms of multiple concrete characteristics, including their physical characteristics, specific interpersonal relationships, and particular abilities (Damon & Hart, 1988; Harter, 2012). A child will typically present all kinds of information about him- or herself, and one is hard-pressed to find connections among the varied statements. Similarly, when asked to tell stories about their lives, young children often string together fragmented bits of information (e.g., Fivush, Habermas, Waters, & Zaman, 2011; Habermas & de Silveira, 2008; Reese et al., 2011). In addition to a lack of integration between and among bits of information about oneself, the bits of information are relatively global or undifferentiated. That

---

Box 3.3 **Overview of Differentiation and Integration during Self/Identity Development**

- Unintegrated and global self-descriptions

- Starting to integrate concrete self-characteristics into wider categories
- Increasing differentiation and integration of events and themes into wider self-stories with plots
- Increasing differentiation of self and others by describing oneself in comparison to others

---

- Starting to differentiate positive and negative self-characteristics and integrating them in relation to contexts
- Temporal/chronological and causal integration of events within self-narratives
- Increasingly differentiated accounts of motives and subjective experience within self-narratives
- Differentiated definitions of oneself in relation to different people

---

- Integrating self-characteristics into wider abstract categories
- Resolving subjective distress about conflicting self-characteristics by integrating differentiated ways of being in relation to differentiated contexts and people
- Resolving subjective distress about conflicting self-characteristics by integrating differentiated ways of being in relation to normative standards

---

- Continuing to differentiate and integrate self-characteristics in relation to new roles and practices
- Continuing to differentiate and integrate self-narratives temporally and thematically

---

- Differentiating and integrating self-narratives in terms of wider emotional themes
- Differentiating self from others and integrating self with others by reminiscing
- Differentiated use of irony in self-narratives and integrating irony with other narrative means

---

is, young children do not typically articulate details about themselves because stated characteristics "are seen as sufficient in themselves" (Damon & Hart, 1988, p. 59). For example, in response to the question "What kind of person are you?" a participant in Damon's and Hart's research claimed to have blue eyes. When asked, "Why is that important?" the child said, "It just is." (1988,

p. 59). Children often explicitly say that they do not know why some stated self-characteristic is important.

During the course of childhood and adolescence, self-constructing activities undergo ongoing differentiation and integration in varied ways. For example, research suggests that the fragmentation just described gives way to "a rudimentary ability to intercoordinate concepts that were previously compartmentalized" (Harter, 2012, p. 51). Rather than only listing varied concrete self-characteristics, children increasingly integrate several characteristics to form a wider category of concrete characteristics, such as "knowing letters, words, and numbers" (Harter, 2012, p. 51). Within children's stories about their lives, events and themes are more clearly articulated or differentiated. For example, in addition to providing some basic facts about an event, children include more information about why they themselves and other people did what they did. Children also increasingly integrate distinct events and themes into an overarching story plot (Fivush et al., 2011). Differentiating oneself from others is apparent, as children increasingly describe themselves in comparison to others (Damon & Hart, 1988). Yet children's self-descriptions typically maintain a rather rigid quality that Harter refers to as "all-or-none-thinking" (Harter, 2012, p. 51). That is, children are reluctant to describe themselves in terms of opposite characteristics, such as good and bad, at the same time. According to Harter, children "may acknowledge that they might be bad at some earlier or later time" but there is a "persistence of self-descriptions laden with virtuosity" (2012, pp. 51–52).

Ongoing development occurs as children integrate concrete self-characteristics into "higher-order generalizations" or increasingly abstract characteristics, such as claiming to be smart because they do well in different subjects at school (Harter, 2012, p. 61). In addition, Harter's research shows that children more flexibly acknowledge that they can be both smart and dumb, or outgoing and shy, or happy and sad, but in different contexts. As such, positive and negative self-characteristics are considered separately and thus remain differentiated from one another, as a child is likely to deny being both smart and dumb, or sad and happy in the same situation. However, this kind of differentiation occurs in conjunction with some connection or integration between self-characteristics and contexts. Thus, there is more integration than in the earlier self-conceptions described above, which involved only possibly acknowledging negative characteristics in past or future circumstances. Harter (2012) argues further that this way of constructing opposing characteristics in relation to context prevents children and young adolescents from viewing themselves as inconsistent, so that opposing self-characteristics are not a source of subjective distress or conflict at this time.

With regard to linking events over time, children increasingly construct "reasonably temporally ordered" self-narratives, which suggests that there is a chronological ordering, or integration, of differentiated events (Reese et al., 2011, p. 433). During adolescence, earlier and later life events are further connected causally, suggesting increasing integration of causality and chronology within a wider self-narrative. In addition, when describing salient life events, adolescents' narratives are increasingly detailed and differentiated in terms of "psychological considerations of motives and subjective reverberations of experience" (Fivush et al., 2011, p. 331). Differentiation and integration continue insofar as adolescents increasingly define themselves differently in relation to varied others, including "father, mother, close friends, romantic partners, and peers, as well as the self in the role of student, on the job, and as an athlete" (Harter, 2012, p. 76). Adolescents are also increasingly likely to think about how their stated self-characteristics affect relationships with varied others, and not only in terms of how they compare to others (Damon & Hart, 1988).

Self-construction can be difficult for some during the course of adolescence. For example, as just discussed, adolescents view themselves differently in relation to varied others. As adolescents reflect on other people's often different perspectives, they sometimes struggle to integrate those varied perspectives. In addition, viewing oneself as different with different people and viewing oneself in terms of opposing self-characteristics may become sources of subjective distress and conflict (Harter, 2012). This issue is typically resolved as adolescents integrate differentiated ways of being in relation to differentiated contexts and in relation to differentiated people. Adolescents are also increasingly likely to integrate opposing ways of being in terms of abstract self-characteristics. For example, viewing oneself as "both introverted and extroverted can be integrated through the construction of a higher-order abstraction that defines the self as 'adaptive.' The observation that one is both depressed and cheerful or optimistic can be integrated under the personal rubric of 'moody'" (Harter, 2012, p. 121). Additionally, adolescents are increasingly likely "to normalize potentially contradictory attributes," as in the following example from Harter's research: "It wouldn't be normal to act the same way with everyone. You act one way with your friends and a different way with your parents. That's the way it should be" (2012, p. 121). Self-constituents are thus connected to or integrated with values and standards for action.

This brief overview indicates that as youngsters leave adolescence, they are constructing verbal accounts of their lives, experiences, and perspectives that are differentiated and integrated along several dimensions. Subsequently, self-construction continues to be an ongoing and dynamic process that involves further differentiation and integration. In varied cultures around the world, what has come to be known as emerging adulthood represents a time of serious and intense self or identity exploration (Arnett, 2000), and it is not always smooth sailing, as "uncertainties, fluctuations, reversals, and see-saws mark young people's lives" (Shulman, Feldman, Blatt, Cohen, & Mahler, 2005, p. 599).

Some research in Israel suggests that there are several "types of emerging adults," characterized by the differing ways "in which they portrayed themselves and understood the changes that they had undergone and were still undergoing" (Shulman et al., 2005, p. 589). The "low integrated" type "did not have clear ideas

about their lives and careers or studies that they pursued," and "difficulties in relationships with significant others were quite common" (p. 589). The "authentic
and competent" type exhibited "a subtle and sensitive perception of themselves
and others." They were able "to present themselves in a coherent manner," marked
by "incorporating different aspects of their personality into a cohesive and integrative view of themselves" (p. 590). The "acting competent/low authenticity"
types "presented a contradictory description of themselves," which "raised some
questions as to the extent to which their accomplishments are consolidated and
authentic" (p. 591). From an organismic-developmental perspective, the first and
third types ("low integrated" and "acting competent/low authenticity") may be
viewed as ways of organizing one's identity that are less differentiated and integrated, relative to what seems to be considered the ideal standard of the second
type ("authentic and competent"). Thus, rather than characterizing emerging
adults in terms of one type, it would be of interest to discern if and how their
self-constructions reflect different types at different times. Then one could identify pathways of differentiation and integration toward cultural expectations
for self-construction. Interestingly, the researchers themselves point out that
the third type "may reflect rather a transitory stage. Reading a number of cases
suggested that possibly these young people are still in a process that has not yet
been completed" (Shulman et al., 2005, p. 592). Insofar as self-construction is an
ongoing process, it can be analyzed developmentally with the tools of organismic-
developmental theory. Moreover, one can also question if self development is ever
completed.

Indeed, during adulthood, self-construction may undergo further differentiation and integration as people encounter new situations and take on new social
roles. As people navigate the often unexpected and sometimes overwhelming
vicissitudes of life, they may struggle to maintain ways of constructing themselves, and they may struggle to construct themselves in new ways. For example,
adults' ways of constructing experience may seem relatively fragmented and/or
undifferentiated compared to other times in their lives. Research suggests that
dealing with conflict among self-characteristics recurs, especially during times
of transition, and thus this process is not settled once and for all during adolescence (e.g., Bell, Wieling, & Watson, 2005). What may be going on is that being
able to resolve the experience of conflicting self-characteristics in different ways
develops during adolescence (as explained earlier). Then, as people face conflicting self-characteristics during adulthood, they do not necessarily immediately
proceed to such developed resolutions, nor do they immediately develop other
ways of resolving identity conflicts. In keeping with the principle of spirality
or variability, they may initially deal with such self-conflicts in less developed
ways, and a hint of spirality during adult self development is evident in some
research. For example, Reese et al. (2011) explain that adults' self-narratives are
more developed than those of children and adolescents with respect to providing

information about context, connecting events chronologically, and articulating themes. They then point out that "contextual and chronological coherence both appear to dip in mid-life" (p. 450). Nevertheless, new ways of differentiating and integrating experiences into a wider self-narrative may emerge subsequently.

Also with regard to spirality, a study of members of an Indian diaspora in the United States indicates that "the events of 9/11 made many Indians rethink their place in the American culture and the implications these events had for their acculturation and identity" (Bhatia & Ram, 2009, p. 143). At the time of September 11th, the Indian participants in this research were mostly professionals living middle- to upper-middle-class American suburban lives, and they readily identified themselves as "white-American" (p. 145). However, after September 11th, "suddenly and quite dramatically, they moved from a comfortable sense of belonging to an uneasy state of being an outsider and a threatening one at that" (p. 146). They were defined by others as potential threats because of their looks, especially their dark skin color. For them, race was being marked as an aspect of identity in new ways, and some participants struggled to integrate their new status into their identity constructions. In this way, their identities were "suddenly destabilized and held up for reexamination" (p. 147). One participant appeared to express a global sense of discomfort and what were once coherent, stable, and articulated identity constructions seemed to be disintegrating and labile.

Some research suggests that identity construction during old age is characterized by globality and disintegration. That is, in comparison to younger adults, older adults (ranging in age from 50 to 85) describe important past events less specifically, and they are less likely to indicate how events are integrated into their overall identities (Singer, Rexhaj, & Baddeley, 2007). However, other research with older adults in naturalistic settings suggests that developmental change continues to occur. For example, analyses of conversations among three female friends (ages 76, 84, 85) indicated that they did indeed sometimes provide numerous specific or differentiated details about past events when common knowledge was not assumed (Underwood, 2010). When common knowledge was assumed, the women were less likely to provide spatial and temporal details, but they differentiated and integrated parts of the story in relation to wider emotional themes. In addition, the women used reminiscing as a means for constructing themselves favorably in relation to each other and sometimes in contrast to younger generations. Such reminiscing is a way of drawing attention to their memory abilities, as well as a way to differentiate themselves from some people and to coordinate with others. Some research also indicates that older people may make increasing use of irony as a means to organize "the disparity of viewpoints and the multiplicity of meaning within the stories of our lives" (Randall, 2013, p. 167). As such, using irony may serve some as a newly differentiated self-construction device that can be integrated with other means for constructing self-narratives that involve differentiated and integrated viewpoints and meanings.

This brief overview of a wide range of research points to the utility of organismic-developmental theory for bringing disparate data into coherence. By defining development in terms of differentiation and integration, we have some consistent criteria for thinking systematically about the developmental changes that may occur during the life span, for any mode and constituent of action. In this discussion, although age and life-phase were mentioned a few times, neither age nor life-phase was the central organizing criterion for thinking systematically about self/identity development. Rather, the focus was first and foremost on the differentiation and integration that occur, and life-phases were used to provide a general indication of the time spans and people involved.

The examples given in this chapter illustrate the overall claims of organismic-developmental theory, but for constituents of action in relative isolation. We now turn to thinking about the development of action in terms of differentiation and integration within and across multiple and interrelated action constituents.

4

Thinking about the Early
Development of Action

Nothing will come of nothing.
—Shakespeare, *King Lear*, Act 1.1

The main goal of this chapter is to illustrate how to think systematically about what happens during the development of action during infancy and early childhood by synthesizing and applying the theoretical claims presented in previous chapters. The theoretical framework presented thus far starts with the forest of human functioning as a whole and claims that much of what develops during human development is cultural action in relation to others. This conceptualization also holds that the development of action occurs in relation to cultural standards and goals, and it involves differentiation and integration within and across action constituents. Insofar as research in developmental psychology has been dominated by analyzing action constituents separately, we can say more about development within constituents of action than we can about the ways in which they are interrelated during development. Nevertheless, we can think systematically about and explore how the development of action involves varied constituents simultaneously.

This chapter draws on studies of middle-class families in the United States, with whom much research in developmental psychology has been conducted. Issues regarding what happens during the development of action in other parts of the world will be considered in Chapter 5. The focus here is on infancy and early childhood, because the development of action is conceptualized in terms of the ongoing, cumulative processes of differentiation and integration. Action does not develop out of nothing, and thus a good place to start thinking systematically about development is with the action that is possible at birth. It is certainly acknowledged that such action also does not come from nothing. It is based on prenatal development, but it is beyond the scope of the book's analysis to delve into prenatal development. Clearly, action also develops beyond infancy and early childhood, and subsequent chapters will include material pertaining to what happens during the development of action beyond these life-phases.

In this chapter, we will emphasize the development of action when children are interacting with adults, especially their caregivers. Much research on parent–child interaction during infancy and early childhood involves asking parents to interact with their children as they would typically, without trying to complete particular tasks (e.g., feeding, bathing). This research has resulted in a wealth of information about development in what can be understood as play contexts, which are central action contexts for middle-class European-American children and parents. Although most of the discussion here is about the development of action during play with caregivers, some research on action beyond play situations will also be mentioned. Some issues regarding the development of acting in relation to peers are raised at the end of the chapter.

Acting in Relation to Caregivers

The analysis of what happens during the development of acting in relation to caregivers is organized in terms of "periods," and each period is characterized by a mode of action that is emerging. More importantly for each period, I will also attempt to describe the differentiation and integration of action constituents that occur during the course of each period. Thus, this chapter's presentation of periods is meant to describe the *ongoing dynamics* of developmental processes, rather than serve as a catalog of static modes of action. Box 4.1 presents highlights of each period's mode(s) of action, as well as highlights of the ongoing differentiation and integration that are occurring throughout the periods.

The sequence of developmental periods posited here is not meant to represent the definitive sequence of action development during infancy and early childhood. Rather, it represents one way of synthesizing a wide range of classic and contemporary research in terms of the current theoretical approach to action and in terms of organismic-developmental theory. The periods include some developmental changes for some, but not necessarily all, modes of action during infancy and early childhood. In addition, the five periods provide a relatively macrolevel or general view of the differentiation and integration that happen during the development of action in relation to adult caregivers. Although this discussion focuses on the broad contours of typical action development, it is recognized that every individual's development is worked out in particular ways, as particular individuals engage with particular others in particular circumstances. The theoretical approach discussed thus far can certainly be applied to discerning what happens during the development of other modes of action in other cultural practices, as well as to discerning the development of action along a microlevel to macrolevel continuum. We will consider some of these applications when discussing implications and future research directions in Chapter 8.

Box 4.1 Overview of Action Development during Infancy and Early Childhood

I. BEGINNING FOUNDATIONS: GLOBAL ACTION IN RELATION TO OTHERS

- Ways of Acting
  - Ceasing crying when soothed by others
  - Erratic imitating
- Ongoing Differentiation and Integration
  - Differentiating physical comfort and discomfort
  - Differentiating among people in terms of sight, sound, smell, and nursing position
  - Differentiating physical self-awareness and physical awareness of self with others
  - Differentiating and integrating bodily/physical movement

II. ESTABLISHING AND MAINTAINING MUTUAL ATTENTION

- Ways of Acting
  - Sustained face-to-face interaction
- Ongoing Differentiation and Integration
  - Differentiating and integrating varied sensorimotor means to establish and maintain interaction
  - Differentiating positive and negative feelings (pleasure–displeasure)
  - Differentiating being attended to and not being attended to by others
  - Integrating positive and negative feelings with being attended to or not
  - Differentiating and integrating cognitive action constituents
  - Differentiating some purposes for being attended to by others (e.g., mutual attention, fatigue, hunger)

III. JOINT ATTENTION: COMMON TOPICS AND ROUTINES

- Ways of Acting
  - Engaging with others about common topics
  - Engaging with others in routines (e.g., peek-a-boo; give and take an object)
- Ongoing Differentiation and Integration
  - Differentiating and integrating acting on objects and acting in relation to people
  - Differentiating and integrating events and roles within routines
  - Differentiating new means for establishing mutual attention and integrating them with previously developed means

IV. ESTABLISHING AND MAINTAINING A COMMON ACTION ORIENTATION

- Ways of Acting
  - Engaging with others beyond the immediate action context
  - Complying with caregiver demands
  - Directing and following another's attention
- Ongoing Differentiation and Integration
  - Differentiating awareness of others' attention
  - Differentiating means and object of pointing
  - Differentiating and integrating words
  - Differentiating and integrating action procedures and action standards
  - Differentiating and integrating awareness of one's own and another's goals

V. NAVIGATING AND NEGOTIATING PERSPECTIVES

- Ways of Acting
  - Monitoring one's own action in relation to absent others
  - Globally explaining one's own action to others
  - Teasing
  - Negotiating common goals and meanings with others
- Ongoing Differentiation and Integration
  - Differentiating and integrating one's own and others' perspectives

Insofar as development occurs in relation to cultural standards and expectations, we begin the discussion with a brief overview of some cultural expectations for acting in relation to others by the end of early childhood, which is when children in the United States start going to school. By this time, children are generally expected to focus on structured activities, pursue goals, and follow sequential instructions, as well as follow basic social standards or rules of conduct, such as taking turns. There are expectations for children to take on different roles (e.g., tagging and avoiding being tagged, hiding and seeking) and to coordinate different roles when they play together. In varied contexts, children may be expected to express themselves verbally, get along with others, cooperate with each other to achieve common goals, and resolve at least some of their own conflicts.

Acting in these ways involves interacting with others by establishing common topics of attention and attuning to what others are doing. It involves considering others' perspectives, as well as constructing and expressing one's own perspective. Such action involves cognition, including making decisions, as well as setting goals and figuring out how to achieve them. It is also fraught with emotions. Clearly, such action is constituted through language as well. Taken together, multiple and interrelated constituents of action comprise cultural ways of acting in relation to others.

I. Beginning Foundations: Global Action in Relation to Others

We begin analyzing neonatal action by considering how some action constituents are organized from the outset to comprise global action in relation to others. Then we will think about the differentiation and integration that occur during the first few months of life that enable infants to move on to acting in relation to others by establishing and maintaining mutual attention.

At birth, newborns are separate and distinct individuals who require others for survival and development. Thus, some individuality and some connectedness characterize infant functioning from the outset. Newborns cry when they experience physical discomfort, indicating that they are differentiating between a global subjective sense of physical comfort and discomfort. At the same time that crying is an automatic or reflexive way of experiencing and expressing individual distress, it also places an infant in relation to others because someone typically comes to the infant's aid. Moreover, infants are responsive to the ministrations of caregivers, who usually succeed in helping to soothe a distressed baby. In this way, ceasing to cry as others comfort them is a way in which neonates act in relation to others. This responsivity is global, or rather undifferentiated, insofar as newborns are not terribly picky about who comes to their aid. However, research shows that during the first days and weeks of life, a newborn is starting to discriminate, or differentiate, among aspects of his or her mother's voice, smell, and face (Bartrip, Morton, & de Schonen, 2001; Cernoch & Porter, 1985; DeCasper & Fifer, 1980; Schaal, Soussignan, & Marlier, 2002). Within the context of soothing, a newborn is not necessarily distinguishing or differentiating among specific people and does not know or conceptualize people as his or her mother, father, grandfather, aunt, older sibling, father's good friend, or next-door neighbor. Nevertheless, some perceptual differentiation among people seems to be occurring. In addition, research suggests that, by the fourth feeding, infants begin to engage in "anticipatory approach movements" when "placed in a nursing position close to the mother's body but prior to actual contact" (Schaffer, 1984, p. 31). If someone else steps in to feed a baby, the pattern that was established with the mother is disrupted and a new one is constructed. These findings also suggest that infants are starting to differentiate among people through sensorimotor action. Integration is evident, as the infant must coordinate body movements to adjust him- or herself physically in relation to specific, or differentiated, others, all within the context of feeding.

There is an abundance of research on infant perception, and the present conceptualization leads to thinking about how ways of perceiving the world function as constituents of global action in relation to others. For example, with regard to vision, newborns tend to focus on objects that are curved, symmetrical, and in motion (Kagan, 2013), which, interestingly, are dimensions of human faces. Of course, when newborns look at people's faces they are not distinguishing conceptually between people and objects, nor are they differentiating among people as specific people with particular roles or characteristics. The point here is that global action in relation to others is possible from the outset, and it partakes of varied action constituents and subconstituents. During the first weeks of life, infants are increasingly able to control their eye movements (due to differentiation and integration of muscles and tissues, among other subconstituents of vision), allowing for smoother visual scanning. Infants increasingly integrate looking and head-turning to track objects (Campos et al., 2000; Moore & Povinelli, 2007; Reddy, 2008). As infants see ever more clearly, they can focus on the internal features of others' faces, such as the eyes, nose, and mouth, which enables them to differentiate facial features and can be a basis for continued differentiation among people and for coordinating with others.

Global action in relation to others also involves self-constituents insofar as varied sensorimotor abilities enable infants to be physically aware of themselves as separate individuals and aware of themselves in relation to others (Butterworth, 1990; Pipp, 1990; Stern, 1985). Individual physical self-awareness is possible because infants experience sensory feedback when they touch their mouths, heads, ears, noses, and eyes with their fingers, all of which occurs already during the first hours of life (Butterworth, 1990). We can infer that an infant's tactile experience is different when the child is held and touched by others. Insofar as self-generated touching and being touched by others provide different kinds of sensory feedback, some differentiation can occur between individual physical self-awareness and being aware of oneself in relation to others (e.g., Pipp, 1990; Stern, 1985). As discussed in Chapter 3, self-construction undergoes development throughout the life span, and in no way am I suggesting that newborns are constructing complex conceptions of themselves. Rather, the point here is that there are sensorimotor forms of self- and other awareness from the outset, and these modes of awareness provide a foundation for ongoing self development to occur. Thus "the self" does not appear out of nothing at a later age.

Discussions of infant functioning also include the controversial issue of neonatal imitation. There are debates over whether newborns are capable of imitating and whether imitating is possible because of a "specialized, innate cognitive mechanism" that is "present in a mature form at birth" (Ray & Heyes, 2011, p. 93). Some research suggests that newborns can imitate varied isolated acts in controlled experimental settings, such as opening their mouths and protruding their tongues (e.g., Meltzoff & Moore, 1983). However, research reviews indicate that infants do not imitate a wide range of other physical movements, including "chin tapping, cheek swelling, close eyes, arm waving, making and unmaking a fist, ear touching" (Ray & Heyes, 2011, p. 94). It is also argued that infants often open their mouths, and they often stick out their tongues when they are excited (e.g., Anisfeld et al., 2001; Jones, 2009). Further research indicates that some newborns (3 hours to 5 days old) are more likely to stick out their tongues when relatively strong forms of tongue protruding are modeled (i.e., sticking out the tongue beyond the lips or maximally extending the tongue), but not in response to the modeling of relatively weak forms of tongue protruding (i.e., opening the mouth, protruding the tongue to the lips but not beyond the lips) (Nagy, Pilling, Orvos, & Molnar, 2013). In addition, in this study, babies were more likely to increase tongue protruding during a modeling session when they were sitting in a baby seat or when they were lying down, but not when they were being held by the experimenter. Taken together, analyses indicate that

> imitation in newborns is not inevitable or even predictable. It does not always occur, either each time the action is observed by the same infant or by all infants. That is, the same infant sometimes imitates and sometimes does [not], and a few perfectly normal and attentive infants never imitate at all. (Reddy, 2008, p. 53)

Moreover, when neonatal imitating occurs, it often gives the "impression of being effortful" and is "often followed by distress" (Trevarthen, 1982, pp. 94–95). Research conducted mostly with middle-class American samples indicates that during the course of the first year of life, it is actually caregivers who do most of the imitating. That is, mothers imitate their infants more than infants imitate their mothers (Jones, 2009; Užgiris, Benson, Kruper, & Vasek, 1989).

Controversies over infant imitation have also recently taken a neurological turn within discussions of mirror neurons. Mirror neurons were originally identified in monkeys and are neurons that fire both when a monkey is engaging in some act, such as reaching for an object, and when a monkey is watching another monkey reach. Such neurons appear to be present in human brains as well (e.g., Cook, Bird, Catmur, Press, & Heyes, 2014). However, there are debates about the function of mirror neurons and the extent to which they mediate people's understanding of each other (Cook et al., 2014; Hickok, 2014). In addition, debates continue over the ways in which human mirror neurons are the genetic result of an evolutionary adaptation and the ways in which they are formed through experience, especially social interaction (Cook et al., 2014). With regard to imitation, there are discussions about the ways in which infant imitation is possible because of innately present mirror neurons and the ways in which mirror neurons themselves develop through imitative experiences (Cook et al., 2014).

Within the context of such controversies, it seems most reasonable at this point to conclude that some kind of imitation is possible early in life. In turn, a developmental perspective leads to conceptualizing and investigating imitating as a form of action that develops (Užgiris, 1999). Indeed, imitating can be viewed as a complex form of action that involves awareness and understanding of what others are doing, awareness and understanding that one can do what others are doing, a reason or reasons to do what the other is doing, and trying to do or approximate what the other is doing. All of this understanding develops, and thus early erratic imitating may serve as a foundation for the development of more complex forms of imitating. For infants during this first period of action development, imitating may be viewed as a way in which infants can (but do not always) act globally in relation to others.

II. Establishing and Maintaining Mutual Attention

This analysis of beginning foundations indicates that infants act in relation to others from the outset in relatively global ways and that during the first few months of life, varied constituents and subconstituents of global action undergo ongoing differentiation and integration. As action constituents undergo differentiation and integration during the first few months, parent–child interaction moves toward sustained episodes of face-to-face interaction. According to Stern (1977), the purpose of such interaction is "to have fun, to interest and delight and be with one another. During these stretches of purely social play . . . there are no tasks to be accomplished, no feeding or changing or bathing on the immediate agenda" (p. 71). They involve establishing and maintaining mutual attention as the infant attends to the caregiver and the caregiver attends to the infant.

During this period, infants increasingly use their "own acts of animation" (Trevarthen & Hubley, 1978, p. 188), such as smiling, shifting gaze, and raising eyebrows, which are integrated with head-turning and reaching, as well as with crying and other vocalizations (e.g., cooing), to engage with others. In this way, crying is no longer only a global expression of subjective discomfort but also an increasingly differentiated action constituent of establishing and maintaining mutual attention. In addition, head-turning, looking, and smiling are all used not only to engage with others but also to disengage from others (Bronson, 2000; Calkins, 2007). In other words, these varied constituents of action are integrated within the wider whole of establishing and maintaining mutual attention. During this period, infants also increasingly imitate adults and often contribute to rounds of imitative exchanges with others (Užgiris, 1991). They imitate acts on objects, vocalizations, emotional expressivity, and "conventional, socially meaningful actions such as waving 'bye'" (Užgiris, 1991, p. 226). Such imitation by the child serves as "a means of initiating and maintaining social interactions" (Užgiris, 1991, p. 238). As such, imitating can be viewed as a means that infants use to establish and maintain mutual attention, and it can be integrated with other means for establishing and maintaining mutual attention. Imitating further involves differentiating and integrating components of the acts that are being imitated.

Action in the form of establishing and maintaining mutual attention also "involve[s] the regulation of affect and excitation" (Stern, 1985, p. 75) within a pleasurable to unpleasurable range. Stern explains further that caregivers use varied means to "regulate the infant's level of arousal and excitation within a tolerable range" (p. 74), including "exaggerated behaviors in a theme and variation format" (p. 73). At the same time,

> the infant also regulates the level of excitation, using gaze aversion to cut out stimulation that has risen above the optimal range and gaze and facial behaviors to seek out and invite new or higher levels of stimulation when the level of excitation has fallen too low. (p. 75)

These findings suggest that infants' subjective experiences are increasingly differentiated into the emotional experiences of pleasure and displeasure, and such development is part of what permits mutual attention to involve emotional responsivity between an adult and infant. It also suggests that emotional experience is being integrated with using varied means to engage with and disengage from others. It further appears that differentiating pleasure and displeasure is increasingly integrated with sensorimotor-based self- and other awareness to comprise mutual attention. That is, if an infant enjoys mutual attention, the emotional constituent of mutual attention is inseparable from differentiating between being attended to and not being attended to by others. In addition, infants are integrating their awareness of others' attention to themselves and their own attention to others.

Taken together, a wide range of research points to how perceiving, moving physically, emotion, self-awareness, other awareness, and interacting with others function inseparably to comprise action in the form of establishing and maintaining mutual attention. This way of acting also involves the ongoing development of sensorimotor cognition, the first stage of cognitive development according to Piaget (1953). Piaget identified six sensorimotor substages that occur during infancy, beginning with reflex acts, including looking, sucking, and grasping. According to Piaget, these reflexes are organized action schemes that enable infants to start constructing ways of understanding the world because they are self-generated and provide sensory feedback. As an infant encounters different aspects of the world, reflex schemes undergo differentiation, and integrative processes also occur as, for example, "the newborn child at once incorporates into the global schema of sucking a number of increasingly varied objects" (Piaget, 1953, p. 34). Integration further involves combining schemes, such as grasping an object and shaking it or sucking it. Such differentiation and integration lead to the second sensorimotor substage, primary circular reactions, when infants are increasingly able to initiate, repeat, and coordinate these schemes on their own.

As children progress from primary circular reactions to the secondary circular reactions of the third sensorimotor substage, their functioning is characterized by combining or integrating schemes in new ways to "make interesting sights last" (p. 153). According to Piaget, such functioning implies the beginning of differentiating between means and ends. Up to this point, means and ends existed as a global whole, insofar as sensorimotor acts or schemes were interesting in and of themselves, and infants engaged in them for their own sake. Now, the sensorimotor schemes are subordinated to the goal of prolonging an interesting result. In other words, schemes are differentiated and integrated in relation to goals that consist of prolonging interesting events. For infants, mutually engaging with others is an interesting event that they may try to prolong or maintain. As discussed earlier, varied means for establishing and maintaining mutual attention are differentiated and integrated during the first months of life. Taken together, we can discern that crying, looking, head-turning, reaching, emotion, and sensorimotor cognition function in relation to each other and are increasingly integrated in the service of establishing and maintaining mutual attention with others.

In addition, development within the motor domain (e.g., crawling, walking) provides further means for establishing and maintaining mutual attention, and motor means are differentiated from and integrated with other means for establishing and maintaining mutual attention. As such, the development of walking is not isolated from other domains of functioning, which *together* comprise developing modes of action in relation to others. In an article on the trials and tribulations of transitioning from crawling to walking, Adolph and Tamis-LeMonda (2014) puzzle over why infants persist in trying to walk when walking is initially so inefficient and dangerous, compared to well-developed crawling. They speculate that there may be varied reasons, and at the end of the article they point out that "once infants begin walking, it alters their interactions with primary caregivers" (p. 190) by enabling them to carry objects to others who may be in different locations and to use their hands to establish and maintain engagement with others. This conclusion is compatible with the current framework's theoretical *starting point* that multiple and interrelated constituents comprise action. This starting point leads to positing that the development of walking does not occur in isolation from other domains of functioning and that it co-contributes to the development of acting in relation to others.

Of course, infants are not always happily willing or eager to engage in playful interactions with others. Sometimes they are tired or upset, or in need of physical caretaking. As Trevarthen (1993/1996) explains:

> The distressed baby pulls away, threshes about, closes eyes firmly, and cries with rejecting (disgusted) movements of the mouth. The hungry

baby avoids eye contact and roots for the nipple. The sleepy baby seeks support and a comfortable contact with the mother and closes mouth, hands, and eyes. (p. 134)

This research indicates that babies differentiate between ways of being attended to by others in terms of varied purposes besides engaging in mutual attention. Throughout the first year of life, ongoing differentiation among action settings occurs and may be part of what enables people to engage in different modes of action in relation to different people, in different cultural practices.

III. Joint Attention: Common Topics and Routines

As infants become adept at establishing and maintaining mutual attention, the constituents of action undergo further differentiation and integration, thereby paving the developmental pathway toward establishing and maintaining joint attention. During the second half of the first year, action in relation to others develops to involve engaging with others about common topics, including engaging with others in routines around a common topic. I refer to such action as "joint attention," to suggest that it is distinct from yet also builds on the mutual attention of the previous period. That is, mutual attention is when engaging with others revolves around mutually attending to each other. To engage in joint attention, mutual attention is integrated as a subsystemic constituent of attending jointly to something else (including another person), beyond each other. The emergence of this form of action indicates that infants are differentiating between attending *to* another person and attending to something else *with* another person. It also involves integrating attending to others and attending to something else.

Establishing and maintaining joint attention during this period increasingly involves objects as the common topic of interaction or the topic of joint attention. Even though objects are part of American children's lives throughout the periods discussed thus far, infants do not necessarily differentiate between people and objects, and distinctions between them are constructed during development (Užgiris, 1996). Infants are often credited with the ability to distinguish between objects and people at around 5 months, when they turn their attention from people to objects (Reddy, 2008; Rochat, 2001/2004; Schaffer, 1984; Stern, 1977). At first, their attention may be divided, as engaging with objects is differentiated from engaging with people.

However, infants' interest in objects does not appear suddenly at 5 months. Again, nothing will come of nothing. Indeed, as mentioned earlier, infants are not continuously engaged in mutual attention with others, and sometimes they attend to other objects that make up their worlds. From an organismic-developmental perspective, the question is not, when does interest in objects begin, but rather: What differentiation and integration are occurring for the constituents of engaging with inanimate objects and human beings? Furthermore, by starting with action in relation to others as the wider whole (or forest) that develops during development, we are led to considering how the cognitive development of object understanding contributes to the development of action in relation to others.

Analyses that elaborate on Piaget's conceptualization of infants' understanding of objects suggest a multistep sequence for the "development of schemes for relating to objects" (Užgiris & Hunt, 1975/1989, p. 122). Initially, "objects serve chiefly to elicit various schemes already present within the infant's repertoire of actions" (Užgiris & Hunt, 1975/1989, p. 122). During this time, features of particular objects are not differentiated, nor are infant sensorimotor acts or schemes integrated in relation to the affordances of particular objects. Instead, "infants appear to be intent upon exercising these familiar schemes regardless of the characteristics of the eliciting objects," as "the manipulative schemes in the repertoires of very young infants are applied to objects indiscriminately" (p. 122). Through continued use, schemes such as "hitting, shaking, [and] waving" are accommodated "to particular characteristics of different objects" (pp. 122–123), which provides a way for infants to differentiate among objects.

In addition, "a rapid differentiation of schemes occurs, and this differentiation takes into account not only the physical characteristics of objects, but their social significance as well" (p. 124). That is, now that objects are increasingly treated as differentiated aspects of the world, they can also be integrated with social interaction to comprise a new mode of action. Thus, objects become a topic of joint attention between infants and others and can be incorporated into their interactions, which in turn is part of what enables infants to develop beyond mutual attention. In other words, action involves engaging with another person about a common topic.

As infants differentiate between inanimate objects and people, and as they integrate objects into interpersonal interaction, they also increasingly engage in interactive or social routines that are about a common topic, including objects. Routines are characterized by a repeated sequence of events that can be carried out in varied specific ways, as well as in terms of turn-taking and distinct roles, such as hiding and seeking, and giving and taking (Bruner, 1983; Martin, 2012; Martin & Gillespie, 2010). It is important to point out that caregivers have been structuring some interactions with infants in routinized ways from the outset (Fogel, 1993; Stern, 1985). As mentioned earlier, Stern (1985) explains that caregivers often use a "theme and variation format" (p. 73) to structure mutual engagement with infants. For example,

> the general game "I'm going to get you," when played in the tickle form
> of "walking fingers," consists of repeated finger marches up the infant's
> legs and torso, ending up with a neck or chin tickle as the punch line. It

is played over and over, but each finger march is distinctly different from the previous one in speed, in suspense, in vocal accompaniment. (Stern, 1985, p. 73)

As infants engage with others in such routines, they become increasingly active participants during the course of this period.

Bruner (1983) explains that hiding routines are made up of sequential segments that can be executed in varied specific ways to achieve the disappearance and reappearance of an object or person. The segments include preparing for disappearance, disappearance, reappearance, and re-establishing interest in the routine. Bruner's classic longitudinal analyses of two mother–child dyads playing peek-a-boo with an object can be analyzed in terms of the differentiation and integration that occur in a child's ways of acting during this period of joint attention.

Bruner (1983) describes how one mother and her son, Jonathan, played a variation of peek-a-boo with "a little toy clown that could be moved so as to rise above or disappear into a cloth cone mounted on a stick" (p. 49). At first, Jonathan "was little more than a smiling spectator as the clown disappeared and then reappeared" (p. 49). In other words, he attended globally to the display, but did not differentiate among the segments of the routine. Nor did he take on either of the differentiated roles (hider and spectator) and integrate it with the other. Between 5 and 9 months, "he paid increasingly more active attention" (p. 51) and he also started trying to grab the clown himself. At 6 months, "he accompanied his attempts to reach or grab the clown with undifferentiated vocalizations" (p. 52). A month later, Jonathan "began responding to the game's predictable rhythm. He lost interest in grabbing and now reacted at appropriate points by smiling and laughter" (p. 53). In other words, he was differentiating among the segments of the routine, by smiling and laughing to mark certain points in the routine. Subsequently (at 8 months), "he was ready to get the clown up out of the cone by himself" (p. 53). When Jonathan was a year and 2 months, he "could participate as agent *or* as experiencer" (p. 54), indicating that he could differentiate between and integrate the roles that comprise the routine, as well as differentiate and integrate varied aspects of the two roles. In this way, he could act flexibly according to the turn-taking demands of each role and in relation to the other's role.

As Mead (1934/1962) pointed out some time ago (relative to the context of contemporary psychology), engaging in such routines involves self- and other awareness because it enables children to be aware of themselves and of others in different roles. Building on Mead, Martin (2012) explains that such

position exchange gradually enables the young child to recall previous experience in one position (e.g., as receiver or hider) while occupying and engaging in another related position (e.g., as giver or seeker). With such rudimentary remembrance and the anticipation of position shifts in the immediate future that it enables, the child effectively is able to "occupy" different positions simultaneously—that is, to anticipate the activity of another in one position while personally occupying a closely related, complementary position. (p. 137)

In these ways, engaging in routines involves differentiating between and integrating distinct, yet complementary social interaction roles, as well as being aware of oneself and others in terms of increasingly differentiated and integrated roles or positions.

During this period, babies are also directing others' attention to themselves in new ways as a topic of joint attention. For example, in some research,

> Parents reported infants of 7 and 8 months to be very aware of others' attention to the things they did, to play up to unusual attention, particularly from strangers, by showing off from their repertoire of tricks, and to seek to repeat actions for signs of approval or appreciation. . . . The showing off at this age often involved extreme actions, shrill shrieks, squeals, or banging and splashing, as well as some newly learned skills, such as clapping, waving, crawling, and pulling oneself up to a standing position. (Reddy, 2008, p. 137)

These antics indicate that the global awareness of others' attention to oneself, of the mutual attention period, is being differentiated to include attention to specific aspects of what one is doing. Children are also further differentiating among and integrating varied means to establish and maintain joint attention to what they are doing. Drawing attention to one's antics, including coming up with new means to elicit others' attention, additionally involves ongoing cognitive development. According to Piaget, during the fourth substage of the sensorimotor stage, the coordination of secondary schemes, children differentiate between means and ends by integrating familiar means in new ways to achieve new goals. Subsequently, the fifth sensorimotor substage, tertiary circular reactions, is characterized by "the discovery of new means through active experimentation" (Piaget, 1953, p. 263.) That is, "the child tries to attain a goal but obstacles (distance, etc.) prevent him. The situation is therefore 'new' and the problem is to discover appropriate means. But . . . no familiar method presents itself to the child any more. It is therefore a question of innovating" (p. 288). Through experimenting, new schemes are differentiated from familiar ones, and they are also integrated to produce novel ways of acting. Thus, children's antics involve inventing varied new means for getting others to pay attention to what they are doing.

Throughout these periods, infants and their caregivers are obviously not engaged in continuous rapt mutual attention or joint attention. Sometimes infants are distracted by something outside of the immediate action context and they attend to it. Adults may try to discern what an infant is attending to, and they may try to interact with the infant about it. As continued development within and across action constituents occurs, infants will also be able to direct themselves in relation to what an adult is attending to beyond what they are doing in the moment. For example, they can follow another person's pointing outside the immediate situation when the pointing is accompanied by gaze and head-turning (Iverson, 2010). As well, they are increasingly able to draw others' attention to some aspect of the world beyond the immediate action context to make it part of the immediate action context. In these ways, action in relation to others is developing toward establishing and maintaining a common action orientation with others. This terminology is perhaps not ideal for this period because the periods posited thus far clearly involve some kind of common action orientation in that even infants are acting in relation to others within a "joint field of experience" (Užgiris, 1996, p. 23). Actually, by definition, all action in relation to others involves some kind of common action orientation. The aspect of action I am trying to emphasize here is that children are engaging with people who may be otherwise occupied in terms of what those people are doing, and not only in terms of what the children themselves are doing. It is difficult to come up with terminology for the periods. For current purposes, I will proceed with this terminology so that we can think about the main issues, which are the dynamics of differentiation and integration occurring during these periods and the structuring of emerging modes of action.

IV. Establishing and Maintaining a Common Action Orientation

Acting in relation to others in terms of a common action orientation involves being aware that when another person is not attending to you, he or she is attending to something else in the world. In this regard, children's self-awareness and other awareness are developing beyond being aware that others are either attending to them or not, as well as beyond being aware of themselves and others in different roles in the immediate action context. They now seem increasingly aware that when others are not attending to them in some way, those people are attending to something else in the world. In other words, children's awareness of others' attention is being differentiated beyond whether attention is directed toward oneself or not. In addition to this developing awareness of what other people may be attending to, acting in relation to others in terms of a common action orientation involves discerning the object of the other person's attention and attending to it as well. It then culminates in interacting with the other person about that aspect of the world, thus integrating the previous period's achievements as subsystemic constituents of sharing a common action orientation. In this way, infants are also integrating their own attention with their increasingly differentiated awareness of the other's attention.

As Reddy (2008) argues, it is commonplace to mark the beginning of being aware of others' attention at around 9 months, when infants "point to things in the world communicatively (that is, checking to make sure an adult is looking)" (p. 91). However, Reddy goes on to explain that using such pointing to mark the beginning of infants' awareness of others' attention "makes infants' earlier engagements with others' attention a bit of a mystery" (p. 91). That is, if previous forms of action do not involve some kind of awareness of oneself and others, including one's own and others' attention, from where does such awareness suddenly appear, full-blown toward the end of the first year? From an organismic-developmental perspective, nothing comes from nothing, meaning that the earlier ways of being aware of others' attention are integrated as subsystemic constituents of children's current other awareness. Thus, to make sense of children's awareness of others' attention toward the end of the first year, we have to discern its roots in earlier periods of action. And that is part of what we have been doing all along in this chapter.

At this point, some readers may wonder why I am discussing action orientations, rather than perspectives. After all, if a child is discerning what others are attending to, one could say that he or she is discerning something about another person's perspective, or taking the other's perspective. I hesitate to use the term *perspective* at this point, because it is important to distinguish between a sensorimotor awareness of oneself and others, and symbolically constructing what a person (including oneself) intends, feels, knows, values, or believes. In this discussion, I use the term *perspective* to refer to the process of symbolically constructing one's own intentions, beliefs, opinions, and knowledge, as well as symbolically considering what others intend, believe, opine, and know. As symbolic constructions, perspectives are knowable separately from particular action contexts, and people can think about their own and others' perspectives in the presence of others, as well as in their absence. However, it is problematic to attribute such perspective-constructing or perspective-taking abilities to children during this period, because symbolically rendering and reflecting on one's own and others' perspectives are beyond their sensorimotor abilities (Dunn, 2008; Reddy, 2008; Stone, Carpendale, Sugarman, & Martin, 2012; Youniss, 2008). Distinguishing between "action orientation" and "perspective" is not semantic pedantry; it is taking development seriously. Indeed, insofar as nothing comes from nothing, perspective taking does not simply start at some point. Instead, it builds on and integrates previous sensorimotor forms of self- and other awareness. That is, rather than reflecting on or theorizing about what other people know or believe or intend, during this period children act in relation to others by attuning to or coordinating with what others are doing (Stone et al., 2012).

Much research suggests that by the end of the first year, children's ways of establishing and maintaining a common action orientation involve following others' gazes and points, as well as directing another's attention through showing, giving, and pointing to objects (Bates, Camaioni, & Volterra, 1975; Behne et al., 2008; Scaife & Bruner, 1975). With regard to following another person's pointing, infants first typically fixate on the person's hand only. Subsequently, they move on to a two-step process of pausing to look at the hand and then attending to the object of the pointing (Butterworth, 1998). These two steps indicate that infants are differentiating between the means of pointing and the object of pointing. Finally, infants stop alighting their gaze on the hand and instead look immediately at the object. They also check back to the other person, as if to make sure they have found the right object to attend to (Tomasello, Carpenter, & Liszkowski, 2007). This checking indicates being aware that there are possibly different objects to look at and that people are looking at and drawing attention to some object(s) in particular. As such, this checking indicates an increasingly differentiated awareness of what others may be attending to.

Shatz's (1994) observations of her grandson, Ricky, provide a rich source of data on the development of action in relation to others throughout infancy and early childhood. With regard to sharing a common action orientation, when Ricky could follow another person's point and direct someone's attention by pointing, he did not initially consider that another person's line of vision could be obstructed, even if he could see something clearly. Nor did he consider that, for another person to see an object, it might have to be positioned differently, which could then obstruct his own view of the object. For example:

> One day he was sitting on the hall stairs looking at a book. Seeing a picture of a butterfly, he ran toward where I was sitting in the living room, shouting "Butterfly, butterfly." He stopped near me, pointing at the butterfly, but he did not turn the book so that I could see the picture. He seemed to have taken proximity but not my line of sight into account. On another occasion, I asked him to show me a duck in a book he was reading with his father. He pointed to it, but again made no effort to turn the book so that I could see it. (Shatz, 1994, p. 31)

Ongoing differentiation and integration of proximity, as well as one's own and another's line of sight, then contribute further to establishing a common action orientation with others.

Although the abundance of research on pointing and gazing makes these constituents of establishing and maintaining a common action orientation quite salient, other developing action constituents also comprise this mode of action. For example, by the end of the first year, ongoing language development enables language to serve as a central means for establishing and maintaining a common action orientation with others (Durkin, 1995; Shatz, 1994; Tomasello, 2003). As Nelson (2007) points out, "the goal for the child is sharing meaning, not the successful solution of a lexical acquisition task. Words are assumed to be tools for sharing meaning, for advancing the process of being with others in shared endeavors" (p. 142). Although children's initial one-word utterances are relatively global, some differentiation is evident as children use single words to achieve different social ends, such as making demands, drawing another person's attention to something, asking and answering questions, commenting on events, and greeting and taking leave of others. Children also use language to mark their own agency in differentiated ways (Budwig, 1989). The development of language comprehension additionally contributes to children's increasing compliance with some caregiver demands, within a given situation (Kopp, 1982). Such compliance involves controlling one's own action in relation to what the other is requesting, thereby entering into and maintaining a common action orientation. I readily recognize that language development is a complex topic in and of itself, and I do not mean to minimize its intricacies or importance. The point here is that differentiation and integration within and across action constituents enable new modes of action to develop.

In addition, establishing and maintaining a common action orientation increasingly involves using others' standards to judge one's own action (Bronson, 2000). As such, shared values and standards can serve as a basis for acting in relation to others in terms of a common action orientation. Using shared standards to judge one's own action is evident in the development of self-conscious emotions, such as pride and shame (Mascolo, Fischer, & Li, 2003). In classic studies, Stipek, Recchia, and McClintic (1992) observed 1- to 5-year-olds during free play with their mothers, and also when the children were instructed to operate a toy in the same way that a researcher had just demonstrated. The results indicated that the older children (2½ years and older) were more likely than the younger children to look at the experimenter when they achieved the demonstrated outcome. They also increasingly called attention to their achievements verbally by saying "look" or "see" (p. 32). In contrast, when the children failed to solve a puzzle, they were more likely to frown, and they avoided contact with the experimenter. Seeking contact and avoiding contact depending on one's performance represent ways of acting in relation to others in terms of a common understanding of standards and meanings. They also involve being able to differentiate between procedures for carrying out a task and standards for accomplishing that task. This research shows further that children are increasingly "likely to call attention to outcomes that they had defined than to outcomes related to goals that their mothers had proposed" (Stipek et al., 1992, p. 33). Such action suggests that children are differentiating between their own and others' goals, as well as sharing or integrating their own and others' goals to establish a common action orientation. They also seem to be integrating self-awareness with an increasingly differentiated awareness of others as people who pursue individual goals.

Ongoing development during this period subsequently leads to sharing a common orientation with others, even when those others are not physically present in the immediate action context. For example, children increasingly follow absent caregivers' commands (Kopp, 1982), such as stopping or not doing what was previously prohibited by a caregiver. In addition, children may use egocentric or private speech to regulate themselves in the caregiver's absence. According to Vygotsky, such speech is derived from social interaction and involves speaking out loud to oneself to regulate one's own action (Vygotsky, 1986/1987). Establishing a common action orientation with someone who is not physically present involves differentiating one's awareness of another's orientation from the here and now of concrete action. Monitoring one's own action in relation to absent others also involves differentiating between and integrating one's own current action orientation and absent others' action orientations.

By acting in relation to absent others, children are, in Meadian terms, "taking the attitude of the other" toward themselves (Mead, 1934/1962, p. 47). With language, a child can apply others' attitudes to his or her own action and thus react to his or her own action in terms of others' attitudes, including when the others are not immediately present. Insofar as such attitudes are constructed symbolically, children's self-awareness and other awareness are developing beyond the common action orientation of the here and now. They are increasingly able to symbolically construct and think about what others are doing, as well as consider what a situation means to themselves and to others. In other words, children are on the way to acting in terms of what others know, believe, intend, and feel, which constitute perspectives as defined earlier.

V. Navigating and Negotiating Perspectives

The continued development of action in relation to others involves being increasingly aware that different people may construct different perspectives on a situation, as well as being aware that others' perspectives may be different from one's own construal of a situation. As such, a child is navigating among individuals' perspectives as well as negotiating common goals and meanings with others. In other words, the common action orientation of the previous period is undergoing differentiation insofar as children are no longer acting in terms of one assumed orientation that everyone shares in the here and now. They are also acting in relation to others in terms of increasingly differentiated perspectives. The differentiation of perspectives includes an initial differentiation between one's own and another's perspective, and continued development occurs as a child's understanding of each perspective (his or her own and another's) undergoes further differentiation and integration.

For example, Dunn's observations of family interaction show that teasing, in the form of trying to deliberately annoy another (often a sibling), increases between 15 and 23 months (Dunn, 2004; Dunn & Munn, 1985). Such teasing is a form of action that involves differentiating among perspectives insofar as one has to understand that what bothers a particular person is not necessarily bothersome either to oneself or to all others. At the same time, there is integration of perspective taking with cognition, which is undergoing differentiation and integration, as varied means may be used to bother another person effectively. Teasing also involves emotional development as one's own and another person's feelings about a situation are differentiated. Continued development within and across varied action constituents would enable teasing to develop beyond this period to include being aware of and negotiating the sometimes narrow and moving line between good-spirited teasing and hurting someone's feelings.

Language is also involved in negotiating common meanings and navigating among people with different perspectives. For example, Shatz (1994) reports that her grandson, Ricky, began to verbally justify his behavior to others in varied situations. She explains:

> He began to justify his refusals to fulfill requests, instead of simply saying "no" or ignoring them as he had in the past when he didn't want to do as asked. One day just after Ricky and his parents had arrived for a visit, Alice [Ricky's mother] invited him to go with her to see a new porch swing. As Ricky began to follow her to the porch, Richard [Ricky's grandfather] appeared and demanded a hug for a greeting. Ricky refused, and continuing to run down the driveway, said, "Grandma got a new swing." (p. 87)

This scenario indicates that Ricky is explaining his action in terms of global reasons. It also indicates that he can differentiate between what he knows and what someone else knows about a given circumstance, as well as use language to coordinate with the other person according to this differentiated awareness of perspectives. In general, "Ricky regularly told people things he thought they did not know. If someone was not physically present during an event, he assumed the person had no knowledge of it" (p. 115).

Along similar lines, Blum-Kulka, Hamo, and Habib (2010) point out that explanations are "a way of conveying sensitivity to the social needs of interlocutors, a responsibility to communicate a message that will be understood, and an awareness that such understanding depends on the way the message is produced" (p. 441). Preschoolers' action reflects such sensitivity to others' perspectives in that they initiate explanations on their own if they think others require clarification or elaboration. Although children (as well as adults) are not always accurate about what others know and do not know, the point is that their action involves differentiating and integrating what they and others know, and such action is linked to language development.

The analysis of this period thus far has focused on children's developing understanding of *others'* perspectives and the mostly positive implications of that understanding for acting in relation to others. However, it is often a rocky road through these years of differentiating among and integrating perspectives. At the same time that children are increasingly able to take others' perspectives, differentiating among perspectives also means that the child's *own* perspective is undergoing development. In addition, children are increasingly able to function on their own, including formulating and pursuing their own increasingly differentiated and integrated goals. When they do so, they often embark on courses of action that caregivers find objectionable (Bronson, 2000; Mascolo & Fischer, 2007). In turn, children find the caregivers' objections to be objectionable, and children often seem to be acting in opposition to others. In other words, the "terrible twos" have arrived.

The so-called terrible twos (which may occur before or after the age of 2, providing an example of how age is not the central issue in development) can be viewed as manifestations of ongoing differentiation between one's own and others' perspectives, as well as attempts to integrate different perspectives. That is, when children disobey their caregivers and test boundaries (sometimes with great delight), they may be actively differentiating between and integrating their own and others' perspectives. The following description by Shatz (1994) of her grandson's attempts at navigating and negotiating perspectives illustrates some of the dynamics of differentiation and integration during this period, as well as how navigating among and negotiating with people involves varied action constituents.

> Ricky had been visiting overnight, and we were waiting for his father to come to pick him up and take him out for supper on the way home. Ricky got hungry and wanted something to eat in the interim. I offered a banana and opened the peel just a little. Ricky's habit was to pull the peel down a bit at a time as he ate the banana, but this night he pulled the peel down too far at once. Annoyed, he tried to throw the banana on the floor, but I intervened. I told Ricky the banana was still good—that it would taste just the same, but he refused to accept it and insisted on another. I said he didn't have to eat the banana—he could have something else, but he wasn't going to have another banana just to play around with. However, there was no compromising. Ricky was angry. He climbed down from his chair and went to stand in a corner, facing the wall. This was his customary response when he wasn't getting his way with his mother. Apparently, it served as a refusal to interact with others when he thought they weren't being fair or good to him. When I ignored him, he took a different tack. He went to climb over to the bunch of bananas on the counter to help

himself, but Richard [the grandfather], who was sitting nearby, moved the bananas out of reach. At that point, Ricky announced huffily, "I going upstairs," and he marched out of the kitchen and up the stairs.

After about 10 minutes, Richard went upstairs to look for him. He found him [and Ricky said]: (Grouchily) "Don't bodder me. I sleeping." Richard did as he was told, and left without a word. A bit later, Ricky came back down to the kitchen and announced, "I eat my banana now." He picked off a small piece from the infamous banana, tossed it away, saying, "Yuck," and then ate the rest. His behavior was a remarkably adaptive way to handle his anger, accommodate me, and save face at the same time. (pp. 128–129)

In this scenario, Ricky differentiated between his own and his grandmother's perspectives, and he also seemed to work hard cognitively to integrate varied means to achieve his goal. His action was emotionally fraught, and he seemed to be struggling to act in accord with standards and values regarding his relationship with his grandmother. He was thus integrating his own goals with an awareness of standards and values. Ultimately, his action involved integrating his own and his grandmother's perspectives so that the conflict was resolved in a way that satisfied them both, and that restored their harmonious relationship.

Although further development of acting in relation to others will certainly continue, we have come a long way from global action to navigating among perspectives and negotiating with people. Conceptualizing action in terms of multiple and interrelated constituents, and conceptualizing development in terms of differentiation and integration, have enabled us to synthesize and think systematically about a wide range of research. The five posited periods refer generally to new modes of action that emerge during infancy and early childhood, but they do not represent milestones that appear at a certain age, and subsequent modes of action do not simply replace previous ones. Rather, insofar as action reflects the genetic principle of spirality, people function within a developmental range, and therefore earlier modes of action can be used even when more developed ones are part of a person's action repertoire. Earlier modes of action also become integrated as subsystemic constituents of subsequent modes. In addition to being characterized by a mode of action, the analysis shows that ongoing differentiation and integration within and across constituents of action take place during these periods. In other words, it is not only the case that development enables a person to engage in different modes of action. It is also the case that development involves the ongoing dynamics of differentiation and integration. Thus, we can think not only about how new modes of action are organized but also about the developmental processes that occur in between the posited periods.

Peer Play

The goals of this brief discussion of peer play are to 1) think about how action in relation to peers during infancy and early childhood involves varied action constituents, 2) think about the development of peer play in terms of differentiation and integration, and 3) think about intraindividual variability or the genetic principle of spirality.

As with the development of any form of action in relation to others, the development of playing with peers reflects cultural expectations or goals of development, and it involves varied action constituents which undergo development, including thinking, feeling, using language, interacting, self-construction, and perspective taking. With regard to emotion, Dunn (2004) points out that "children of three and four rarely have elaborate conversations about what they feel or fear. But they do explore the issues that make them afraid or excited, when they are playing pretend with their close friends" (pp. 28–29). Clearly, language is required in varied ways during play, from negotiating play themes, to explaining play moves, to resolving conflicts. Cognitive processes also comprise play as children set goals, make plans, and use varied means to achieve their ends. Self and perspective-taking constituents are involved as children take on varied roles during play and negotiate among each others' varied feelings, intentions, goals, and ideas.

In the previous section of this chapter, we saw that young infants engage in mutual attention and joint attention with adult caregivers during the course of the first year of life. However, children who engage in these modes of action with adults may act rather differently with peers, thus pointing to how social processes partly contribute to the emergence of a person's action. In addition, these differences illustrate one of systems theory's main claims, as well as organismic-developmental theory's genetic principle of spirality, namely that people's functioning can be characterized by varied developmental patterns of action simultaneously. Infants and young children certainly contribute in critical ways to acting in relation to their adult caregivers during the periods of mutual attention and joint attention, but adults bear primary responsibility for structuring the ongoing flow of interaction. Children are thus full but not equally responsible participants in a system of acting in relation to others (Užgiris, 1989, 1996). It is however different between peers, because the relative equality of their action abilities shapes different pathways for the development of action in relation to peers. These differing developmental pathways may be especially likely among peers of the same age, and peer play among middle-class European-American children often occurs in preschool and school settings, where children are grouped by age.

During infancy, acting in relation to peers is relatively short-lived and rather infrequent. When it does occur, it is typically characterized by one child looking, smiling, and/or making noises at the other and perhaps holding out a toy or object to the other child (Dunn, 2004; Howes, 1980; Howes & Matheson, 1992). The other child may or may not do the same. If children are in the same room, they may play near each other (or parallel to each other), and they may be engaged in similar types of play, but they are not typically cooperating to achieve a common play goal. Subsequently, children "engage in the same or similar activity and talk, smile, offer and receive toys" (Howes & Matheson, 1992, p. 964). They also increasingly act in relation to each other through mutual imitation and turn-taking. Cooperative play is ultimately evident when "children demonstrate action-based role reversals in social games such as run and chase or peek-a-boo" (Howes & Matheson, 1992, p. 964). Cooperative play also involves making individual contributions to common play goals. For example, cooperating in a playroom's block area means that rather than only building separate structures, each child is contributing to constructing a collective block structure.

During the course of the third and fourth years, symbolic or pretend play becomes an increasingly prevalent form of cooperative play. As with non-pretend play, pretend play is initially relatively solitary. That is, it "consists of the child performing a pretend action outside of the context of joint play but in the presence of a partner" (Howes, Unger, & Matheson, 1992, p. 14). Subsequently, children engage in the same forms of pretend next to each other. Children then move on to enacting pretend play scripts whereby each child acts out different parts of the script. However, the differentiated parts of the script are not integrated, and there "is little or no joint organization of pretend" (Howes et al., 1992, p. 18). Cooperative symbolic play occurs when children take on complementary pretend roles, communicate about pretend meanings, and make "independent contributions to a shared pretend theme" (Dunn, 2004, p. 22).

Much differentiation and integration within and among action constituents occur as children go from relatively isolated play to engaging in cooperative play, which encapsulates cultural expectations for children's play. There is likely differentiation among one's own and others' play goals, as well as integration among varied play goals. Play roles are also differentiated and integrated. Negotiating goals is further inseparable from developing cognitive processes, as children may be using increasingly differentiated and integrated means to achieve goals. Taking on different roles during play involves differentiating among and integrating varied emotions that partly constitute different social roles (e.g., an angry parent, a distressed sibling).

Being able to engage in social pretend play also reflects the continued development of children's awareness of themselves and others as well as their burgeoning perspective-taking abilities. Dunn (2004) explains:

> The significance of the development of this capacity for sharing an imaginative world lies partly in what it tells us about children's capacity to

recognize the intentions of another person, sharing their focus of attention, and coordinating their communications about these shared intentions. (pp. 23–24)

Recognizing another person's intentions implies differentiating between one's own and the other's intentions. Sharing attention with another implies integrating one's own and another's attention. Coordinating is a synonym for integration, and coordinated communication about intentions involves integrating what one is saying with what the other is saying.

Cooperative play (pretend or otherwise) does not simply happen just because children are capable of such action. Research shows that in preschool settings, children who are capable of cooperative play do not actually spend most of their time playing cooperatively. Rather, their action is distributed among varied forms of play (Howes & Matheson, 1992), pointing once again to the genetic principle of spirality. Insofar as preschool worlds are dynamic and varied, children often work hard to establish and maintain cooperative play with each other. Corsaro's (1986, 2003) ethnographic observations in American preschools provide further insights into the challenges and drama of playing cooperatively during the preschool years.

Corsaro argues that children are concerned with protecting interactive space, or maintaining cooperative play once it is occurring. However, for varied reasons, interactive space is precarious for preschoolers. Corsaro (2003) explains that

> the social ecology of most preschools increases the fragility of peer interaction. A preschool play area is a multiparty setting much like a cocktail party with lots of clusters of kids playing together. Kids know from experience that at any moment a dispute might arise over the nature of play ("Who should be the mother and who the baby?" "Should the blocks go this way or that?"), other kids might want to play or take needed materials, or a teacher might announce "clean-up time." Kids work hard to get things going and then, just like that, someone always messes things up. (p. 40)

Given the precariousness of interactive space, preschool children are sometimes unwilling to allow newcomers into an already established play setting.

For example, Corsaro (2003) describes the following incident in which a girl, Linda, is trying to join two other girls, Barbara and Betty, who, as zookeepers, are building houses for toy animals. Linda has just picked up a toy animal.

> Barbara takes the animal away from Linda and says, "You can't play."
> "Yes, I can," Linda retorts. "I can have some animals too!" "No, you

can't," responds Barbara. "We don't like you today." "You're not our friend," says Betty in support of Barbara's exclusion of Linda. "I can play here, too," says Linda refusing to back down. "No, her can't. . . . Her can't play. Right, Betty?" asks Barbara. "Right," Betty confirms. (pp. 38–39)

Corsaro then explains that he himself is "bothered by this talk. However, in line with my ethnographic vow to not act like a typical adult, I try to stay out of the dispute" (p. 39). But Linda draws him in, and he asks Barbara why Linda is being excluded even though they "played with her yesterday. 'Well, we hate her today,' snaps Betty" (p. 39). Although he was initially taken aback by this statement, Corsaro argues that in such instances, children "are not refusing to share, rather they want to keep sharing what they are already sharing" (p. 40). Thus, Barbara and Betty see Linda as a threat to their play and they are working to maintain their interactive space. If joining other children who are already at play is viewed as a potential threat, the burden is then on the one who is joining to do so in a way that does not disrupt what the others are doing.

Corsaro (2003) describes another scenario in which Betty and Jenny are playing in a sandbox, and Debbie is trying to join them.

> First, Debbie merely places herself in the area of play, a strategy I call *nonverbal entry*. Receiving no response, Debbie keeps watching the play, but now physically circles the sandbox (what I term *encirclement*). . . . In this case, Debbie, when stationary and on the move, carefully makes note of what the other kids are doing. With this information she is able to enter the area and do something in line with the other kids' play (that is, pick up a teapot). Although often a successful access strategy, it is initially resisted in this instance. Not giving up, however, Debbie watches some more, again enters the area, and makes a verbal reference to affiliation ("We're friends, right?"). Betty responds positively, but does not explicitly invite Debbie to play. Debbie then repeats her earlier strategy of doing something similar to what the other kids are doing, this time verbally describing her play ("I'm making coffee"). Betty now responds in a way that includes Debbie in the play, noting that she is also making something (cupcakes). (pp. 42–43)

From the perspective of organismic-developmental theory, Linda's attempt at entering into cooperative play with Barbara and Betty is not as developed as Debbie's attempt to play with Betty and Jenny. Linda does not appear to have differentiated her own goals from Barbara's and Betty's goals, and she does not use differentiated and integrated means to join their play. She also seems to rather rigidly use the same strategy of asserting her right to play with the animals. In contrast, when Debbie carefully observes the others, she seems to be trying to discern what the others are doing. After her first attempt at engagement does not work, she does not give up. She watches again, and then she does something similar to what Betty and Jenny are doing, and she verbally describes what she is doing. Taken together, she seems to be flexibly constructing differentiated and integrated means to engage with the others. Moreover, those means are integrated with her awareness of the others' goals.

It is interesting to note that Debbie initially watched Betty and Jenny for "about five minutes" before she "circles the sandbox three times and stops again" to watch for "a few more minutes" (p. 41). Much time is certainly devoted to joining Betty and Jenny, and the description suggests that Debbie is working hard at carefully considering what to do. Accordingly, Corsaro (2003) wonders why Debbie did not directly ask the others what they are doing or if she can play. He explains that

> preschool children rarely use such direct strategies. One reason is that they call for an immediate response, and that response is very often negative. . . . Kids fear that others may disrupt the cherished but fragile sharing they have achieved. Direct entry bids like "What ya doing?" or "Can I play?" or the frequently heard "You have to share!" actually signal that one does not know what is going on and, therefore, might cause trouble. (p. 43)

Instead, discerning what the others are doing and doing what is relevant to their ongoing play comprise a nondisruptive way to engage with them. Other research corroborates this pattern of discerning what others are doing and then joining them. For example, classic sequential analyses show that parallel play often precedes cooperative play among 2½- to 3½-year-olds (Bakeman & Brownlee, 1980). Such parallel play enables children to figure out what others are doing before they attempt to enter into cooperative play. As such, parallel play functions as a means of achieving the goal of coordinating with others, and it involves differentiating among and integrating play goals.

As children play together, conflicts among them are inevitable, and resolving conflicts is also a form of action that develops during the early childhood years (and beyond). Dunn (2004) explains, "Instead of simply insisting on their own way, or wailing, grumbling, protesting or threatening the other child . . . four- to five-year-olds often now offer compromises . . . they bargain . . . or they attempt outright conciliation" (p. 37). This brief description indicates that children develop increasingly differentiated and integrated means for resolving conflicts that are used flexibly. Using such means also implies differentiating between one's own and others' perspectives as well as working to integrate varied perspectives.

Moreover, Dunn's (2004) research shows that "what is especially clear is that children make these conciliatory moves and compromises more frequently in disputes with their friends than they do with their siblings, or with children about whom they do not much care" (p. 37). In addition, with friends rather than siblings, children are "more likely to use reasoning that took account of the other person's point of view or feelings" (p. 38). Thus, children who are perfectly capable of more developed forms of conflict resolution do not always engage in such action. Dunn (2004) offers the following example:

> five-year-old Shirley (taking part in our London research) who dealt with disputes with her sister by simply screaming and reiterating what she wanted (and eventually pulling hair) went to some lengths to compromise or bargain when she was in conflict with her friend. "Let's take it in turns—I'll go first then you can have two goes.". . . "How about we both do it?" (pp. 38–39)

In other words, there is intraindividual variability as children engage in different developmentally organized modes of action in relation to different people.

This brief overview of peer play shows that varied action constituents are interrelated to comprise modes of acting in relation to peers during early childhood. As differentiation and integration within and across action constituents occur, new modes of acting in relation to others develop. In addition, this overview points to some of the different ways in which intraindividual variability or spirality characterizes human action and development. For example, a person may act differently in relation to different people in different situations, and sometimes those different ways of acting vary in terms of their developmental organization and complexity. In addition, even when people are capable of different modes of action that vary in terms of developmental complexity, they do not necessarily always act in the most developed ways immediately. They may begin with less developed modes of action before engaging in the more developed modes of action, or vice versa, depending on the vicissitudes of particular circumstances.

Some General Remarks

This chapter's analysis of children's action in relation to caregivers and peers illustrates how the theoretical framework presented here can be used to think systematically about what happens during the development of action during infancy and early childhood. I have posited some ways in which multiple and simultaneously occurring domains of functioning undergo differentiation and integration to comprise the development of action in relation to some cultural goals of development. In addition, it is evident that action during infancy and early childhood follows the genetic principle of spirality insofar as children act in more and less developed ways in relation to different people and in different action circumstances. This chapter's developmental analysis also illustrates how organismic-developmental theory enables us to think about development in terms of ongoing processes, rather than as a series of static stages. Thus, we have gone beyond positing a sequence of different modes of action to thinking about some of the differentiation and integration that occur along the way or in between the periods that are characterized by different modes of action.

The differentiation and integration constructs provide more specific criteria for defining development than change over time or age-based change. For this chapter, these constructs have provided a theoretical framework for synthesizing and thinking systematically about a wide range of research and for thinking systematically about some of the broad contours of development during infancy and early childhood. Nevertheless, identifying even more specific aspects of differentiation and integration could enhance our understanding of the complexities of what happens during development at any time during the life span.

In dynamic skills theory (e.g., Fischer, 1980; Fischer & Bidell, 2006; Mascolo & Fischer, 2010, 2015), Fischer posits a more specific scale for identifying increasing differentiation and integration that could potentially be adapted to the development of action as conceptualized here. Dynamic skills theory originally focused on cognitive development but has been extended to emotional and self development as well. The scale assesses development through four general tiers and through four levels within each tier. The four tiers include "reflexes (i.e., innate action elements that require stimulation for their activation and uses), sensorimotor actions (i.e., controlled actions performed on physical and social objects), representations (i.e., signs and symbols), and abstractions (i.e., representations of generalized, intangible meanings)" (Mascolo & Fischer, 2015, p. 12). Within the tiers, development is taken to proceed from differentiating single sets to integrating single sets into mappings, to integrating differentiated mappings into systems, which can be integrated into systems of systems.

With regard to the periods of action posited in this chapter, it is possible to identify some movement from single sets to mappings to systems for varied constituents of action, mostly within the sensorimotor tier. For example, mutual attention occurs when infants use a system of sensorimotor means (e.g., gazing, head-turning, crying, cooing, reaching) to engage with and disengage from others. During mutual attention, the infant's emotional expressivity is differentiated into single sets consisting of pleasure and displeasure. The self constituent of mutual attention involves the single sets of being attended to by another and not being attended to by another. When an infant is mutually engaged with someone, he or she is mapping attending to the other with being attended to by the other. In addition, other awareness includes the single sets of familiar and unfamiliar people. During the course of this period, infants are differentiating between physical objects and people, treating them as single sets by engaging with either objects or people separately.

As action develops from mutual attention to joint attention, infants are constructing mappings between objects and people as they engage with others about a common topic. During this period, the system of means to engage with others is further differentiated to include drawing attention to one's behavioral antics. Sharing a common action orientation during the fourth period becomes possible as children realize that when someone is not attending to them, the person is attending to something else in the world. There is thus differentiation of other awareness into subsets. To construct a common topic of interaction during the common action orientation period, a child is mapping his or her own attention and what the other is attending to.

Identifying more specific aspects of differentiation and integration in the organization of action requires research that is explicitly designed from an organismic-developmental perspective and on the basis of this book's conceptualization of action in relation to others. We will discuss some implications for such research in Chapter 8. At this juncture in the discussion, however, the point to be made is that the principle of increasing differentiation and integration can be elaborated in relation to specific cultural practices and modes of action.

Given the importance of culture to the current theoretical approach to action as well as to what happens during the development of action, we are led to going beyond research with middle-class European-Americans to exploring and thinking about what happens during the development of action in varied cultures. Some research suggests that action in relation to others may be structured in different ways around the world. For example, in some cultures parents and young children do not engage primarily in face-to-face interaction; in some cultures eye contact is avoided throughout the life span; in some cultures there are no terrible twos; and in some cultures children participate primarily in mixed-age peer groups (e.g., Dixon, Tronick, Keefer, & Brazelton, 1981; LeVine, 2004; LeVine et al., 1994/1998; Nsamenang, 1992; Ochs & Schieffelin, 1984/1988; Rogoff, 2003). Such research suggests that what happens during the development of action occurs in culturally particular ways, some of which we will explore in Chapter 5.

5

Thinking about the Development of Action around the World

[D]ifferent sociocultural groups may have different notions as to what constitutes ideal human development.... It is human beings who introduce teloi and values and construe development in terms of such teloi and values.... Now if teloi are "culture relative" or "culture bound," and claims about the development of some aspect of human functioning or human functioning itself depend on the teloi, then it makes no sense to speak tout court or to assume a priori that human development is everywhere the same. Any change in the telos, or the order of value of the teloi, will entail different developmental sequences and different interpretations and evaluations of what human beings are doing.

—Bernard Kaplan (1986, pp. 92–93)

Ideally, the goal of this chapter is to posit some sequences for the development of action in different cultures during infancy and early childhood, as was done in Chapter 4 on the basis of research in the United States. It would actually be ideal to have several chapters, with each one positing periods of development for action in a different culture. Unfortunately, these goals cannot be realized for at least two reasons.

First, a great deal of research on culture and development remains dominated by a dichotomous approach to individualism or independence and collectivism or interdependence. As explained in Chapter 2, a dichotomous approach treats individualism and collectivism mostly as opposing dimensions of culture and behavior. As such, cultures and the people who populate them end up being characterized in terms of either individualism/independence or collectivism/interdependence. Such research presents problems for our current enterprise because it starts from a premise that is antithetical to the current theoretical framework, which assumes that independence and interdependence are universal dimensions of human action. Indeed, this conceptualization of action in relation to others is derived from the premise that all people are separate individuals or independent or individualistic and *also* connected to others or interdependent or collectivistic. Moreover, both independence and interdependence are taken to be 100% necessary for action to occur, and cultural differences are taken to lie in how they are understood and particularized as people act in relation to others in all corners of the world. Moreover, as discussed in Chapter 2, research clearly shows that it is problematic to characterize cultures in terms of either individualism or collectivism because such characterizations obscure the ways in which both independence and interdependence are played out in culturally particular ways.

A second reason our discussion of non–European-American cultures is limited to one chapter is that there is simply not the sheer volume of research in particular cultures that one finds for research with European-Americans in the United States. In a wide-ranging *Handbook of Cultural Developmental Science* (Bornstein, 2010), several chapters include laments about the paucity of research in varied cultures. For example, "few studies have been conducted in developing countries, and evidence from South America is even scarcer" (Ribas, 2010, p. 323). There is "limited information" about development in Russia (Nelson, Hart, Keister, & Piassetskaia, 2010, p. 409). In Asia, "there are also cultural disparities in the depth and breadth of developmental science; Japan has more developmental scientists than any country outside the United States and Europe, but Vietnam and Indonesia have no distinct developmental scientific field" (Shwalb et al., 2010, p. 446). Nsamenang (2011) comments on the "sparseness and unsystematic nature of published research on African childhoods and adolescences" (p. 236) and points out that "Africa's developmental grids are largely uncharted" (Nsamenang & Lo-Oh, 2010, p. 383). Around the world, there may be a few studies that are relevant to the development of action, but a few studies here and there do not provide the depth and breadth needed to posit periods of differentiation and integration for varied modes of action at any time during the life span.

But we will not despair! By using the theoretical tools presented in Chapters 2 and 3, it is possible to start thinking systematically about what happens during the development of action in varied cultures. Indeed, this theoretical approach enables us to synthesize a wide range of research and to bring disparate research findings from disparate cultures into coherence. Once again, the current theoretical approach to development enables us to find the forest among the trees. In this case, the trees represent the scattered studies and bits of information about what happens during development in different cultures. When we see only the trees or read isolated studies about this or that culture, development seems to be a hodge-podge of unsystematic changes. By considering research from the perspective of the forest, some coherence and systematicity about development in any culture can be constructed. The forest here includes the wider whole of action in relation to others. According to the current theoretical perspective, it is assumed that all people develop ways of acting in relation to others, and such action is taken to be structured or organized in culturally particular ways. The forest also includes the current conceptualization of what happens during development, which provides consistent theoretical tools for thinking systematically about the development of action in varied cultures in terms of differentiation and integration in relation to cultural meanings and goals of development.

This chapter begins with the wide range of classic and contemporary research on development in cultures where there is little formal schooling and where life revolves around subsistence work. Thinking about development in such cultures further includes research on the widespread practice of sibling caregiving. In addition, this chapter considers research on the development of storytelling for middle-class and working-class children in the United States, as well as for middle-class families in Taipei, Taiwan. Research on the development of action in Japan is also presented. The chapter ends with a brief discussion of development in relation to cultural change. The research discussed in this chapter is included here because it provides information about modes of action in different cultures and/or because it provides some glimpses of developmental pathways for action in different cultures. Throughout this chapter, the discussion is directed toward discerning and thinking about some of the ways in which action is understood and organized around the world, as well as some of the ways in which development-as-differentiation-and-integration is played out around the world. Because the available research is not specifically derived from organismic-developmental theory, it can provide only glimpses of differentiation and integration. Accordingly, the chapter's analysis provides a broad overview of some of the ways in which development-as-differentiation-and-integration is evident around the world. Discerning the details awaits future research.

Lifelong Work

Over and over, classic and recent research in a wide range of cultures points to expectations that are already in force during early childhood for becoming a productive member of one's family and community through subsistence work. Participating in family and community work practices is not to be equated with the exploitation of children that occurs all too much around the world. The news is filled with reports of street children, child prostitutes, and child soldiers, as well as children being forced into hard labor in dangerous conditions. In contrast to these cases, the focus here is on work practices that can promote children's development through opportunities for "self-paced learning, playful and rich interaction with other children, and initiative or problem-solving" (Edwards, de Guzman, Brown, & Kumru, 2006, p. 43).

Development toward subsistence work goals begins during early childhood in many rural and relatively nonindustrialized communities around the world. For example, Whiting and Edwards (1988) describe varied work-related goals for children, in their classic analyses of life in towns and villages in Kenya, India, Mexico, the Philippines, Japan, and the United States. They write that mothers in

> Sub-Saharan Africa believe that responsibility and obedience can and should be taught to young children. They begin teaching household, gardening, and animal husbandry skills at a comparatively early age. The Ngecha mothers [in Kenya] we interviewed are typical: they believe that they should train a child to be a competent farmer, herdsman, and child nurse and that a child from age 2 on should be assigned chores that increase in complexity and arduousness with age. (pp. 94–95)

Gaskins (2000) argues that in a Mexican Yucatec Mayan village the "first cultural principle is primacy of adult work. . . . Children are legitimate cultural participants in adult work, even as they are learning how to participate appropriately" (p. 379). Within this context, "all children older than 1½ or 2 years are expected to do whatever chores they are asked to do quickly and effectively" (p. 385). In addition:

> By the ages of 3 to 5, children spend over 15% of the day working. . . . From 6 to 8, children spend 35% of the day working. . . . By 9 to 11, children spend the most time working of children of any age—50%. (Gaskins, Haight, & Lancy, 2007, p. 193)

Research in Bemni, India indicates that "children's seemingly constant absorption in different forms of work was one of the most remarkable aspects of the social life of Bemni" (Dyson, 2014, p. 42). In this village,

> by the age of five, children—boys and girls—could often look after younger siblings and prepare water for washing their face and hands. They could pick nits out of younger children's hair. . . . By seven, children were able to clean the house and surrounding yard and collect water or wash dishes at the nearest tap. By the age of ten. . . . they could hand-wash their own clothes, light fires, cook, clean dishes and deliver meals to other family members outside the home. They could keep the house, cattle stalls and courtyard clean. (p. 44)

In an analysis of a wide range of anthropological research, Lancy (2008/2010) identifies varied work curricula that shape developmental experiences in cultures around the world. There is the chores curriculum, whereby children are assigned tasks "that are 'just right' for a given child's age and strength" (p. 235). For example, "in Tanzania, a group of Hadza children heads out to the savannah to look for baobab fruits. From the age of four, they gather, haul back to camp, and process these nourishing snacks" (p. 235). Lancy notes that "pigs are of central importance throughout much of New Guinea as they provide both food and a store of capital" (p. 235). Within this context, "Kwoma children of six eagerly embrace the piglets they are given to protect, raise, and train" (p. 235). Where such practices occur, children's work achievements and "assumption of responsibility are widely acknowledged within the community" (p. 235), and development is marked not only by age but also in terms of "the chores that are typical for that age" (p. 235). Lancy additionally identifies the errand curriculum, which "incorporates many 'grades' from carrying messages (at age five) to marketing produce, hard bargaining, and making change for customers (by age eleven)" (p. 238). In many cultures, there are expectations for boys to become hunters and/or to complete a fishing curriculum, while girls (and sometimes boys) become adept at caring for younger siblings (Lancy, 2008/2010; Whiting & Edwards, 1988). Lancy (2008/2010) further identifies a craft curriculum that is "entirely voluntary" in contrast to the "often compulsory" chore curriculum (p. 251).

Undoubtedly, the physical skills and specialized knowledge that comprise these varied forms of work undergo development, and such development could be analyzed in terms of differentiation and integration. Moreover, as explained in Chapter 2, specialized skills and knowledge are constituents of modes of action that comprise work practices, which further involve varied other action constituents, including interacting with others. Cognition is also involved as children and adults pay attention, remember, and construct varied means to solve problems. Their action further involves language, emotion, self-direction, and identity processes. For example, Whiting (2004) explains that women in Ngecha, Kenya

> had acquired the intellectual and emotional skills they needed to work long hours, take initiative, and solve multifaceted problems. They had developed self-confidence as they succeeded in accomplishing the share of the work assigned to them by their own mothers. They had learned to take pleasure when they succeeded as members of the family work team. They had learned to cooperate with others and coordinate their actions to fit planned outcomes and to find enjoyment in seeing group goals accomplished. As they had grown up and become more responsible, they had learned how to organize their younger siblings and to manage the household in their mothers' absence. They had become practiced in planning, leading, and giving orders to others younger than themselves. (p. 103)

In other words, they had developed ways of acting in relation to others, and such action involves interrelations among varied action constituents.

Taken together, this research provides a basis for starting to think about the development of action in subsistence cultures by enabling us to discern some of the ways in which action is structured in relation to cultural values and expectations for development, as well as how action consists of varied domains of action. From the theoretical perspective presented in previous chapters, such ethnographic research is replete with relatively general descriptions of what happens during development. For example, we have learned that children are expected to engage in and take responsibility for increasingly complex forms of work. Using organismic-developmental theory, we can posit that differentiation and integration occur along the way, although research is not specifically directed toward discerning pathways of differentiation and integration in relation to cultural expectations and standards. Nevertheless, some research provides some hints of possible pathways of differentiation and integration in relation to cultural goals of development (Lancy, 2008/2010).

For example, ethnographic research on the Marquesas Islands indicates that "daily life is organized around work for the household" (Martini & Kirkpatrick, 1992/1994, p. 207), and development occurs in relation to varied cultural goals, including "how to be competent householders; how to establish and maintain intimate relations at home and elsewhere; how to manage distant relations in the community; and, how to exercise autonomy in a world of consociates" (pp. 207–208). Martini and Kirkpatrick describe how these goals are played out during infancy, childhood, adolescence, and early adulthood. Our theoretical perspective leads to thinking about Marquesan development in terms of how achieving these goals of development involves modes of action that undergo differentiation and integration.

During the first 2 months of life, Marquesan infants are cared for primarily by their mothers, and when infants can sit, mothers "turn them to face outward and encourage them to attend to others" (p. 209). When babies are able to walk, "mothers release them into the care of preschool siblings who play with them near the house" (p. 208). From 18 months to 3 years, children learn to feed and dress themselves, and they become increasingly self-reliant. Caregivers also "begin to expect children to be compliant and nondemanding when they are busy or irritable. This is a major shift from the earlier period in which caregivers met nearly every infant demand" (p. 210). In addition, children are increasingly expected to comfort themselves. At the same time, however, in some situations "caregivers enjoy toddlers who make demands, tease, chatter, and make mischief" and during this period, children "learn to read contextual cues to know when to be obedient and when not" (p. 210). Toddlers remain on the periphery of peer group activities, and older siblings expect them to "keep themselves safe, stay out of the way of the group activity, and make few demands on the older siblings" (p. 211).

The development of such modes of action may involve differentiation and integration within and across action constituents in varied ways. For example, children seem to be differentiating among and integrating emotions, as well as differentiating between their own and other people's perspectives in order to discern when someone else is busy or irritable or to tease another person effectively. Children may also be differentiating among and integrating varied means to comfort themselves and to keep themselves safe. Knowing when to act in different ways (e.g., to obey or to make mischief) likely requires differentiating among social situations and using differentiated and integrated means to act in relation to others in those different situations.

During the preschool period, children "learn simple household skills . . . and may be expected to gather wood, pick up leaves, sweep, and run to the store on errands" (p. 211). They also become the older siblings who take care of younger children. Within the peer group, 3- and 4-year-olds move from the periphery to the center of group activity. Accordingly, "they learn to attend to other children's cues . . . they must scan others to learn what the shared activity is" (p. 212). Such action involves the continued differentiation and integration of perspectives. Subsequently, "after a year or two, they will shape the definition of the situation to which younger children must adapt" (p. 212). Also during this period, children learn to "relate to distant others" (p. 212), which suggests that they are making distinctions, or differentiating among people and ways of acting in relation to different people. They may also be integrating differentiated relationship roles into a wider view of themselves in relation to others.

During the school years, children continue to master household tasks, which likely involve continued differentiation and integration of physical skills and specialized knowledge. In addition, they

> are considered to be competent conversational partners and adults draw on children's superior knowledge of valley events. At home, children sit near adults and participate in all but the most serious conversations. They initiate topics, take long speaking turns, and adults listen to their input. (p. 213)

Many Marquesan children go to boarding schools, where they may be able to continue developing ways of acting in relation to varied others while maintaining ties to peers from their home valley. Finally, during adolescence and young adulthood, "young people develop cross-sex liaisons and learn to maintain dyadic commitments despite competing demands from the peer group and, in some cases, their households" (p. 214). Ultimately "they establish their own households, and can 'direct themselves'" (p. 215). This description suggests that young adults are positioning themselves in terms of increasingly differentiated social roles and may be working out ways to integrate them.

Sibling Caregiving

Sibling caregiving has long been a common practice around the world, especially in subsistence cultures where there is little or no formal schooling, and it continues to be practiced around the world today. At any time during the life span, caregiving involves modes of action in relation to others that partake of varied constituents, including interpersonal interaction, perspective taking, thinking, feeling, and self-construction. As Gaskins (2006) explains, when older children take care of younger siblings,

> they are required to take into account the needs, abilities, and emotions of someone else. They must be able to put their own desires second to those of others. They practice arts of cajoling, distracting, asserting authority, serving as ombudsman and judge, and directing. They have the pleasure of receiving trust, affection, cooperation, and dependency of someone who needs them. They recognize their own competencies and power compared with those they take care of. They learn the rules they have been taught more completely as they try to teach them to others. They bear responsibilities with direct consequences for people they love. And they know that their efforts at child care are a true contribution to the work of the compound and are thereby valued by the adults who are important to them. (p. 298)

It is readily acknowledged that there is cultural variability in the organization of sibling caregiving (Weisner & Gallimore, 1977). Nevertheless, research points to some general patterns of sibling caregiving that provide glimpses of the differentiation and integration that may occur during the development of varied modes of action that comprise caregiving practices.

Once again, we turn to Whiting's and Edward's (1988) classic synthesis of research in a wide range of cultures. They report that mothers often encourage young children to "entertain babies for short periods of time and to help stop their fussing" (p. 172). Even 2- and 3-year-olds "are seen to smile at, pat, or imitate lap babies, to give them objects, play peek-a-boo games, tickle them, make faces to entertain them, and try to guess their needs or wants when the infants show distress" (p. 163). Sometimes, young children of 4 or 5 years carry out caregiving responsibilities, but mothers seem to prefer caregivers who are between 6 or 7 and 10 years old (Rogoff, 2003; Whiting & Edwards, 1988; Zukow-Goldring, 2002). From an organismic-developmental perspective, we are not so much concerned with the age of sibling caregivers, but rather with what sibling caregivers do, and whether there is differentiation and integration in the modes of action that comprise caregiving.

Initially, younger caregivers tend to "overdo their hilarious play and overstimulate the lap child, which causes crying that the baby tender is then unable to quiet" (Whiting & Edwards, 1988, p. 172). In response, the young caregivers may become "impatient and antagonistic—shaking, punching or slapping the baby in exasperation" (p. 172). Such action suggests a global reaction to the infant that does not involve a clear differentiation between perspectives. In addition, different techniques for tending to an infant, depending on his or her needs, are neither differentiated nor integrated. Subsequently, the preferred older caregivers are "more consistently and appropriately nurturant and less overstimulating" (p. 176). This consistency is linked to being able to better understand the needs and feelings of their charges, as well as being more adept at comforting them. In other words, the caregivers seem to be differentiating between perspectives in terms of different needs and feelings, and both differentiating and integrating means to comfort their charges. In addition, there is increasing flexibility in action insofar as the ideal caregivers "can see more than one way to resolve a problem, and can put another's needs before their own" (Zukow-Goldring, 2002, p. 266). It is also argued that children are assigned caregiving responsibilities when they can "carry out a sequence of acts in an exact order without supervision" and when they know "the goals and rules of everyday life" (Zukow-Goldring, 2002, p. 262). This description points to cognitive development in that children are differentiating and integrating means to solve problems, and differentiating among parts of a task as well as integrating them into a temporal sequence.

Some research suggests that sibling caregiving includes teaching (Maynard, 2002; Maynard & Tovote, 2010/2012; Rabain-Jamin, Maynard, & Greenfield, 2003). For example, in a Mexican Mayan community, sibling interactions were analyzed in terms of "the Zinacantec model of teaching" which involves "expectation of obedience, scaffolded help, observational learning, contextualized talk, [and] teacher and learner bodily closeness" (Maynard, 2002, p. 971). The sibling caregivers "taught everyday tasks such as washing, cooking, taking care of baby dolls, and making tortillas" (p. 973). Observations of 3- to 11-year-old sibling caregivers indicated that the youngest sibling caregivers were likely to do the tasks themselves, while allowing their charges to "join in right next to them" (p. 978). This description suggests that the sibling caregiver is treating both the task and teaching as a global whole, and that the caregiver is unable to integrate what he or she and his or her charge are doing beyond physical proximity. Sibling caregivers between 6 and 7 years old "gave a lot of commands" but ended up doing the task by themselves if their 2-year-old charges "didn't do enough" (p. 978). From the perspective of organismic-developmental theory, this description is rather vague, and it is not clear if some of the commands provide clearly articulated (i.e., differentiated) information that accommodates the charge's perspective. It is also not clear if the commands are integrated temporally or in relation to the components of a particular task. Between the ages of 8 and 11, sibling caregivers increasingly accompany their activities with explanations and descriptions, provide appropriate feedback, and simplify the task into subgoals for the younger children to carry out. Providing appropriate feedback suggests that the sibling caregiver is taking the younger child's perspective into consideration, thereby differentiating between and integrating perspectives. In addition, constructing subgoals involves differentiating among and integrating task components.

Research on life in subsistence settings enables us to think about what happens during development in cultures that differ markedly from the culture of middle-class Americans who populate so much of developmental research. In particular, it shows how people's action in relation to others can be structured in some very different ways within different cultural practices. At the same time however, there are also similarities among people around the world, and cultural differences are often variations on common themes and practices (e.g., Rogoff, 2003). In the next section we will explore what happens during the development of storytelling in different cultures.

Telling Stories

Research on storytelling provides further insight into cultural expectations for life span development and cultural ways of structuring action, as well as glimpses of development-as-differentiation-and-integration. Storytelling is ubiquitous around the world and "much of what passes for everyday conversation among people is storytelling" (McAdams, 1993, p. 28). When people tell stories they do not merely or dispassionately recount the facts of an event. Rather, they interpret and give meaning to their own and others' behavior through the prism of cultural beliefs and values (Bamberg, 2012; Bruner, 1990, 2002; McAdams, 1993). Furthermore, "storytelling functions span the wide territory from entertainment to attributions of blame or accounts of personal transgression" (Bamberg, 2011, p. 102). Bamberg argues that whereas researchers typically call upon people to tell "big" stories or autobiographical accounts of themselves, people often tell "small" stories about themselves and others within the ongoing flow of action in relation to others (Bamberg & Georgakopoulou, 2008). Taken together, storytelling can be understood as a form of action that involves varied action constituents, including language, social interaction, cognition, emotion, and self-construction. Storytelling additionally includes skills such as organizing themes and plots and using varied rhetorical devices and means to create an interesting story and maintain listeners' interest. As a form of action, storytelling also develops. According to Bruner, "negotiating and renegotiating meanings by the mediation of narrative interpretation is . . . one of the crowning achievements of human development" (1990, p. 67).

We begin thinking about what happens during the development of storytelling with Heath's (1983/1992) classic ethnographic research on language development for children in two working-class rural towns in the southern United States. Heath "lived, worked, and played with the children and their families and friends" in these towns between 1969 and 1978 (Heath, 1983/1992, p. 5). In Roadville, populated by European-Americans, stories were used to uphold community standards and emphasize group membership. People told stories that "maintain a strict chronicity" and "reaffirm their commitment to community and church values by giving factual accounts of their own weaknesses and the lessons learned in overcoming these" (p. 185). In Trackton, populated by African-Americans, storytelling expectations were quite different.

African-American storytelling has its roots in African cultural traditions, which have long emphasized expressing individuality through "verbal facility" (Levine, 1977, p. 128). With regard to cultural expectations, Heath (1983/1992) observes that among rural working-class African-Americans, individual creativity is a criterion for a good story. In addition, "the 'best stories' often call forth highly diverse additional stories, all designed . . . to set out the individual merits of each member of the group" (p. 185). At the same time, these stories "are intended to intensify social interactions and to give all parties an opportunity to share in . . . the unity of the common experience on which the story may be based" (p. 166). Varied specific linguistic means may be used to tell stories, including "imitations of other community members or TV personalities, dramatic gestures and shifts of voice quality, and rhetorical questions and expressions of emotional evaluations" (p. 186). This description points to differentiating between oneself and others, as well as coordinating with others in culturally particular ways. In addition, organismic-developmental theory leads to positing that the development of storytelling involves differentiating among and integrating the varied linguistic means taken to comprise a good story.

Within this context, children are encouraged to tell stories about themselves as a way to "assert individual strengths and powers" (p. 184). Heath found that children "tell story-poems from the age of two" (p. 187), and they initially tell stories in the form of monologues, meaning that they do not necessarily "make an effort to attract the attention of listeners before they begin the story" (p. 170). Heath notes that children "gradually learn to work their way into any on-going discourse with their stories," which requires being "highly creative and entertaining to win a way into an on-going conversation" (p. 187). It would seem that children are differentiating between telling stories and other modes of action, and then integrating storytelling with ongoing action. In addition, children presumably differentiate among and integrate varied narrative devices as they "embellish [monologues] with gestures, *inclusios* [bracketing a section of narrative], questions asked of the audience, and repetitions with variations" (p. 187).

For over two decades, Miller and colleagues have conducted research on narrative practices among working-class and middle-class European-Americans, and more recently among middle-class families in Taipei, Taiwan. Storytelling occurred frequently during naturalistic observations of family interaction in these cultural communities, and interviews with parents indicated that storytelling is valued by the adults in all of these groups. Our consideration of this research begins in the United States, and then turns to Miller's analyses of storytelling in Taipei.

In the United States, the working-class participants told stories more frequently than the middle-class participants did, and "when the working-class children were 3 years old, they produced nearly three times as many stories as their middle-class counterparts" (Cho & Miller, 2004, p. 82). In addition, personal storytelling in working-class communities

> privileges the individual's right to have a voice, to celebrate his or her own unique experiences and perspectives on the world. This version allows people to see that each person—however humble his or her resources, status, and place in the world—has had many story worthy experiences; that each person has the right to tell these experiences from his or her own perspective; that it is fun, entertaining, and enlightening to tell and listen to such stories; and that while some people are especially talented narrators, almost everyone can become a competent storyteller. (Miller, Cho, & Bracey, 2005, p. 125)

A key goal of life span storytelling among the working-class participants in Miller's research is to "defend one's own point of view" (Miller, Cho, & Bracey, 2005, p. 129). Thus, development involves differentiating one's point of view or perspective from others. In addition, particularly pleasing stories are constructed through using varied narrative devices, including changing intonations, shifting verb tenses, and nonverbal accompaniments. From an organismic-developmental perspective, developmental analyses would involve discerning pathways of differentiation and integration in the use of these narrative devices.

Miller's analyses show that relative to their middle-class counterparts, working-class mothers and children "produced more stories of negative experience, narrated a wider range of negative experiences, and shared more extreme negative experiences" (Miller, Cho, & Bracey, 2005, p. 127). Within the category of negative narratives, "one of the most popular subgenres of personal narrative in a South Baltimore working-class community was stories of anger and aggression. These stories consistently invoked a self-protagonist who valiantly and effectively stood up for herself" (p. 129). Longitudinal observations of young mothers (18 to 20 years old) and their daughters in South Baltimore included interviews with the mothers about their childrearing beliefs, values, and goals (Miller & Sperry, 1987).

The mothers emphasized "the qualities of strength, pride, and self-control. . . . The abilities to stand up for oneself and to 'take' pain and suffering without betraying hurt feelings were highly valued. . . . The mothers also disapproved of overindulging or 'spoiling' children" (Miller & Sperry, 1987, p. 15). Moreover, children had to "learn to distinguish between justifiable anger (anger in self-defense) and unjustifiable anger (self-indulgent anger)" (p. 18). This description indicates that stories about anger and aggression occurred in relation to developmental expectations, and involved differentiating among types of anger that reflect cultural meanings.

Analyses further provide glimpses of an early developmental sequence for telling stories about anger and aggression. In the reported observations, which began when the girls were between 18 and 25 months old, they initially expressed their anger through both verbal and nonverbal means. For example, the following scene is described:

> When Cousin Kris (age 5) took Amy's doll, Amy (25 months) responded by screaming, swatting at, and hitting Kris and by loudly protesting ("No!"), asserting and demanding ("My baby! Give my baby! a want that!"), and accusing ("Kris, my baby"). (p. 23)

In this case, screaming, swatting, and hitting seem to be relatively global means that Amy used to express anger and defend herself. With language, she showed some beginning differentiation among asserting, demanding, and accusing. The brief description does not indicate if or how these speech acts were integrated, but Miller and Sperry explain that subsequently, the children used language "quite articulately" to express anger and to defend themselves against the objects of their anger:

> They protested or refused to comply with an instigating act. . . . They demanded or asserted their own plans or goals. . . . They responded to the instigating act with an overt verbal action, such as a threat or insult. . . . They gave reasons for their angry response by accusing the target of anger. (p. 24)

These responses imply that children use language to differentiate among varied ways of expressing anger and defending oneself, namely demanding, asserting, threatening, insulting, and accusing. Miller and Sperry report further that subsequently "accusations were elaborated into narrative accounts of events of aggression by one of the children" (p. 25), which could include differentiating among and integrating the details of different accusation instances, as well as integrating accusations into a wider narrative. In many stories, one child "provided additional details about the alleged transgression" (p. 25), suggesting that there is differentiation within the events that comprise the wider story.

Miller's and colleagues' (Miller, Fung, Lin, Chen, & Boldt, 2012) comparative longitudinal analyses of middle-class families in Taipei and Chicago point to the value of storytelling across cultures, as well as to culturally particular ways of structuring storytelling. The children in the families were 2 years old at the outset of the study and 4 years old when observations ended. The focus here is on the findings from Taipei, where life is rooted in Confucian values and goals of development, including "obedience to elders, proper behavior, good habits, and 'learning virtues' such as persistence in completing tasks, patience in learning, and the ability to concentrate for extended periods of time" (pp. 44–45).

Analyses focused specifically on when children contributed to telling stories about their own personal experiences. The participants told such stories frequently, and they covered varied topics, from physical harm, to enjoyable family events, to unusual events. In addition, the families in Taipei emphasized transgression stories in which "the child was portrayed as violating a social or moral rule in the past, as interpreted from the perspective of at least one of the narrating participants" (p. 32). Miller et al. explain that "for these families, the past misdeeds of very young children required assiduous attention, but vigilance could be leavened with affection and humor" (p. 81). In contrast, the American families downplayed children's misdeeds and instead emphasized stories that promoted children's self-esteem, thus reflecting culturally particular values and developmental expectations.

Children participated in telling stories as co-narrators and bystanders. As a co-narrator, "the child contributed at least two substantive, on-topic utterances," and as a bystander, "the child was present within earshot of a narration that a family member addressed to another person(s), primarily referring to the child in the third person" (p. 59). In Taipei, children acted as bystanders more often than as co-narrators throughout the years of the study. When the study started, the children participated in storytelling with others mostly by following

> along with narrations that were structured primarily by older, more competent narrators. Caregivers and siblings structured the stories so as to focus the child's attention on the misdeed: They stated what the child had done wrong, pointed out its consequences, and rehearsed how such situations should be handled in the future. (p. 78)

The 2-year-olds listened to often repeated stories about their transgressions and answered others' questions nonverbally and verbally "with simple utterances" (p. 81).

When they were 3 years old, the children were increasingly likely to initiate stories about varied topics by "vigorously pursuing those topics, introducing the issue of intentionality, mitigating their own misdeeds, and even challenging moral rules" (p. 86). Going beyond answering others' questions to initiating stories in these ways indicates that the children were differentiating between their roles as listeners and co-narrators. These moves also indicate that the children were differentiating among and integrating varied story elements. There may also be ongoing differentiation and integration of one's own intentionality into goals and subgoals. During this observation period, children offered their own ideas, sometimes refused to participate in a narration, defended themselves by challenging "a co-narrator's accuracy or interpretation" (p. 65), and "supplied information that their co-narrators lacked" (p. 84). These findings suggest that children were differentiating among and integrating their own and others' perspectives, which were increasingly differentiated in terms of ideas and knowledge.

Ultimately, by the last observation, at the age of 4, the children initiated narratives and were "taking a substantial role in steering the conversation toward" narratives about "their own past experiences" (p. 87). They also judged their own and others' behavior in terms of the "standards upheld by adults" (p. 87), which suggests that cultural standards were being differentiated as a dimension of action. Moreover, they "began to treat *not* transgressing as a reportable event" (p. 87), which suggests that they increasingly differentiated among different types of narrative events. Differentiating between oneself and others was also apparent as the children used "invidious comparisons as a way of extolling their own virtuous conduct" (p. 87). It is interesting to note that whereas the European-American parents eschewed making invidious comparisons among children, the Taiwanese parents did so frequently. Thus, the children's use of invidious comparisons reflects culturally particular ways of positioning oneself in relation to others. Miller et al. also describe how one precocious girl used varied, or differentiated, means to resist her aunt, who wanted her to tell a particular story about her birthday. The child used "silence, explicit refusals to tell, displays of embarrassment, creation of a diversion, a brief, ambiguous confession/accusation, and finally a successful attempt to steer the story to the fun activities on her birthday" (p. 89). Although the analyses do not speak to issues of integration, this storytelling incident points to the differentiation of narrative means and topics.

Taken together, these research findings show that storytelling is structured in culturally particular and meaningful ways, and that differentiation and integration during the development of storytelling are played out in culturally particular ways. Insofar as developmental research on storytelling is not explicitly informed by organismic-developmental theory, we have only been able to discern glimpses of differentiation and integration. Thus, further research is required to identify more specific cultural pathways of differentiation and integration for the development of storytelling. The analysis here points to the utility of conceptualizing what happens during development in terms of differentiation and integration for thinking systematically about storytelling in a way that preserves cultural specificity. It also provides a common framework for systematically comparing and contrasting varied developmental pathways.

Thinking about Development in Japan

As an industrialized democracy, Japan provides an important cultural contrast to the United States where there is an abundance of research with European-Americans. In this section, we consider some research on inner and outer action circumstances as well as some research on group action in Japan.

Inner and Outer Action Circumstances

Research in Japan has long pointed to the important distinction between outer or public, and inner or private settings (Bachnik, 1992/1995, 1994; Doi, 1985/ 1988; Hendry, 1986; Rosenberger, 2001; Tobin, 1992/1995). From our current perspective, outer and inner settings can be understood in terms of culturally particular ways of acting in relation to others. According to Doi:

> Like their Latin counterparts *recto* and *verso*, *omote* and *ura* are paired opposing concepts. We speak of the *omote-ura* of things, referring to the two sides of everything, and we also use them as opposing concepts in various combinations with other words. An *omote-dōri* is a busy main street; an *ura- dōri* is a lonely back alley. *Omote-muki* refers to that which is public, open, official; *ura-muki* suggests something private, closed, personal. (1985/1988, p. 23)

With regard to cultural expectations for life span development, "to be Japanese is to be aware of the fact that things have an *omote* and an *ura*, and a person is not considered to be an adult until he or she has grasped this distinction" (Doi, 1985/ 1988, p. 33).

Outer or public modes of action are particularly salient in school and work settings and are characterized by formal and indirect communication patterns that enable people to avoid overt conflict. In addition, action in outer circumstances involves self-control, including refraining from expressing opposing opinions. According to Lebra (1992/1995), action in public settings involves "self-effacement and modesty" (p. 108). At the same time, there are also expectations for developing inner or private modes of action at home and among friends. Inner/private modes of action are characterized by informal language, as well as directly expressing one's individual opinions and feelings (Bachnik, 1994; Lebra, 1992/1995; Mathews, 1996). It is argued that "in one's inner circle there is no need to . . . worry about consequences of one's actions toward others. There is no need to hold back one's desires" (Kondo, 1990, pp. 149–150). As with any form of action, inner and outer modes of action involve multiple and interrelated domains of functioning, including interacting with others, perspective taking, speaking, feeling, and self-construction. According to the approach to action presented here, these action constituents are taken to be structured and interrelated in different ways for inner and outer modes of action. We can posit that during development, the constituents of action for inner and outer modes of action would undergo differentiation and integration.

Inner action circumstances further involve Japanese ways of acting known as *amae* (Behrens, 2004; Doi, 1973/2001; Marshall, Chuong, & Aikawa, 2011; Yamaguchi & Ariizumi, 2006). According to Doi, whose early treatment of *amae* continues to inform research on this issue, *amae* "is the noun form of *amaeru*, an intransitive verb that means 'to depend and presume upon another's benevolence'" (1974/1986, p. 121). Although many treatments of *amae* focus on how it is played out within parent–child relationships (especially mother–child relationships), attention has also been paid to *amae* as a life span developmental issue that characterizes action within friendships as well as within adult romantic relationships (Marshall, Chuong, & Aikawa, 2011; Yamaguchi & Ariizumi, 2006). According to Peak (1991/1993), the home is an inner or private context "where one can freely demonstrate feelings of *amae*, or the desire to be indulged. This legitimate desire for indulgence encompasses the free display of feelings that in other settings would be termed selfishness, regressive dependence, irritability, and even petty tyranny" (pp. 5–6). *Amae* may also be understood in terms of reciprocal and interchangeable roles, meaning that sometimes a person engages in *amae*, and sometimes he or she indulges another person's *amae*. Accordingly, the development of *amae* would involve differentiating between and integrating these two roles, as well as differentiating among and integrating means to achieve them. The development of *amae* also likely involves differentiating among perspectives, as well as differentiating and integrating emotional action constituents.

Although inner and outer modes of action are distinguished or differentiated, they are also interrelated ways of acting. Accordingly, development is "more complex than simply distinguishing inside from outside, front from back, public from private, and family from strangers" (Tobin, 1992/1995, p. 24). That is,

> one must learn to make much more fluid and subtle distinctions, learn to step back and forth across the gap dividing *omote* from *ura* in the course of a single conversation, or indeed, even in the midst of a single phrase, as a slight wink of an eye or a change in the level of politeness of a verb ending suddenly signals a slight but crucial warming up or cooling down of relations. (Tobin, 1992/1995, p. 24)

Developing these abilities begins early, even in preschool, where "the most crucial lesson to be learned is ... the knowledge needed to shift fluidly back and forth between *omote* and *ura*" (Tobin, 1992/1995, p. 24). In other words, inner and outer modes of action may be differentiated, but they are also integrated within particular action circumstances.

Group Action

Varied analyses of Japanese culture and development point to the importance of acting in relation to others in different group settings, such as at home, school, and work. Already in preschool, children are identified as members of a particular class (Tobin et al., 1989), and "competition among classes in a school is often used to encourage group effort and promote a sense of group identification and pride" (p. 41). In elementary school, children continue to be part of a class and they also spend a great deal of time in small groups of four to eight to work on school activities, as well as to eat and play together and to keep the school clean (Hoffman, 2000; Lewis, 1995/1999). For adults, work in a company is often viewed in terms of responsibility to the company-as-family, which "means above all accepting the burden of membership in the group. By carrying out their responsibilities, managers allow the group to survive and prosper" (Todeschini, 2011, p. 49).

When people participate together in group practices in Japan, they are not necessarily all acting in the same way, and thus seem to be both differentiating themselves from others as well as coordinating with others. As Rosenberger puts it, "personhood linked with the group" includes "consensus hammered out of individual expressions" (2001, p. 6). Or, as a Japanese preschool principal pointed out, despite strong group norms, "Everyone doing the same thing at the same time isn't the same as real group life, is it" (Tobin et al., 1989, p. 39). Beginning in preschool, group functioning and harmonious relationships are established and maintained in part by supporting individual perspectives and goals, which would seem to involve differentiating among goals as well as integrating them. With regard to school practices, during some group activities, "each child in the school is given an opportunity to participate in his or her own fashion" (Tobin et al., 1989, pp. 41–42). Observations in first-grade classrooms indicate that students "listened and responded to one another's ideas—clapping for one another, correcting, congratulating, devising explanations for students who were having difficulty" (Lewis, 1995/1999, p. 177). Students are also often asked to "reflect privately on questions such as, 'Did today's class discussions involve all classmates or just a few classmates?' and 'Did I volunteer my ideas sometime today?'" (Lewis, 1995/1999, p. 113).

In addition, ethnographic research in a Japanese middle school indicates that "the basic task of maturation involves creating strong individual goals. ... Adolescent development requires finding some goal or dream that will provide organization in one's life" (Letendre, 2000, p. 95). These goals can then be enacted in social settings, which suggests that individuals are integrating their goals with others who are also pursuing individual goals. Similarly, adults at early morning work ceremonies in a company setting "took turns in telling the audience what they had done for the company" (Todeschini, 2011, p. 49). These practices point to the importance of valuing each individual's perspective and contributions and of developing one's own ways of contributing to the group. Taken together, development seems to involve differentiating among and integrating one's own and others' perspectives, as well as discerning how one's differentiated individual goals can be integrated with others to pursue wider group goals.

Research in Japan points to varied cultural goals and expectations for the development of action throughout the life span. It also provides a basis for thinking about differentiation and integration within and across action constituents. As with the other cultures considered in this chapter, we have glimpses of differentiation and integration. More research is needed to discern specific pathways for the development of inner and outer modes of action in Japan, as well as for modes of action within group practices.

Cultural Change

This chapter's analysis of what happens during the development of action in varied cultures indicates that people act in relation to others in culturally particular ways and that the development of cultural modes of action can be fruitfully understood in terms of differentiation and integration within and across action constituents. But of course cultures are dynamic and undergo ongoing change for a wide range of multiple and interrelated reasons. Insofar as human action emerges and develops in relation to ongoing cultural change, our current consideration represents a fleeting view of what happens during development in the cultures discussed. The point here and in Chapter 4 is not to tell THE story of development in any particular culture. That would be an impossible undertaking, in part because cultures change. Rather, the point is to think systematically about what happens during development in varied cultures, by applying our current systems conceptualization of action as well as the theoretical tools of organismic-developmental theory. The fact that cultures change does not invalidate this theoretical approach to action and development. While it may be impossible to construct a definitive catalog of the developmental changes that people experience, this theoretical approach facilitates thinking systematically about what is going on during development, when it does happen, whatever the cultural circumstances may be. Indeed, it is precisely because people's developmental experiences change as cultures change that we need a way to think systematically about development in terms of dynamic processes. Organismic-developmental theory provides a way of doing so by conceptualizing development in terms of the ongo-ing processes of differentiation and integration.

This conceptualization leads to discerning how cultural change is reflected in the emergence of new cultural goals for development and in the development of new modes of action. We would posit that as cultures change, development involves potentially new pathways of differentiation and integration in relation to new cultural goals for development. Thinking about development in relation to cultural change is a topic for a volume in and of itself that requires histori-cal analysis, as well as analyses of different sources of cultural change. Although such analyses are beyond the scope of this book, a brief consideration of some research enables us to explore some issues about development in relation to cul-tural change and to further illustrate how to use the theoretical framework pre-sented here to think systematically about what happens during the development of action.

Some of the starkest examples of changing developmental pathways in the midst of cultural change are described in research conducted in subsistence cul-tures that have undergone varied changes with the introduction of formal school-ing and wage labor. Indeed, some of the subsistence cultures discussed earlier in this chapter have undergone such changes. With regard to the introduction of formal schooling, increasing school attendance may bring new modes of action for both children and adults, and some analyses indicate that children and adults differentiate between modes of action considered appropriate at home and at school (Rogoff, 2003; Whiting et al., 2004). For example, research conducted in Ngecha, Kenya, from 1968 to 1973, as Kenya was emerging from British colonial rule, points to changing modes of action for children who were going to school for the first time, as well as for their parents. Children had

> to get used to new rules about the role of questions in discourse. Being questioned by an adult who knows the answer was a new experience. Questions in the home setting were for seeking information, not for test-ing knowledge. Adults questioned children frequently, but children sel-dom initiated conversations with adults. Asking questions of the teacher was considered rude. (Whiting et al., 2004, p. 127)

As children spent more time in school, Ngecha mothers increasingly endorsed new developmental goals and values, such as "cleverness, confidence, inquisitive-ness, and bravery or boldness" (Whiting et al., 2004, p. 144).

Beyond academic lessons, "children had to learn to manage competition within a large peer group of children who were not kin-related, who had not been their constant companions since early childhood, and whose relative age was not their most striking ordering characteristic" (Edwards et al., 2006, p. 39). School attendance also brought children in contact with other children of "different conventions and lifestyles" (p. 39). They thus likely had opportunities to develop new ways of acting in relation to varied, or differentiated, others.

Economic and technological changes also occurred in Ngecha that profoundly "reorganized the daily lives of men, women, and children" (Whiting, 2004, p. 93). For example, the time that women spent fetching water was dramatically reduced with the construction of a town well and pump. At the same time, women were given "a garden plot by assignment on her husband's or father-in-law's homestead" (p. 99), which became a source of "cash that they could control themselves from the sale of surplus vegetables" (p. 100). In addition:

> The women of Ngecha were quick to catch the entrepreneurial spirit and to try new ventures. . . . They learned how to raise chickens in order to sell pullets and eggs. They made baskets for sale through a basket cooperative and invested in sweater-making machines. They followed closely the farm reports broadcast on the radio and were eager to gather useful information and hear of new opportunities. (pp. 103–104)

A notable change for men's action involved increasing interaction with babies and young children. These new modes of action suggest possible developmental changes for both men and women in the organization of multiple action constituents, including cognition, as well as interacting with varied others both within and beyond the family and community. In addition, these new modes of action may involve constructing oneself in terms of differentiated roles, as Ngecha women "derived a sense of importance from their roles as mothers, farmers, and entrepreneurs" (p. 116).

Cultural changes through education and a cash economy may also involve the development of using new symbolic means and technologies. Saxe's (2012) research with the Oksapmin of Papua New Guinea shows that they adapted their body-based counting method over a period of three decades to allow for adding and subtracting, which became necessary when a cash economy was introduced in the 1960s. Saxe explains that the Oksapmin body-based counting method "includes 27 body parts" (p. 44), and counting

> begins with the thumb of one hand and enumerates the 27 places around the upper periphery of the body (with accompanying body-part names), ending on the little finger of the opposite hand. . . . To count past the 27th body part . . . the counter loops from the little finger (27) to the wrist, then proceeds to the forearm, and on up and around the body. . . . To indicate a particular number, the counter points to the appropriate body part and says the body-part name. . . . To create a cardinal representation, he or she uses the morpheme "*hai*" after the body-part word. (pp. 45–46)

Saxe explains further that this counting method was "well-tailored to solving numerical problems in traditional life," such as "counting valuables, measuring string bags (a common artifact), and indicating ordinal position (such as ordinal relations along a path)" (p. 47). It did not provide means for adding and subtracting, but before the introduction of cash-based economic exchange and wage labor, there was no need for the Oksapmin to add and subtract.

Establishing a cash economy did not mean that counting body parts was simply replaced suddenly with a new counting method. Part of what happened during the course of this cultural change is that some people's ways of counting changed and presumably developed. In 2001, the body-part counting method was on the decline and was used with most facility by community elders who had not experienced formal schooling. The Hindu-Arabic counting method was increasingly prevalent among younger adults, adolescents, and children in relation to their economic and educational experiences. From our theoretical approach we can posit that individuals' ways of using Hindu-Arabic numbers underwent differentiation and integration. It is also important to point out that such development is not about math in isolation from development within and across other domains of functioning. Rather, doing math with the new way of counting can be seen as a cognitive subconstituent of action insofar as it is used in part to conduct business in commercial settings. Such action also involves interacting with others, and we can posit that it includes viewing oneself as someone who can use the new counting method as well as viewing oneself as a member of a cultural community with a particular history of counting and commerce.

Research in a Mexican Mayan village indicates that development for the first villagers to attend university has included constructing new modes of action in relation to new cultural meanings and developmental goals (Manago, 2012). For women in particular, there are more job options and social roles beyond the family, which also bring opportunities for independent decision making. These changes appear to be related to constructing increasingly differentiated opinions and perspectives, as well as to integrating them with the perspectives of others. Some study participants talked about burgeoning friendships beyond their families and communities, suggesting that they are constructing differentiated conceptions of relationships and new ways of coordinating with others. At the same time that family obligations remain strong, family relationships are also becoming less hierarchical and increasingly egalitarian, which involves integrating individuals' differentiated points of view. While students are making their ways in the world beyond the village, they are not necessarily abandoning traditional ways of acting. Instead, it seems that there is differentiation among action circumstances and the ways of acting that are differentially appropriate to them. In addition, the study participants are working to integrate new ways of acting with traditional modes of action. For example, the students discussed ways of "harmonizing increased role options and individual choice with family obligation" (p. 679).

However, living in the midst of cultural change is not necessarily a happy or harmonious developmental experience for everyone all the time. The kinds of differentiation and integration suggested in the examples just discussed and in other changing cultures are not inevitable, because people may resist cultural change and some of the new modes of action it brings. Thus, we return to a point raised in Chapter 3: cultural expectations and standards for development are contested phenomena linked to power and authority. As such, new modes of action may be privileged by some, but not others. In turn, one's position in relation to changing forces of power and authority in a culture may lead to varied pathways of development during times of cultural change for different people. Taken together, development in relation to cultural change is not simply a matter of shedding old forms of action and taking on new ones. There may be varied new developmental goals, and people may experience varied pathways of differentiation and integration in relation to them. And sometimes those experiences may be difficult and painful, with some people sometimes feeling trapped between the past and the present and uncertain about the future. Given these kinds of complexities, encountering new modes of action may sometimes lead to nondevelopmental changes, or modes of action that reflect decreasing differentiation and integration. By distinguishing development from any kind of change in functioning, and by defining development in terms of differentiation and integration, it becomes possible to think systematically about and ultimately investigate the different patterns of change that action may undergo for individuals in relation to cultural change. It also becomes possible to identify connections among different patterns of change.

Of course, insofar as cultures differ in some ways, patterns of cultural change may differ in some ways as well. In turn, the vicissitudes of development in relation to cultural change may also differ across cultures. Even the ostensibly "same" cultural changes, such as new economic and educational opportunities, may play out differently in different cultures. For example, Gaskins (2003) argues that although the move from subsistence work to wage labor and cash crops in the Mexican Mayan community where she has conducted research for decades has led to a whole host of daily life changes, some aspects of children's development remain remarkably similar. She argues that in this community,

> an important goal . . . was the maintenance of the family as the central social and economic unit and the direct engagement of children as members of that unit. . . . No matter which of the economic options were being used in the households in 2000, both boys and girls were still intimately involved in the daily work of their parents and still had significant responsibility for and engagement with their younger siblings. (p. 269)

Dyson (2014) has returned to Bemni, India several times since conducting her original research in 2003, and during the course of 10 years, many villagers have

gone to school beyond elementary school and a few are pursuing higher education. There is a new road to the village, as well as some electrical service and cell
phone service. Dyson points out: "The implications of these infrastructural and
educational changes are complex and manifold, affecting employment strategies
and aspirations, upsetting labour availability and the agricultural cycle and bringing repercussions for intergenerational relations and even the ways in which marriages are arranged" (p. 148). Yet, at the same time, she cautions that "one should
also not overemphasize the extent to which everyday life in the village has been
transformed" (p. 148). Due to limited employment opportunities beyond the village, many young men work in and near the village, and women continue to work
in the village as well. Ultimately, "it was what they know and what many continue
to want for their own children" (p. 148).

While examples of development in relation to cultural change in traditional
cultures are readily accessible, I do not mean to imply that traditional cultures are
the only ones that undergo cultural change. In addition, by providing examples
of certain kinds of cultural change, namely expanding economic and educational
opportunities, I do not mean to suggest that they are the only kinds of cultural
changes that occur. Indeed, sometimes cultural change involves economic stress,
rather than economic opportunity. Individuals also experience cultural change
when they immigrate, and not only when some kind of change occurs within a
cultural community. Again, I readily recognize that cultural change is complex,
and that the links between cultural change and the development of individual
action are complex. The point here is that organismic-developmental theory provides consistent tools for systematically conceptualizing and investigating the
development of action in relation to different patterns of cultural change, anywhere in the world.

We have taken a whirlwind trip through varied cultures, and whirlwind travel
often leaves one with an uneasy feeling that something is missing. Perhaps the
trip was a bit superficial and lacking in details. Maybe I should have stayed
longer in this or that place to really see it and to really get to know the people.
Although the goal of this book is to offer a theoretical framework for thinking systematically about human development without getting bogged down
in minutiae, I end this chapter fully cognizant that the discussion of development in different cultures has been very general and at times speculative.
I think we are in this predicament partly because research on what happens
during development around the world is spotty and at best provides some fleeting glimpses of pathways of differentiation and integration for cultural modes
of action. Plus, I have been limited to research that is published in English.
Research is also not typically informed by a clear a priori definition of development that is applicable across varied contexts and cultures. Fortunately, our
current systems approach to action in relation to others, in conjunction with
organismic-developmental theory, provides ways to redress this predicament.

More specifically, the research discussed in this chapter indicates that even though cultures differ and even though cultures change, people act in relation to others in cultural practices around the world. The research discussed in this chapter further illustrates some of the ways in which action involves multiple and interrelated constituent domains—from thinking, to feeling, to interacting with others, to pursuing goals, to perspective taking, to using language, to self-construction. In addition, the research discussed in this chapter illustrates some of the varied cultural ways in which action may undergo differentiation and integration. We thus have systematic and consistent theoretical tools for thinking about what happens during development that can be flexibly applied in varied cultures at any time. As such, organismic-developmental theory provides a common, yet culturally sensitive, language for comparing and contrasting development within and across varied cultures.

6

How Does Development Happen?

Some Preliminaries: Nature and Nurture

> We can't partition the responsibility for aggression, altruism, or cha-
> risma between DNA and upbringing. In many such cases, trying to
> separate the contributions of nature and nurture to an attribute is
> rather like trying to separate the contributions of length and width to
> the area of a rectangle, which at first glance also seems easy. When you
> think about it carefully, though, it proves impossible.
> —Paul R. Ehrlich (2000, p. 6)

> Explanation of action by redescription, by citing agential reasons, or
> by specifying the agent's motives . . . are not replaceable, even in prin-
> ciple, by explanations in terms of neural events in the brain. This is not
> an empirical matter at all, but a logical or conceptual one. The type
> of explanation is categorically different, and explanations in terms of
> agential reasons and motives, goals and purposes, are not reducible to
> explanations of muscular contractions produced as a consequence of
> neural events.
> —M. R. Bennett and P. M. S. Hacker (2003, p. 64)

How does development happen? How does a person's action in relation to others undergo differentiation and integration? What causes development to happen? Trying to understand how development happens has occupied many people
for many centuries. It has been a difficult enterprise because action and development are complex. From a systems perspective, thinking about how development happens requires considering the contributions of multiple and interrelated
processes. Making sense of how development happens in terms of multiple and
interrelated processes is encapsulated in the claim that development happens
through interactions between nature and nurture. A consideration of nature and
nurture—both complex processes in and of themselves—is a good place to start
a discussion of how development happens. Once some issues regarding aspects of

nature and nurture have been raised, this chapter will turn to a consideration of sociocultural theory and its central point that development happens as a person participates with others in cultural practices. Subsequently, in Chapter 7, sociocultural theory and organismic-developmental theory are synthesized to provide a systematic way of thinking about how development-as-differentiation-and-integration happens through individual, social, and cultural processes which, not coincidentally, are the same processes through which action emerges in general.

Nature and Nurture

From a systems perspective, understanding the roles of nature and nurture involves considering how nature and nurture interact. Although it is widely understood that nature and nurture interact to produce development, there is a tendency in psychology, as well as in popular treatments, to see one or the other as dominant, and the pendulum has shifted between them over the years. Currently, with advances in both genome mapping and neuroimaging, many contemporary discussions of development revolve around genes and the brain, thus putting issues of nature at the forefront of many analyses. How often does one hear claims such as "it's genetic" or "that's how her brain is wired" as explanations for a person's behavior or development? However, despite the promise of genome mapping, no genes "for" any particular form of behavior or personality trait have been identified (Krimsky, 2013; Wahlsten, 2013). In 2013, the two annual volumes of the *Advances in Child Development and Behavior* series were devoted to explaining the "logical and empirical shortcomings of split, biological reductionist (genetic or neuronal) models . . . and methods (e.g., adoption designs, MZ and DZ twin research, or heritability analysis)" (Lerner & Benson, 2013, p. 4).

Rather than attributing much of development to one dominant factor, such as the brain or genes, a systems perspective leads to recognizing that not only are there multiple causes of development, but those multiple causes are interrelated and made up of their own multiple and interrelated subconstituent processes. Let us begin this discussion of how development happens by considering some of the ways in which genetic and environmental processes are interrelated. Issues of the brain and development will be taken up subsequently.

Genes and Environments, Environments and Genes

Because I am neither a geneticist nor a biologist, this exploration of how development happens through interactions or interrelations between genetic and environmental processes will not be terribly technical, and it is not meant to be exhaustive. The goal here is to make some basic points about how action and development emerge through interrelations between genetic and environmental processes.

It is difficult to begin this discussion because it is tempting to resort to starting with one process and thus to implicitly prioritize it. A way out of this predicament is to start with the gene–environment *system*, or the environment–gene *system*, thereby recognizing that genes come with environments and environments come with genes. One can speak of genes and environments or environments and genes. As such, it is theoretically problematic to separate the roles that genetic and environmental processes play in an individual's action because they are utterly interrelated (Ehrlich, 2000; Goldhaber, 2012; Gottlieb, 1991, 2003, 2007; Gottlieb, Wahlsten, & Lickliter, 1998; Ho, 2013; Johnston & Lickliter, 2009; Lewontin, 2000; Meaney, 2010; Mistry, 2013; Overton, 2011; Oyama, 2000; Rutter, 2006; Wahlsten, 2003). More specifically,

> because genes and environments always collaborate in the production of any phenotype in a continuous interplay of bidirectional influences over time, it is not possible to say that a certain component (or a certain fraction) of the phenotype was caused exclusively by genes (independent of environmental considerations) and some other component (or fraction) was caused exclusively by environment (independent of a genetic contribution). (Gottlieb & Halpern, 2002, p. 421)

The roles of genes and environments may be qualitatively distinct, but both genes and environments are completely involved during development, and both are 100% necessary for development (Figure 6.1). In keeping with basic systems premises, insofar as both genes and environments are necessary for the development of all forms of action, all forms of action are completely genetic and also completely environmental. Moreover, from a systems perspective, genetic and

Figure 6.1 Genes and the environment, or the environment and genes, are inseparable and mutually constitutive. Both contribute 100% to development. Neither is prior or primary.

environmental processes cannot function separately or make development happen separately. Neither is prior to the other, and neither has primacy over the other. Taken together, an "understanding of developmental phenomena demands a relational or coactive concept of causality as opposed to singular causes acting in supposed isolation" (Gottlieb & Halpern, 2002, p. 421).

The gene–environment system/environment–gene system includes genes which

> are sequences of nucleotides within the DNA. The sequences of bases along each strand of DNA provide the templates for gene expression. Gene expression occurs through the processes of DNA transcription and RNA translation. The primary product of gene expression is the formation of proteins. (Stiles, 2008, p. 47)

Gottlieb (2007) explains further that these genetic processes are inseparable from environmental processes because "the fact that DNA is an inert molecule means that genes can't turn themselves on and off; they require intracellular signals, some of which originate from outside the cell and, indeed, outside the organism" (p. 2). Furthermore, although genes produce proteins, there are no one-to-one correspondences between genes and proteins, because proteins can function in different ways depending on the cellular environment (Gottlieb, 1991; Gottlieb, 2007; Gottlieb et al., 1998; Krimsky, 2013; Wahlsten, 2013). If there are no one-to-one correspondences even between genes and proteins, it is reasonable to question whether there can be a one-to-one correspondence between genes and some complex form of action.

It is worth repeating the same basic point about what genes do: "The gene codes or programs for the sequence of amino acids in a specific kind of protein, not a brain structure or behavioral phenotype" (Wahlsten, 2003, p. 37). Thus, "genes themselves do not participate in developmental processes" (Stiles, 2008, p. 384), and "the immediate consequences of genetic activity are confined to the cell" (Gottlieb, 2003, p. 349). The proteins go on to

> enter into complex signaling cascades. It is these signaling cascades that serve to direct the development of cells, assemblies of cells, and connections among cells. The formation of these neural networks underpins and supports the behavior of the organism, and the behavior of the organism, in turn, influences the organization and functioning of the neural system. (Stiles, 2008, p. 65)

These claims are rather amazing, especially when one is used to thinking that genes can be independent and ultimate causes of behavior and development. The researchers cited here are not simply saying that there is more to development than genes. They are explaining that genes produce proteins, and it is those proteins that contribute to the development of cells, which contribute to further biochemical processes, all of which occur in relation to environmental and experiential processes (Johnston & Lickliter, 2009; Meaney, 2010). In other words, human functioning requires more than biochemical processes. Moreover, genes can and do change in relation to environmental circumstances, and genes may also function differently at different times during a person's life (Krimsky, 2013; Meaney, 2010). Thus, once genes have produced proteins, it is still a long and winding road to the complex forms of action that we see in human beings, even in neonates (Karmiloff-Smith, 2006; Krimsky, 2013).

In addition, even if there is a genetic predisposition for some constituents and modes of action, ways of acting still *develop* (van Geert, 1998). Oyama (2000) points out that the metaphor of genetic trait transmission from parents to children is problematic because it implies that ways of acting go from parents to children full-fledged. The transmission metaphor thus ignores, and at times even denies, any developmental process. For example, being artistic may run in families, but not simply because family members share a genetic heritage. In order for any family member to develop into an accomplished artist, his or her artistry requires nurture, and it is likely that the person will participate in artistic activities with others. In addition, what counts as an accomplished artist is partly cultural. As Oyama (2000) explains: "Traits do not pass from one organism to another like batons in a relay race. They must be constructed in ontogeny. This is true whether or not they are invariant in the population or have a traceable phylogenetic history" (p. 87).

The genetic transmission metaphor can lead to all sorts of misconceptions about how development happens. For example, I remember a student in one of my classes saying that her mother is always telling her that she (the student) inherited her personality from her aunt because they are so alike. When behavior is taken to be transmitted directly through the genes, it has to be transmitted from someone, and if not the person's parents, then the relative whom the person most seems to resemble. However, not only do we get our genes from our parents, but this transmission story also bypasses any process of development that occurred during the course of this person's life.

These points about interrelations between genetic and environmental processes also have implications for conceptions of what is innate or "natural" to human beings. The modes of functioning that are possible at birth may be viewed as part of a person's innate nature and hence not subject to development through experience. However, that position ignores the development that took place to get to the modes of functioning that are possible at birth (Oyama, 2000; Stiles, 2008, 2009). Referring to the period prior to birth as prenatal "development" highlights the point that neonatal functioning does not simply appear full-fledged out of nothing. After all, nothing will come of nothing. Even though prenatal development generally follows a species-specific genetic sequence, it still requires environmental processes, and prenatal development is shaped by what is going on in the intrauterine and extrauterine environments. Thus, newborn functioning is emergent rather than preprogrammed and can be understood as the developmental product of systemic interactions between inseparable genetic and environmental processes.

A nondevelopmental view of nature is further evident in the tendency to view it as fixed or immutable. For example, it may be considered difficult to change a person's initial behavioral inclinations, which are taken to reflect his or her nature. Apparently, the great lefty tennis player, Rafael Nadal, started out as a right-handed player, suggesting that playing right-handed was "natural" to him. However, his initial right-handed inclination was neither fixed nor immutable, and Nadal developed into a formidable left-handed tennis player. One could even say that it is now Nadal's nature to play lefty tennis, suggesting that a person's nature develops (van Geert, 1998; Oyama, 2000).

Research on temperament is instructive for considering the dynamics of "nature" and why it may be neither fixed nor immutable, as well as for considering interrelations between genetic and environmental processes. Although temperament is defined somewhat differently by different researchers, there is some consensus that it emerges partly through genetic processes. According to Kagan, temperament refers to "an inherited physiology that is preferentially linked to an envelope of emotions and behaviors" (Kagan & Snidman, 2004, p. 5). Rothbart defines temperament in terms of "constitutionally based individual differences in reactivity and self-regulation. . . . By the term constitutional, we refer to the biological bases of temperament, influenced over time by heredity, maturation, and experience" (Rothbart & Bates, 2006, p. 100). Insofar as genetic processes interact with environmental processes, it is not surprising that research on temperament generally shows that there is only about 20% to 30% stability in temperament ratings during the first years of life.

More specifically, over the course of 25 years of conducting research on temperament, Kagan and his colleagues identified four temperament types, based on placing 4-month-old infants in situations "that were discrepant from the infant's past experience" (Kagan & Snidman, 2004, p. 12). For example, "the examiner, standing in back of the infant, presented a set of mobiles composed of 1, 3, or 7 unfamiliar colorful toys that moved back and forth in front of the infant's face for nine 20-second trials" (p. 13). The researcher also "dipped a cotton swab into very dilute butyl alcohol and presented it close to the infant's nostrils" (p. 13). The high-reactive temperament classification included approximately 20% of the infants who "showed crying and vigorous pumping of the legs and arms, sometimes with arching of the back, on at least 40% of the trials" (p. 13). Approximately 40% of the babies comprised the low-reactive temperament type, and they "showed the opposite pattern—minimal motor activity and minimal distress . . . and appeared minimally aroused" (p. 13). In addition, 25% of infants were distressed, showing "low levels of motor activity but were very irritable" (pp. 13–14). A small group (10%) of aroused babies "showed vigorous motor activity, usually pumping of arms and legs but no arching of the back, and rarely cried" (p. 14). About 5% of the infants "were difficult to classify" (p. 14). Longitudinal assessments of the children's behavior as well as biological assessments were conducted five times, ending when the children were 11 years old. Kagan and colleagues hypothesized that highly reactive infants would be "biased to become inhibited children," whereas less reactive infants "were likely to become uninhibited children" (p. 12).

By the time of the last assessment, 25% of the high-reactives "developed an expected pattern of behavior and biology" (p. 23). That is, they were "quiet and subdued with the examiner" (p. 23). Similarly, 25% of the low-reactives "preserved their expected behavioral and biological profile" between 4 months and 11 years (p. 23). At the same time, however, Kagan and Snidman point out that "because 11-year-olds have considerable control over their public behavior, only a modest proportion of high-reactive preadolescents behaved in ways an observer would characterize as extremely shy, fearful, or timid" (p. 23). In other words, the "nature" of these children was not fixed, and their temperament type "had not prevented them from learning ways to cope with strangers and new challenges," even though "it did prevent them from displaying the relaxed spontaneity and low level of cortical and autonomic arousal characteristic of many low-reactive children" (p. 23). Analyzing the findings as a whole, Kagan and Snidman concluded that "most children displayed behavioral and biological patterns more characteristic of randomly selected middle-class Caucasian children" (p. 196). Furthermore, "the most accurate summary of this evidence is that an early temperamental bias prevented the development of a contrasting profile. . . . An infant's temperament was more effective in constraining the development of a certain profile than in determining a particular profile" (p. 196). The infants' initial temperaments did not determine their future ways of acting because the children's initial ways of acting were inseparable from their environments and experiences.

It is also interesting to point out that some research suggests that temperament types can be played out differently in different cultures. Some studies indicate that Chinese and Japanese infants are generally less reactive and less likely to cry than Caucasian infants (Kagan & Snidman, 2004). However, when these babies "grow up, they do not show the attraction to novelty and exuberance characteristic of many low-reactive Caucasian children. . . . Thus, we confront the paradox of low-reactive 4-month-old Chinese infants becoming subdued older children, while low-reactive Caucasian infants become exuberant" (p. 227). Such findings are not necessarily paradoxical when the biogenetic aspects of infant temperament are understood as fundamentally inseparable from cultural processes. Thus, the same temperament type can contribute to different patterns of behavior in different environments (Krimsky, 2013; Meaney, 2010; Wahlsten, 2013).

Another important example of the complexities of the gene–environment/environment–gene system can be found in the controversial issue of how intelligence develops in relation to genetic and environmental processes. First, it is important to point out that defining and assessing intelligence have been incredibly difficult and messy endeavors. There are debates about the ways in which intelligence is a general characteristic and the ways in which intelligence involves varied specific abilities. In addition, there are cultural differences in how intelligence is defined. For example, the American researchers who conducted a classic study of preschool in Japan, China, and the United States wondered if a Japanese preschooler was gifted because he seemed to be misbehaving out of boredom with class activities (Tobin, Wu, & Davidson, 1989). A school staff member responded that the child's "intelligence is about average, about the same as most other children," and another pointed out that "entertaining the other children by singing all those songs is a reflection not so much of intelligence as it is of his great need for attention" (p. 24). Tobin et al. explain that, in Japan, young children are considered to be smart or intelligent when they are well-behaved and obedient. Misbehavior in social situations is thus "more likely to be associated with being not smart enough" (p. 26). In addition, what is referred to as socially responsible intelligence is valued and promoted in varied cultures. For example, according to Nsamenang, cultural conceptions of socially responsible intelligence are key to understanding development in Africa (Nsamenang, 1992, 2006, 2011). Such intelligence "includes a quick and perceptive quality of the intellect, a sympathetic understanding of the social world, and a readiness to act" (Super, Harkness, Barry, & Zeitlin, 2011, p. 122). It is also argued that the meaning of dementia differs culturally and that in India "the forgetful aged are far less likely [than Westerners] to attract a diagnosis of dementia" (Hashmi, 2009, p. 210).

In the 1960s and 1970s, researchers started going to far-flung corners of the world with Piagetian tasks (e.g., conservation tasks to assess understanding that the amount of some substance is conserved despite changes to its appearance or location) and other Western assessments of cognition (e.g., free recall tasks in which people are presented with decontextualized lists of words and asked to remember as many words as possible). Over and over again, researchers found that children and adults had trouble with the tasks, yet seemed to engage in complex forms of thinking in their daily lives (for reviews, see Cole, 1996; Rogoff, 1990). In one case, when Kpelle rice farmers in Liberia did poorly on free recall tasks, the researchers tried out different ways of assessing memory. For example, participants were paid "for each word they recalled" and they then "*said* a lot more words at recall time, but their recall did not improve" (Cole, 1996, p. 64). Finally, in an effort to create a memory task that was representative of the ways in which Kpelle rice farmers actually remembered in the context of their daily-life cultural practices, the researchers asked, "When, if ever, would these people encounter a task where they were required to commit a list of words or objects to memory simply for the purposes of remembering" (p. 65)? When the task involved remembering words that were part of a story, the participants remembered quite well. Such research points to how thinking does not occur in the abstract but involves thinking about something in particular as a person acts in relation to others in particular cultural practices.

Given these kinds of cultural complexities, it is at least problematic if not impossible to attribute the development of a person's intelligence primarily to genetic processes. Moreover, from a systems perspective it is conceptually unsound to focus on discerning how much of an individual's intelligence is genetic and how much is environmental, because both genetic and environmental processes are completely involved and 100% necessary. Indeed, research points to complex interactions between genes and environment in the development of intelligence (e.g., Ho, 2013; Nisbett, 2009; Wahlsten, 2003, 2013). Much research on the development of intelligence revolves around investigations of heritability, which refers to the proportion of total variation (or differences between individuals) for some characteristic within an identified population that can be attributed to genetic factors. As such, heritability is a quantitative statement about populations or groups of people who are categorized by investigators according to some criterion, such as socioeconomic status, race, or gender. With regard to intelligence, heritability is not a statement about how genes function during the development of individual intelligence. Instead, it is a quantitative rendering of the total variation in intelligence between individuals within a group that can be attributed to genetic factors (Rutter, 2006). Heritability is also not a statement about differences between individuals from different groups, and therefore we must guard against lapsing into "blithe cross inference from populations to individuals and back again" (Oyama, 2000, p. 53). While estimating what proportion of the total variation in a group's intelligence can be attributed to genes may be a worthy enterprise, it is not the same as discerning how individuals develop (Griffiths & Tabery, 2013; Overton, 2011). In other words, "the question of the difference between two states is not the same as a question about the causation of either of them" (Lewontin, 2000, pp. 28–29). Or as Gottlieb explains: "The finding of variance between individuals cannot be validly applied to an explanation of variation within individuals: Inter-individual variation does not explain intra-individual variation" (Gottlieb, 2003, p. 338). Thus "generalizations from individual differences do not illuminate individual development" (Gottlieb, 2003, p. 339).

The Brain, Action, and Development

Just as there are efforts to attribute behavior and development to genetics, there are also efforts to attribute behavior and development to the brain. There are claims that behavior occurs in the brain, creating the problematic view that "psychological processes" are "either isomorphic to or, at best, epiphenomenal byproducts of the brain's neurochemistry. Under these circumstances, brains themselves become agentive overseers of organismic functioning, assuming causal primacy" (Witherington & Heying, 2013, p. 162). Cognitive activities in particular seem to be equated with brain processes or are taken to occur "in the head" or "in the brain." For example, a person might say, "I figured it out in my head," or "I had it all planned out in my head." Instead of saying that action, including its cognitive constituents, occurs in the brain or in the head, I prefer to say that action occurs *with* the brain and head, along with the heart, lungs, liver, and other body parts and organs. In addition, action occurs or emerges through interactions among individual, social, and cultural processes, and therefore human thinking involves cultural categories and symbol systems as well as a human brain. It is interesting that sometimes the heart is viewed as the location of emotional activity, and thus we may say that our hearts are heavy when we are sad, and we feel lighthearted when we are happy. However, these statements do not mean that a person's heart causes his or her emotions or that a person's feelings occur in the heart. Rather, the heart is a *metaphoric* location for emotion. Similarly, the inside of the head can be understood as a metaphoric location for cognition and action more generally, which also require other processes in addition to neurological ones.

Certainly, the brain is involved in all that we do, and it is necessary for human action, but it is not an independent or singularly deterministic cause of action. Thus,

> if we wish to know why A signed a cheque for £200, no answer in terms of brain functions is likely to satisfy us. We want to know whether A was discharging a debt, making a purchase, donating money to charity, or betting on a horse—and once we know which of these is the case, we may also want to know what A's reasons were. A description of the neural events in A's brain could not possibly explain to us what we want to have explained. (Bennett & Hacker, 2003, p. 64)

Describing neurological events can tell us about some of the processes that co-constitute a person's action, but that is not the same as equating the person's functioning with brain processes. The neurological events partly constitute the action, but not independently of the other processes through which action emerges. Moreover, brains do not act; people with brains act (Bennett & Hacker, 2003).

Neuroimaging enables us to identify blood-flow changes that occur in different parts of the brain when a person does different tasks, thus providing useful information about some neurological processes that occur when people behave (Bennett & Hacker, 2003). However, there is a lot of information about behavior that neuroimaging does not provide. It does not necessarily tell us about the cultural meaning of a form of behavior, or about what the situation means to the individual under scrutiny. It does not allow us to know the particulars of what a person is thinking or feeling or with whom he or she is interacting. In other words, "attempts to explain a psychological event with sentences containing only biological words leads to a situation in which the psychological phenomenon vanishes into a long description of neuronal firings" (Kagan, 2008b, p. 5). Thus, "the devout Jew's commitment to fasting on Yom Kippur or the devout Muslim's commitment to Ramadan is not captured by a recital of the physiology of hunger" (Bruner, 1990, pp. 21–22). Although these commitments are made by human beings with brains, these commitments also require social and cultural processes.

Just as the brain is sometimes viewed as the rock-bottom cause of behavior in general, it is also not unusual to hear that the brain causes behavior to develop. For example, I remember once listening to a mother lament her 7-year-old daughter's inability to control herself. The mother asked, "When will she get some impulse control?" The child's father replied, "When her frontal lobes develop." The mother asked, "When will that happen?" These statements imply that the brain changes will cause the desired behavioral changes. Asking when the brain changes will occur further implies that the changes occur on their own, over time somehow. However, the passage of time does not guarantee development, and it is likely necessary for the child to engage in practices that involve impulse control in order for the associated brain connections to be established and maintained (Ho, 2013; Johnson, 2005). Of course, engaging in such practices occurs over time, but the passage of time is not the central issue. Thus, the developmental question to ask is not so much about when impulse control is attained, but how it is attained.

Consider the following description of a child who seems well able to control herself:

> Yanira stood waiting with a small pot and a bundle with two dresses and a change of underwear in hand. A member of the Matsigenka people of the Peruvian Amazon, she asked to accompany anthropologist Carolina Izquierdo and a local family on a fishing and leaf gathering expedition down river. Over five days away from the village, Yanira was self-sufficient and attuned to the needs of the group. She helped to stack and carry leaves to bring back to the village for roofing. Mornings and late afternoons she swept sand off the sleeping mats, fished for slippery black crustaceans, cleaned and boiled them in her pot along with manioc then served them to the group. At night her cloth bundle served as blanket and her dresses as her pillow. Calm and self-possessed, she asked for nothing. Yanira is six years old. (Ochs & Izquierdo, 2009, p. 394)

In this case, I suspect that Yanira's development resulted in part from practicing varied modes of action, and from engaging with others in cultural practices that involve these modes of action. Indeed, Ochs and Izquierdo report:

> Self-sufficiency in accomplishing daily tasks coupled with sociability lie at the heart of what it means to be a competent member of the Matsigenka family and society. These basic tenets are socialized early in a child's development and permeate daily life. . . . Three-year-olds frequently practice cutting wood and grass with machetes and knives. . . . Toddlers carry out numerous small tasks in proximity to their mothers. Many of these tasks are self-initiated, whereas others are in response to mothers' commands. (p. 395)

Yanira's frontal lobes may or may not be well developed already at the age of 6. However, the analysis of cultural practices in her community suggests that the development of her brain, as well as the development of her action, are emerging from practicing varied modes of action that involve what we might refer to as impulse control.

Note that the previous paragraphs point out that the brain *develops*. This point is significant because it forces us to recognize that the brain is undergoing development, just as a person's action undergoes development. Moreover, a person's developing action contributes to the brain's development, just as the developing brain contributes to the development of action (Ho, 2013; Johnson, 2005). In other words, there is a brain–action system, or an action–brain system, whereby the brain and action mutually sustain and contribute to each other's development. They are interrelated, and neither has primacy or priority over the other. Indeed, the formation of neural connections at any time during the life span depends in part on stimulation through action.

Some developmental complexities of brain←→action/action←→brain interrelations during development are highlighted in research suggesting that the brains of adolescents (aged 14 to 18) who engage in some forms of risky behavior (e.g., drinking, smoking, taking drugs, unprotected sex) may actually be more developed than the brains of adolescents who report fewer instances of risk taking (Berns, Moore, & Capra, 2009). These findings seem counterintuitive when the brain is taken to cause development and when risky behavior is considered to be less developed than responsible behavior. In other words, it seems odd that more developed brains are associated with less developed behavior. A systems perspective leads to thinking about other causal constituents of behavior. For example, we can recognize that risky behavior by adolescents is not a purely neurological issue because adolescence in Western cultures is typically viewed as a time for identity exploration, which easily lends itself to taking risks (Lightfoot, 1997). Other research suggests that risk taking continues beyond adolescence and actually peaks during emerging adulthood, around the ages of 21 to 22 (Arnett, 2000). Analyses suggest that varied sociocultural issues are involved in the continued occurrence of risk taking, such as lifting legal restrictions on drinking, greater access to drugs, and less parental supervision.

In addition, some behavior that is considered problematic for adolescents is acceptable for adults, such as drinking alcohol, which further occurs in relation to individual and cultural ideas about acceptable alcohol consumption. Thus, youthful risk taking can be seen as exploring adult forms of action, which are linked to more mature brains. Furthermore, a review of research on adolescent functioning points out that it is not even clear that adolescents are more prone to risk taking or more prone to generally irrational behavior than adults. Nor is there clear evidence for qualitative differences between adolescent and adult brains (Moshman, 2013). Rather, adolescence is a culturally stipulated life-phase that was not set off from adulthood in some cultures until the late 1800s. Prior to that "individuals we would now call 'adolescents' or 'teenagers' worked, married, had children, ran households and participated in the social and cultural life of the community" (Moshman, 2013, p. 158). That young people could engage in such action responsibly in the past also raises questions about attributing adolescent behavior to immature brains. For example, if adolescent brains are immature today, what was going on neurologically in the past that enabled people of the same age to function as adults? Has the brain changed so significantly since the late 1800s? If not, why is the brain seen as a source of immature behavior today, whereas in the past it would have been associated with mature functioning? If the brain has changed, why and in what ways are adolescent brains less developed today than in the past? If contemporary adolescents are incapable of the kind of mature functioning that was possible in the past, could it be because they are not participating in cultural practices that enable them to develop relevant modes of action? Are they developing different modes of action in relation to different cultural expectations? Taken together, it is important to consider what is going on in the brain in relation to social and cultural processes.

It is also possible that engaging in risky behavior leads to brain development because it provides young people with opportunities to practice some adult or more mature ways of acting. Berns et al. (2009) point out that "adolescent engagement in dangerous activities is associated with more mature frontal white matter tracts, but it could be the case that precocious brain development leads to precocious behavior, or participation in these activities accelerates the maturation of the brain" (p. 9). The data are also ambiguous about causality because there was generally a lot of variability between participants in the study, much of which could not be statistically accounted for by brain development. Thus, it is necessary to consider other causal processes and how they are interrelated to comprise adolescents' behavior.

A final point about the brain and development parallels our earlier discussion of how attributing development to genetics can lead to bypassing developmental processes. That is, analyses may also bypass developmental processes when some mode of functioning is taken to be "hardwired" in human brains generally, or in an individual specifically. For example, there are arguments about whether human beings are hardwired to empathize with others or to be altruistic. Or, when I marveled recently about how and why some people pursue passions despite knowing they will die some day and it may all amount to nothing in the grand scheme of things, someone responded that we are hardwired to do so. From a developmental perspective, I was wholly unsatisfied with that response. Saying that we are hardwired to do X, Y, or Z connotes such finality. Our brains are hardwired to do X, and that is all there is to it. It is the way we are; it is human nature. However, the way we are has certainly changed over the course of history, and as suggested earlier, what is natural to human beings is highly debatable and dynamic. Moreover, saying that we are neurologically programmed or hardwired to do X, Y, or Z distracts us from thinking about how X, Y, or Z *develops*. Empathizing with others and doing for others can be viewed as modes of action that develop, and they are subject to all of the developmental complexities discussed in this book. In addition, empathy and altruism are by definition directed toward other people, which suggests that in order to develop empathic or altruistic ways of acting, one must engage with other people. Acting empathically and altruistically may also be understood and played out differently in different cultures. Similarly, even though people may pursue passions in a wide range of circumstances, the ability to do something one is passionate about develops. The point here is that rather than reducing the complexities of human functioning and development to neurological hardwiring (or to any other single factor), the theoretical perspective presented here leads to thinking about how development happens through multiple and interrelated processes. Those multiple and interrelated processes very much include but are not limited to neurological processes. In addition, the metaphor of hardwiring may be limited in the context of research on neural plasticity, which indicates that the brain undergoes ongoing change in relation to a person's experience and changing behavior (e.g., Pascual-Leone, Amedi, Fregni, & Merabet, 2005).

The Environment and Experience

We have just explored some aspects of nature and nurture. Nature was discussed in terms of genes and the brain. Nurture was identified rather vaguely as the environment and experience and at times social and cultural processes were invoked. But what more specifically do "the environment" and "experience" involve? Developmental analyses reveal an overwhelming array of experiential and environmental factors that influence development, such as socioeconomic status, healthcare, geographic location, and culture; parental beliefs, siblings, extended-family members, and household density; peers and neighborhoods; daycare and school; TV, video games, and the Internet; community resources and opportunities; work experience and stress; amount of talk directed to a child and type of talk directed to a child, to name but a few factors.

Not only could this list continue on for pages, but each item in the list could be discussed at length. Indeed, many of them have been discussed at length. For example, volumes of research have been produced on the roles of parents in children's development. Studies address a wide range of issues, including styles or patterns of childrearing; childrearing goals and values; the roles of discipline and attachment; adoption; and parents' status, including single, divorced, widowed, step-parents, working mothers, or gay or lesbian parents. Again, the list goes on and on.

It is enough to make one's head spin. We seem to be going from one possible, relatively independent aspect of experience and the environment to another in a rather haphazard way. Plus, we have not even mentioned how these varied factors are related to development-as-differentiation-and-integration. We are lost among the trees, in a dense thicket of factors. We need to find a way out of this thicket and get our bearings in the wider forest. In my view, we need a more organized and systematic framework for thinking about how development happens that can encompass biological processes (e.g., genetics, brain functioning) as well as multiple and interrelated aspects of experience and environments. To that end, we turn to sociocultural theory, which offers a systems-compatible approach to how development happens. Sociocultural theory also ultimately offers ways to link considerations of how development happens with our fundamental theoretical premise that human beings are separate individuals who act in relation to others in cultural practices.

Before proceeding, it is necessary to point out that research informed by sociocultural theory is decidedly child centered, and the discussion of sociocultural theory and research will reflect this emphasis. Nevertheless, the basic premises of sociocultural theory are fully applicable to development throughout the life span. Thus in Chapter 7, which links sociocultural theory and organismic-developmental theory, we will think about how development-as-differentiation-and-integration occurs at any time during the life span.

Sociocultural Theory

Contemporary sociocultural perspectives are based on Lev Vygotsky's early 20th-century theory of how development happens through dynamic social and cultural processes (Cole, 1996; Rogoff, 2003; Valsiner, 1997; Vygotsky, 1978,

1986/1987; Wertsch, 1985, 1991, 1998). Vygotsky lived from 1896 to 1934 and spent the bulk of his career in Moscow, Russia and Kharkov, Ukraine, which both became part of the Soviet Union during that time. Vygotsky was concerned with explicating how "higher mental functions" (e.g., memory, attention, reasoning, concept formation) occur and develop in social contexts, and how they are mediated by cultural symbols, especially language. Although Vygotsky focused on cognitive development, he offered an overall conceptualization of how development happens that is applicable to varied domains of functioning and to action more generally. From a Vygotskian perspective, by actually engaging in modes of action with others, those modes of action can become part of the developing person's intrapsychological functioning, or part of an individual's ways of acting. As Vygotsky (1978) famously put it:

> An interpersonal process is transformed into an intrapersonal one. Every function in the child's cultural development appears twice: first, on the social level, and later, on the individual level; first between people (interpsychological), and then inside the child (intrapsychological). This applies equally to voluntary attention, to logical memory, and to the formation of concepts. All the higher functions originate as actual relations between human individuals. (p. 57)

Contemporary sociocultural theorists posit that development happens as an individual participates with others in cultural practices. According to this approach, development does not happen to a passive person. Instead, human development is conceptualized as an active, constructive process that involves contributions by the developing individual, as well as concrete interactions with others, all in the context of particular cultural practices. By participating in cultural practices with others, people have opportunities to practice, and thereby potentially develop, varied modes of action. For example, we can go back to the research on Girl Scout cookie sales discussed in Chapter 2 (Rogoff et al., 1995). A key point of that research is to show that it is through actually participating with others in selling Girl Scout cookies that Girl Scouts develop ways of selling cookies. As discussed earlier, selling Girl Scout cookies involves modes of action that are made up of multiple and interrelated action constituents. During the course of selling cookies, differentiation and integration can occur within and across those constituents, ideally in ways that make effective cookie selling possible. Based on the research discussed in Chapter 5, we can posit that the development of subsistence work occurs as children actually do some of the work. In Chapter 5 we also saw how adults embark on new pathways of differentiation and integration during times of cultural change by participating in new cultural practices that entail new modes of action in relation to others.

Guided Participation

Sociocultural approaches to how development happens emphasize the ways in which others, especially more competent cultural actors, guide someone's participation in cultural practices. More specifically, guided participation refers to when a developing individual participates in cultural practices with another person (or people) who guides him or her through the activity (Rogoff, 1990, 2003). It may seem rather banal, and even unnecessary, to point out that one can learn a lot by interacting with someone who already knows how to engage in the modes of action relevant to some cultural practice. The insights here are that interacting with others is part of a complex developmental process that is carried out in culturally specific ways and involves active contributions on the part of the developing person. In addition, sociocultural theory emphasizes the systems premise that interacting with others, active individual participation, and cultural processes are all interrelated causal constituents of development.

Around the world, people develop through guided participation as they interact with varied guides in varied cultural practices. Guided participation may occur in practices explicitly designed for teaching particular constituents and forms of action, such as in formal school settings. However, guided participation does not have to be set up formally or consciously by a more competent person. Indeed, guided participation can occur in the mess of daily life as people engage in all kinds of everyday cultural practices with others who may be more, less, or equally competent. Guided participation can occur throughout the life span, and as we will see, it comes in varied forms that involve varied specific strategies, depending in part on the practice, the culture, and the people involved (Rogoff, 1990, 2003; Rogoff, Moore, Najafi, Dexter, Correa-Chávez, & Solis, 2007).

For example, Lareau's (2003) ethnographic research provides insight into the different guided participation opportunities that American children of varying socioeconomic circumstances experience. She describes how middle-class parents guided their children in terms of a "concerted cultivation" model, whereby "parents actively fostered and assessed their children's talents, opinions, and skills. They scheduled their children for activities. They reasoned with them. They hovered over them and outside the home they did not hesitate to intervene on the children's behalf" (p. 238). In contrast, low-income families favored a "natural growth" approach whereby "parents viewed children's development as unfolding spontaneously, as long as they were provided with comfort, food, shelter, and other basic support" (p. 238). Within the natural growth approach, parents

> organized their children's lives so they spent time in and around home, in informal play with peers, siblings, and cousins. As a result, the children had more autonomy regarding leisure time and more opportunities for child-initiated play. They also were more responsible for their lives

outside the home. Unlike in middle-class families, adult-organized activities were uncommon. Instead of the relentless focus on reasoning and negotiation that took place in middle-class families, there was less speech (including less whining and badgering) in working-class and poor homes. (p. 238)

The natural growth approach is in keeping with varied accounts of childrearing around the world, including studies of some traditional cultures where it is rare for adults to directly instruct children or to play with them (e.g., Göncü, Mistry, & Mosier, 2000; Lancy, 2007, 2010; Rogoff, 2003).

It is also interesting to consider that the children from the different socioeconomic groups participated in some of the same general cultural practices, such as sports. However, Lareau points out that some of the particulars of their participation in those practices were quite different, thereby guiding them along different developmental pathways for acting in relation to others. For the higher socioeconomic status children, participating in sports was actively arranged and supervised by their parents. Children and parents spent a lot of time driving to and from sporting events, often staying overnight in other towns. Lareau (2003) points out that these children

> meet and interact with adults acting as coaches, assistant coaches, car pool drivers. . . . This contact with relative strangers . . . provides work-related skills. For instance, as Garrett [a 10-year-old study participant] shakes the hand of a stranger and looks him or her in the eye, he is being groomed, in an effortless fashion, for job interviews he will have as an adult. (pp. 244–245)

The lower socioeconomic status children played pickup sports games and other games that involved several other children in the neighborhood, but without adult supervision. Lareau reports: One child "plays over and over with a relatively stable group of boys. Because the group functions without adult monitoring, he learns how to construct and sustain friendships on his own and how to organize and negotiate" (p. 79). In addition, children "often play games they have devised themselves, complete with rules and systems of enforcement" (p. 80).

These different kinds of participation experiences are associated with the development of different ways of acting in relation to others. Lareau points out that the middle-class children excelled athletically. They "learn to handle moments of humiliation on the field as well as moments of glory" (p. 241) and "they learn to perform. They learn to present themselves" (p. 242). In addition, they became adept at interacting comfortably with authority figures in institutional settings (e.g., teachers, doctors). The working-class and poor children "learned to entertain themselves. They played outside, creating their own games. . . . They did not complain of being bored ... family ties were very strong, particularly among siblings [and they] also developed very close ties with their cousins and other extended family members" (p. 242). While they took responsibility for themselves and also developed ways of resolving conflicts, they did not seem at ease with adults, especially teachers and doctors. With a doctor, one working-class child "appeared cautious, displaying an emerging sense of constraint" (p. 243). In contrast, a middle-class counterpart "was used to extensive conversation at home; with the doctor, he was at ease initiating questions" (p. 243). Taken together, Lareau's research suggests that development differs for children of different socioeconomic circumstances, in part because they experience different forms of guided participation. This research indicates how socioeconomic status is associated with different ways of structuring and guiding children's participation in cultural practices.

The analysis thus far suggests that the children of lower socioeconomic circumstances experience rather little in the way of adult instruction, especially in comparison to their higher socioeconomic counterparts. Moreover, as alluded to earlier, a wide range of research around the world indicates that a lot of child development seems to occur without much direct adult instruction at all (Lancy, 2007, 2010; Rogoff, 2003). In varied cultures around the world, adults do not talk much to infants, and adults are not necessarily children's primary play partners (e.g., Gaskins, Haight, & Lancy, 2007; LeVine, 2004; Ochs & Schieffelin, 1984/1988). In parts of the world where infant mortality is high, "parents tend not to actively teach or stimulate their infants and are rarely seen playing with them" (Lancy, 2010, p. 83). In many traditional cultures, "the child is expected to develop, *unaided*, a fascination with the activities of those older than herself and a powerful desire to emulate them" (Lancy, 2007, p. 276, italics added). It is up to the child to observe, imitate, and practice (Lancy, 2010; Ochs & Izquierdo, 2009; Odden & Rochat, 2004; Rogoff, 2003). Lancy (1996) provides the following description of the development of trapping among the Kpelle of Liberia:

> At first, the boy merely tags along, as his father checks his traps, learning to attend to the salient stimuli of game and bush. Later, he will help his father gather materials to make the trap, then he assists in making and setting them. All this while, there is little verbal interchange between the two. The father expects the boy to learn by observing. Then, the son will try to make his own trap. He can expect to get some advice and criticism from his father but not much. ... At age 7, a boy may be able to construct a simple trap for catching small birds. Each year thereafter, he will probably take on one or two new traps until he has mastered the whole arsenal of 15+ traps. (pp. 146–147)

These research findings compel us to think more specifically about what guided participation involves and how it may be structured in varied ways to promote development. I must acknowledge that I was initially terribly thrown by these findings, and my confusion undoubtedly stemmed in part from my own middle-class Western assumptions and values. I understood that observing and imitating play important roles in how development happens, but I did not understand how they could be virtually exclusive sources of development. These findings led me to question the position that development happens through guided participation, and I puzzled over how children could develop when left so completely to their own devices to observe and imitate. Guided participation did not seem to be occurring, and I wondered how anyone, especially young children, could develop "unaided." I kept reading and delved into more research.

How one goes about making sense of these issues depends a lot on how the guidance of guided participation is defined. Guidance does not have to be defined in terms of the middle-class Western approach to guidance that is exemplified in Lareau's descriptions of concerted cultivation. It does not have to only involve direct instruction, boosting self-esteem, and generally hovering over children as contemporary middle-class American "helicopter parents" are known to do. According to Rogoff (2003), who initiated the widespread use of the term *guided participation,*

> Guided participation provides a perspective to help us focus on the *varied ways* that children learn as they participate in and are guided by the values and practices of their cultural communities. It is *not a particular method* of support for learning. For example, one form of guided participation is explanation; another is teasing and shaming, when adults and peers point out children's foibles and missteps by holding their behavior up to social evaluation. . . . The term "guided" in the concept of guided participation is thus meant broadly, to include but go beyond interactions that are intended as instructional. In addition to instructional interactions, guided participation focuses on the side-by-side or distal arrangements in which children participate in the values, skills, and practices of their communities. (pp. 283–284)

This general definition of guided participation provides a way to think about how people develop through varied patterns of social interaction, in varied cultural settings. For example, Rogoff describes guided participation in the form of intent community participation through which "people learn by actively observing and 'listening in' during ongoing community activities and contributing when ready, to activities as varied as weaving, conversing, reading, using statistics, or programming computers" (Rogoff et al., 2007, p. 497). Assembly-line instruction "involves transmission of information from experts, in specialized exercises outside the context of productive, purposive activity" (p. 499), and guided repetition "involves modeling by the expert and imitation of the model by a novice, with memorization through rehearsal and performance by the novice" (p. 502).

It is also important to consider that even in cultures where direct instruction is not ubiquitous and occurs less frequently than among middle-class Americans, it does not necessarily mean that direct instruction does not contribute significantly to development when it does occur. Furthermore, even in cultures where there is relatively little direct instruction, research reports are replete with statements about how development is supported through interacting with others who engage in varied forms of guidance. These findings suggest that even when there is little direct instruction, observing and imitating are not the whole story, because they may occur in conjunction with *some* direct instruction, as well as with other forms of guidance.

For example, a review of ethnographic research on childhood indicates that in many cultures when a child "engages in a carefully constructed make-believe replication of scenes of adult work" adults "may enable it by giving the child cast-off tools and materials to use" (Lancy, 2010, p. 87) as well as smaller versions of varied tools. Among Kpelle rice farmers of Liberia, once children attempt to imitate an expert's work, "the expert intervenes as teacher to correct mistakes, to offer advice, and to consciously 'demonstrate' the skill" (Lancy, 1996, p. 162). When interviewed, one Kpelle father said, "If a child listens to you and you explain things to him, he will give you no cause for anger" (Lancy, 1996, p. 76). Mayan 1- to 2-year-olds in Guatemala

> observe their mothers making tortillas and attempt to follow suit. Mothers give children a small piece of dough to use and facilitate their efforts by rolling the dough into a ball and starting to flatten it. . . . As the child gains skill in shaping tortillas, the mother adds pointers and demonstrates how to hold the dough. (Rogoff, 1990, p. 128)

During the development of weaving, some research indicates that an experienced weaver typically offers "spoken and nonverbal pointers to a learner during the weaving process itself, highlighting, drawing distinctions, or explaining the ongoing process" (Paradise & Rogoff, 2009, p. 118).

Some research suggests that when it comes to the development of some modes of action, direct instruction does sometimes serve as a form of guidance in varied cultures. For example, on the Solomon Islands, within the Kwara'ae culture, "three-year-olds undergo intensive instruction on how to speak and behave, with heavy dosages of imperatives, corrections, and explanations for behavior, accompanied by praise for adultlike behavior and criticism for childish behavior"

(Watson-Gegeo & Gegeo, 1986/1992, p. 19). Subsequently, Kwara'ae "children learn primarily through observation, practice, and counseling sessions held by the parents after dinner in the evenings" (p. 19). Lancy explains that around the world, there seems to be "one area in which nearly all parents seemed to take on the didactic role of teacher, namely, in teaching manners, polite speech formulas, and respect for the child's age and class superiors" (1996, p. 23). Among the Kaluli of Papua New Guinea, mothers are known to directly instruct their children in order "to teach the social uses of assertive language (teasing, shaming, requesting, challenging, reporting)" (Ochs & Schieffelin, 1984/1988, p. 292).

In addition to guided interaction between adults and children, the research discussed in Chapter 5 shows that children around the world spend a great deal of time with their siblings and other children, including in mixed-age peer groups. Nsamenang (1992) explains that in many African villages, "multiage, dual-sex teams of children ranging in age from 20 months to 6 or 7 years of age are often found together in the neighborhood under the guidance and mentorship of one or two elder siblings" (pp. 151–152). In addition to observing and imitating, varied forms of guided participation can occur in such circumstances as well. In cultures where sibling caregiving is practiced, sibling caregivers often serve as guides for their younger charges (Weisner & Gallimore, 1977; Zukow-Goldring, 2002). In Chapter 5, we considered teaching younger siblings to be a form of action that undergoes development. Research on the structuring of sibling teaching points to how older siblings guide their younger siblings in varied ways, including by explaining, describing, and providing appropriate feedback.

This overview of research on different forms of guidance in varied cultures indicates that observing and imitating may occur along with other forms of guidance, including some direct instruction. Clearly, observing and imitating play important roles in how development happens in varied cultural settings, and they can promote development at any time during the life span. However, as pointed out in Chapter 4, imitating can be understood as a form of action that develops, and the same can be said for observing. Thus, I keep wondering how children develop ways of observing and imitating. Within the current conceptualization, observing and imitating are taken to develop partly through participating in cultural practices with people who are guiding the developing person's ways of observing and imitating. Indeed, it is interesting to note that there are some reports of adults guiding children to observe and imitate. For example, parents may ask children questions about community events as a way to indicate which events are important to observe (Rogoff, 2003). When Kwara'ae children learn to engage in repeating routines, they monitor adult activity, and

> they sometimes repeat spontaneously when adults are engaged in conversation with them or with other adults. . . . Then, assuming the circumstances to be informal, the caregivers will usually turn to the infant at

once and give it more sentences to repeat. Children are thus rewarded
for voluntarily repeating. (Watson-Gegeo & Gegeo, 1986/1992, p. 27)

Some analyses of middle-class Western mother–infant interaction suggest that
mothers guide infant imitation by imitating infants frequently and by encouraging infants to imitate them (Ray & Heyes, 2011). Such reports suggest that
being able to observe and imitate develop in part through guidance, and that a
person can then observe and imitate to promote further development of varied
modes of action. In other words, in order to develop through observing and
imitating others, observing and imitating develop in ways that enable them
to become part of what an individual does to contribute to his or her own
development.

Taken together, research suggests that people around the world participate
with others in cultural practices in ways that shape the development of their
action in relation to others. This conclusion is commensurate with the position that guided participation, as a general process, occurs around the world.
Cultural differences lie in the structuring of particular forms of guided participation, or in some of the particular ways in which a developing person
participates with others in cultural practices. However, what goes on when
individuals—at any time during the life span—participate with others in cultural practices that specifically facilitates or supports development requires
further elaboration. In keeping with organismic-developmental theory, we
need to be able to think systematically about how participating with others in
cultural practices can provide developing individuals with opportunities for
development-as-differentiation-and-integration.

Thinking about How Development Happens through Individual, Social, and Cultural Processes

> It seems easier to adopt static definitions of competencies in order to study their realization in different contexts. But human competencies are not static. They have the potential for development—and not only during childhood. A focus on how incipient competencies are practiced, particularized, and perfected may best reveal the subtleties of the workings of the human mind.
>
> —Ina Č. Užgiris (1989, p. 306)

According to the systems approach presented here, action emerges through interrelated individual, social, and cultural processes, and development represents a kind of emergence. That is, new forms of action can emerge when action constituents undergo differentiation and integration. But how do differentiation and integration happen? What causes differentiation and integration to happen? If action generally emerges through interrelated individual, social, and cultural processes, and if development refers to a particular kind of action emergence, then the development of action can also be understood more specifically in terms of individual, social, and cultural processes. Indeed, we can discern individual, social, and cultural processes in sociocultural theory's claim that development happens as an individual participates with others in cultural practices. Individual processes are involved because it is an individual who is participating in some way in order for his or her action to develop. In addition, individual processes contribute to development because any participating person acts as a separate individual, is a source of his or her own action, and construes the world from a unique subjective position. Social processes are involved insofar as the developing person is engaging with others. Cultural processes are involved insofar as the developing individual is participating in cultural practices that are made up of culturally particular modes of action that reflect cultural meanings, including cultural conceptions of development.

Our task now is to link sociocultural theory and organismic-developmental theory by thinking about how development-as-differentiation-and-integration occurs through individual, social, and cultural processes as people participate with others in cultural practices (Raeff, 2011). In keeping with basic systems premises, insofar as individual, social, and cultural processes are interrelated, no one process is viewed as prior to the others, nor is any one process viewed as more foundational or essential than the others. Individual, social, and cultural processes are distinguished here for analytic purposes, but we remain ever mindful of their fundamental interrelatedness. Box 7.1 provides an overview of how cultural, social, and individual processes shape development.

Box 7.1 **Overview of How Development Happens through Cultural, Social, and Individual Processes**

CULTURAL PROCESSES

- Common and contested goals of development
- Opportunities for participating in cultural practices
- Structuring action constituents that undergo development
- Cultural change

SOCIAL PROCESSES

- Overall structuring of interaction in a situation
- Interactions that promote differentiation and integration
- Varied forms of guidance, such as scaffolding, directing attention, demonstrating, hinting, explaining, instructing, asking questions, physical guidance
- Peer collaboration
- Peer play
- Mild interpersonal conflict

INDIVIDUAL PROCESSES

- Participating in cultural practices
- Setting and pursuing goals
- Constructing subjective meaning
- Practicing
- Shifting attention
- Asking questions
- Choosing some cultural practices and social partners
- Current ways of acting

Cultural Processes

As was the case in Chapter 2, I find it useful to start with Miller's and Goodnow's definition of culture in terms of action that is "invested with normative expectations and with meanings or significances that go beyond the immediate goals of the action" (1995, p. 7). To the extent that human action always reflects historically based cultural meanings, culture shapes how development happens because people are developing cultural modes of action. That is, they are developing ways of acting that reflect culturally particular meanings, including beliefs, values, standards for action, and goals of development. Such meanings can be known and contemplated explicitly and separately from concrete action, but they are also implicit in people's ways of acting, or in the manner of action. Cultural processes additionally refer to the more specific structuring of action constituents that comprise modes of action, as well as the symbolic means and technologies through which such action is achieved. Culture can also be defined in terms of the structuring of power and authority in cultural practices as well as in terms of political and economic processes. Cultural processes shape development in many ways, and in this section we consider how development happens in relation to cultural participation opportunities, the cultural structuring of action, and cultural change.

Cultural Opportunities for Participating in Cultural Practices

In order to develop cultural modes of action through participating with others in cultural practices, people have to have opportunities to engage in cultural practices that promote cultural expectations for development. For example, in his analysis of identity formation, Erikson points out that if adolescents are expected to make their own identity choices, then there have to be cultural opportunities for "free role experimentation" which enables them to forge unique identities that are simultaneously "in accordance with the roles offered by some wider section of society" (Erikson, 1959/1980, p. 120). The same point can be extended to emerging adulthood, which is characterized in part by intense identity exploration with regard to relationships, work, and worldview (Arnett, 2000). Adult education practices provide opportunities for adults to develop, and the independent living communities for older adults that have proliferated in some cultures in recent years ideally provide opportunities for participating in varied practices. Providing opportunities for participating in cultural practices is a complex issue, in part because action within cultural practices reflects common and contested cultural meanings, including expectations for life span development. Thus, people within a cultural community do not necessarily always agree on how to structure opportunities for participating in cultural practices. For example, there may be disagreements about whether to cut a school's arts, foreign language, or sports programs or about what kinds of after school programs should be available to children and adolescents. People may argue about setting up academic or training programs in prisons. Discussions and disagreements about how to structure opportunities for participating in cultural practices can contribute to the ongoing dynamics of how development happens through cultural processes because they may lead to constructing new opportunities for participation, as well as to constructing new cultural goals of development. They may also lead to declining opportunities for participating in some cultural practices that are no longer deemed worthy for one reason or another.

Cultural opportunities for development occur in relation to cultural constraints on development. That is, by encouraging participation in some cultural practices, developing individuals are potentially steered away from other practices, which may be implicitly or explicitly denigrated. In addition, people may or may not have access to some cultural practices for varied reasons, such as gender, race, and/or socioeconomic status. In these ways, opportunities to participate in cultural practices are inevitably linked to issues of power and authority because not everyone has equal access to varied practices, even in cultures where serious efforts are made to ensure equal access. Thinking about development in relation to cultural processes also involves thinking about the different interests that are served, as well as those undermined, by structuring access to cultural practices in particular ways.

Considering the general cultural structuring of opportunities to participate in varied cultural practices provides a starting point for thinking systematically about how cultural processes shape development by linking development to cultural goals of development and to cultural practices, which entail modes of action that reflect cultural meanings. When a developing person is participating in cultural practices, he or she is developing with regard to modes of action that are structured or organized in culturally particular and meaningful ways. Accordingly, we can move on to thinking about how development happens through the cultural structuring of action.

The Cultural Structuring of Action

Cultural processes are played out in human experience partly through particular ways of structuring or organizing the action constituents that comprise modes of action that undergo development. As such, cultural processes are part of how development happens, because development involves the differentiation and integration of culturally specific ways of structuring action constituents in relation to cultural goals of development. In Chapter 4, we considered pathways of differentiation and integration in the structuring of action constituents for middle-class American infants and young children. However, insofar as there may be different cultural goals of development, and insofar as action may be structured differently in different cultures, sequences of action development may differ around the world. For example, classic ethnographic observations of the Gusii in Kenya point to how infant development occurs as babies interact with others in ways that reflect cultural values and expectations for action in relation to others (Dixon, Tronick, Keefer, & Brazelton, 1981; LeVine, 2004; LeVine et al., 1994/1998).

More specifically, Gusii social relationships and social roles are structured hierarchically and throughout the life span, people act according to "a code of restraint" (LeVine et al., 1994/1998, p. 47) or "avoidance" (p. 66). Within this context,

> the houses of co-wives in a homestead were separated from each other by a cultivated field—a distance believed to minimize the possibility of disputes between them. When the patriarch had died and the brothers quarreled over the inheritance of cattle or land, they moved quickly to divide the homestead as a spatial and social unit and thereby reduce interaction (sometimes by emigration to another area), so that overt conflict could be avoided. (p. 68)

Avoidance is further evident in routine interactions among adults who are unlikely to talk in a face-to-face position. Rather, they

> tend to speak side by side, back to back or at a 90-degree angle, in which one looks at the ground while the other speaks. Mutual gaze usually occurs at the moment of greeting and is avoided during the interaction that follows. Excessive eye contact is interpreted as disrespectful familiarity or improper intrusiveness with sexual or aggressive intent. (LeVine et al., 1994/1998, p. 222)

During the first few months of life in this cultural context, mothers are infants' primary caregivers, and babies spend much of the day in their mothers' laps or arms. During this time, there is little face-to-face interaction or mutual gaze, and mutual gaze decreases further when children are between 3 and 6 months old. Claiming that it is "silly to talk to a baby" (Dixon et al., 1981, p. 155), mothers hold babies and respond to them through touch, rather than by engaging them verbally or visually. Moreover, observations indicate that mothers "responded by jiggling or breast-feeding at the child's first fret before it became a full-blown cry" (LeVine, 2004, pp. 154–155). In contrast to the emotional excitation that is characteristic of European-American parent–infant interaction, Gusii mothers engage babies in ways that serve to "dampen, diffuse or diminish the affective level of the interaction" (Dixon et al., 1981, p. 165). To these ends, mothers use "a repertoire of repetitive vocalizations, taps, head nods and fixed facial expressions.

These stylized behaviors give an evenness, a flatness to the interactions" (p. 165). Play periods tend to be short, and when infants show positive or negative excitement, mothers may look away so that "the interaction remains contained within a narrow range of affect and attention" (p. 165). Insofar as the constituents of action are organized differently in relation to different cultural meanings than they are for middle-class American babies, it is possible that the development of action for Gusii babies would be characterized by a different sequence of periods than the one posited in Chapter 4 for middle-class Americans. At the same time, insofar as cultural processes shape both similarities and differences in human action and development, it is possible that some aspects of the developmental sequences in these two cultural contexts would be similar.

In Chapter 5, we saw that throughout the life span, people around the world sometimes participate in different cultural practices, which can put them on different pathways of differentiation and integration for different modes of action that involve different ways of organizing action constituents. We have also seen that there can be different cultural pathways of development across and within cultures for the ostensibly "same" practices, because there are different ways of structuring or organizing the constituents of action within those practices that reflect different cultural goals, values, and standards. For example, in Chapter 5 we saw that even though storytelling seems to occur around the world, there are culturally specific expectations and standards for storytelling, and action constituents for storytelling are structured in culturally particular ways. Thus, people experience culturally particular pathways of differentiation and integration for the development of storytelling. Regarding within-culture differences, as pointed out in Chapter 6, American children of varied socioeconomic circumstances play sports, but their action within sports practices is organized in different ways.

As the sports example indicates, thinking about how development happens through cultural processes involves not only comparing and contrasting pathways of differentiation and integration across different cultures; it also involves thinking about the ways in which cultural processes co-constitute development within particular cultures. It is sometimes problematic to talk about particular cultures or "a" culture, because cultures do not have clear or static physical boundaries and thus cannot be facilely equated with countries. It is also problematic to talk about particular cultures, because contact among cultures throughout history has led to all kinds of combinations of cultural traditions. Indeed, people have long lived at the crossroads of several, and sometimes shifting, cultural traditions (e.g., Chinese-Americans, Mexican migrant workers in the U.S., Turkish guest workers in Austria). Yet, because human action is always culturally constituted, we can say that all people act and develop in relation to *some* cultural meanings. Also, insofar as people engage *with others* in varied cultural practices, they act within some cultural group or groups, and thus it becomes possible to speak of "a" culture, or a cultural community, while recognizing the fluidity and fuzziness of the concept. According to Gutiérrez and Rogoff (2003), a *cultural community* refers to a "coordinated group of people with some traditions and understandings in common, extending across several generations, with varied roles and practices and continual change among participants as well as transformation in the community's practices" (p. 21). This definition is in keeping with our theoretical framework because it involves what people do together, or in relation to each other, as well as dynamic cultural meanings and ways of understanding the world.

As already pointed out, cultural meanings are both common and contested within a culture, thus virtually ensuring both interindividual similarity and variability during development among participants in a cultural community. (See Box 7.2 for an overview of cultural sources of developmental variability.) In addition, interindividual variability within a culture can occur because not everyone in a cultural community is equally involved in the same cultural practices and individuals may participate in several cultural communities (Rogoff, 2003). Insofar as people within cultures may be participating in some different cultural practices in which different cultural meanings are enacted in different modes of action, some of their developmental experiences may differ as well. Moreover, not everyone chooses to participate in the same practices, and as just explained, not everyone enjoys the same access to cultural practices. In Chapters 5 and 6, we saw that American children of different socioeconomic circumstances in the United States participate in some cultural practices in which different cultural meanings and developmental expectations are enacted. These examples also illustrate how cultural meanings and modes of action are not neutral, but are associated with issues of power and authority beyond who has access to varied cultural practices. That is, some cultural meanings and ways of structuring action may be more or less privileged by different groups within a wider culture (Bronfenbrenner, 1979; Wertsch, 1998). For example, in the United States, some modes of action that are

---

Box 7.2 **Some Cultural Sources of Developmental Variability**

INTERINDIVIDUAL DEVELOPMENTAL VARIABILITY

- People have differential access to cultural practices.
- People participate in different cultural practices involving different modes of action that reflect different meanings and goals of development.

INTRAINDIVIDUAL DEVELOPMENTAL VARIABILITY

- A person participates in varied cultural practices involving different modes of action that reflect different meanings and goals of development.
- A person experiences cultural change that involves developing new modes of action.

typical for people of higher socioeconomic circumstances are privileged in contexts such as school or going to the doctor. The research discussed in previous chapters shows that children from lower socioeconomic classes may struggle to act in such contexts when the privileged modes of action are different from and/or conflict with their typical patterns of action in other contexts. According to our current theoretical approach to thinking about how development happens, we can posit that people of different socioeconomic circumstances may undergo some different pathways of differentiation and integration, in part because they participate in different cultural practices that involve different modes of action, which reflect sometimes different cultural meanings and developmental expectations. It is important to point out that the focus here on cultural sources of variability does not mean that cultural processes only shape cultural differences in development. Research is required to discern patterns of similarities and differences in the cultural structuring of action and the development of action within and across cultures.

As pointed out in Chapter 3, individuals do not always act in the same way, and thus individuals can experience intraindividual developmental variability. One way that cultural processes contribute to intraindividual developmental variability is when a person participates in different cultural practices that reflect varied, and sometimes conflicting, cultural meanings (Bronfenbrenner, 1979). For example, in some cultures, it is possible to speak of a peer culture, which implies that the cultural practices and modes of action that children and adolescents engage in are different in some ways from, and sometimes at odds with, the cultural practices and modes of action preferred by adults. Children and adolescents may become adept at acting differently in relation to peers and in relation to adults. In varied cultures, people may sometimes struggle with inconsistent values and expectations for action at home and at work. Throughout the life span, people of heterogeneous cultural backgrounds may encounter varied, sometimes conflicting cultural meanings in different contexts and cultural practices. Insofar as the action contexts in which a developing person participates are interrelated, conflict and harmony among the varied contexts may affect developing individuals in varied ways (Bronfenbrenner, 1979). Whether in harmony or in conflict, a person may develop different modes of action in relation to different cultural meanings and expectations. According to the conceptualization presented here, we would posit that the development of such different modes of action involves different pathways of differentiation and integration for the constituents of action as a person participates in these different contexts.

Cultural Change

A fundamental truism about human culture is that it changes. This point has already been made in previous chapters, and we have considered some of the ways in which cultural change and development are interrelated. For example, in Chapter 5 we considered some of the ways in which changing cultural opportunities for education and wage labor are related to the development of new modes of action. As the examples from Chapter 5 show, one aspect of the complex process of cultural change that is relevant to our current purposes is that it involves the development of new modes of action that reflect new cultural meanings. New cultural modes of action sometimes arise in relation to dramatic events or circumstances, such as political upheaval, war, or changing economic circumstances. New modes of action can emerge as individuals and/or groups resist and/ or subvert dominant or privileged cultural ideologies (e.g., Turiel, 2003; Turiel & Perkins, 2004). New modes of action may also be created without fanfare by people as they engage together in the thick of daily life throughout the life span.

Insofar as culture refers to ways of acting, then cultural change includes changes in people's ways of acting, and some of those changes can be developmental changes. Therefore, cultural change cannot be isolated from the development of individual action, and the development of individual action cannot be isolated from dynamic cultural practices and meanings (Saxe, 2012). For example, I remember a class discussion in graduate school in which the instructor seemed skeptical that cultural change in the United States would involve men becoming more engaged in and adept at taking care of young children. Someone in the class suggested that men could certainly become quite capable of taking care of children, if they had opportunities to take care of children and if they then actually took care of some children. Unbeknownst to the student at the time, she was basically taking the participation approach to how development happens that I am using here. The student was positing that men could indeed develop childrearing abilities by actually taking care of children or by participating in childrearing practices. This claim further implies that cultural changes regarding who takes care of children would occur in conjunction with the development of varied relevant modes of action for men as they took care of children. And now there is the cultural phenomenon of "stay-at-home fathers." Perhaps both men and women have come a long way. Over the course of centuries, there have clearly been cultural changes in male and female action, and those changes have included the development of new modes of action for both men and women. The conceptualization of development presented here leads to thinking about and analyzing the culturally particular pathways of differentiation and integration that have occurred (and are still occurring) in men's and women's ways of acting.

Historically, cultural change is not limited to gender issues, and our current theoretical approach leads to thinking about how any kind of cultural change may be reciprocally linked to development-as-differentiation-and-integration for new cultural modes of action. For example, as I write these words, we live in times known for rapid and massive technological change around the world, especially in the electronic realm. These cultural changes have implications for the development of individual action because cultural constituents of action include the symbolic means and technologies that are used to achieve varied modes of action.

In addition to language, cultural processes include varied tools or technologies used to mediate action, such as books and computers, maps and musical scores, street signs and smartphones, counting procedures and cooking recipes, iPads and the Internet, to name but a few. Some of these technologies involve language and other symbols, and many also have a more

> clear-cut materiality in that they are physical objects that can be touched and manipulated. Furthermore, they can continue to exist across time and space, and they can continue to exist as physical objects even when not incorporated into the flow of action. (Wertsch, 1998, p. 30)

Rogoff's analyses of Girl Scout cookie sales (discussed in Chapter 2) emphasize how selling cookies revolves around the sales form which has changed over the course of decades. Without the sales form, or with a different sales form, selling Girl Scout cookies would be a different enterprise, or a different cultural practice involving some different ways of structuring action. In addition, the changes that have been made to the sales form have led to new ways of selling cookies, and new ways of selling cookies have contributed to further changes in the form. In Chapter 5, we considered Saxe's research on how changing economic circumstances and the development of counting on the part of individuals were reciprocally related for the Oksapmin of Papua New Guinea.

Current changes in computer and Internet technologies are shaping the development of our action in significant ways. However, it is not only a matter of developing the physical skills and specialized knowledge associated with varied technologies, such as how to navigate the Internet or how to add an app to your smartphone. It is also a matter of how these new cultural technologies are linked to developing new cultural modes of action in relation to others. For example, when someone uses a social networking site, or creates a blog, or texts someone, that person is acting in relation to others in a way that simply did not exist in the recent past. Of course, there are debates within and across cultures about the virtues and vices of varied Internet technologies, including whether becoming adept at using social media is a worthy goal of development. Such debates take us back to the point that cultural meanings, including conceptions of development, are both common and contested. Whatever one's stance on the value of Internet technologies may be, using them involves some standards as well as varied constituents, and a person's ability to use them can be analyzed from a developmental perspective in terms of differentiation and integration.

For example, research on adolescents' use of social networking sites (e.g., Manago, Graham, Greenfield, & Salimkhan, 2008; Williams & Merten,

2008) suggests that they are sites for identity exploration. When adolescents try out different identities or present themselves in different ways on the Internet, they have opportunities to differentiate among and integrate identity positions. They may also use others' feedback to further differentiate among identity positions, as well as integrate others' feedback into future posts. In doing so, identity development involves interrelations among cultural, social, and individual processes. In addition, adolescents can be differentiating their own perspectives from others, as well as integrating them. Cognitive differentiation and integration may occur as adolescents think about how to organize and categorize their online profiles and posts. Taken together, not only do the physical skills and specialized knowledge for using new cultural technologies develop, but such development is reciprocally related to the development of other action constituents, all of which may shape the development of new cultural modes of acting in relation to others. At the same time that the new cultural technologies contribute to such development, developing new modes of action may also contribute to ongoing cultural change, including constructing yet more new electronic technologies.

Social Processes

Clearly, human infants cannot survive, much less develop, without being cared for by at least one other person, and thus life span development happens partly through social processes from the outset. A wide range of social processes may provide opportunities for development throughout the life span as individuals engage with others in cultural practices. Let us begin with some general social processes, and then we can move on to thinking about how some more specific social processes may shape development-as-differentiation-and-integration.

Generally speaking, the overall social organization of cultural practices can support differentiating among modes of action in different contexts and cultural practices. For example, even though we may act in relation to some of the same people day in and day out, our action in relation to them is not always exactly the same. Sometimes we engage in different cultural practices and modes of action with the same people. Sometimes we are cranky, and sometimes the others with whom we interact are cranky. Sometimes we understand each other immediately; sometimes we almost give up on connecting. As Užgiris (1996) puts it: "Because there are contrasts between times of sadness and times of happiness, between easy understanding and baffled giving up, and between encouraged initiatives and abruptly denied intentions, the relations of joy, puzzlement, success, and denial can be constructed" (p. 35). Such varying interpersonal situations may provide varied opportunities for development, including to construct oneself in relation to others in differentiated ways, to differentiate among and integrate varied means to establish and maintain interaction, to differentiate among and integrate perspectives, and to differentiate among and integrate emotional sub-constituents of action. They also provide opportunities to construct the manner of action for different situations, which involves differentiating among and integrating values and standards regarding how to act in relation to others in different situations.

The claim that development happens through social processes also refers to the more specific patterning of people's interactions with others that provide opportunities for the differentiation and integration of action constituents. Interaction that involves making distinctions within and across action constituents has the potential to facilitate differentiation, and interaction that involves making connections within and across action constituents has the potential to facilitate integration (Raeff, 2011). Such interaction may be played out in varied ways throughout the life span. Thus, there are varied possible ways to organize this discussion of how development happens through social processes. This discussion is by no means exhaustive, and the point is to think about and illustrate how development-as-differentiation-and-integration can happen through some specific social processes. We begin by exploring how development happens through interacting with others who guide developing individuals in varied ways as they participate together in cultural practices. The discussion then turns to thinking about how development happens through interacting with peers. The section ends with a consideration of how development can occur through mild interpersonal conflict.

Varied Forms of Guidance

This discussion builds on some of the points made in Chapter 6 about guided participation, by focusing on how varied forms of guidance can promote differentiation and integration. Although there is abundant research on how others' guidance promotes children's development, social guidance can promote development throughout the life span. The theoretical approach presented here does not deny that there may be differences in developmental experiences during the life span, and it is fully recognized that different ways of structuring guidance may be more or less effective in promoting development at different times. In addition, different ways of structuring guidance may be more or less effective for different developing individuals, for different modes of action within different cultural practices, and in the context of different relationships between the developing person and the guide. It is also important to point out that age is not viewed as a central issue in the structuring of guidance. The guide may be older, younger, or the same age as the developing person. In Chapter 5, we saw that in many cultures around the world, slightly older siblings often guide children. In immigrant families, children often guide adults in the ways of the new culture. And who often shows adults how to use the latest computer technologies?

A key form of guidance, referred to as *scaffolding*, occurs when the guide breaks action down into simpler chunks (Wood, Bruner, & Ross, 1976). The ways in which action is broken down depend in part on the practice in which it is embedded, and also on the developing person's ways of acting at the time. Through scaffolding, the guide can focus the developing person's attention on certain parts of a task and he or she can also assist the developing person with some aspects of action while being responsible for the rest. Scaffolding in this way can promote differentiation, because cultural practices and modes of action are not being treated globally but in terms of distinct segments and constituents. As the person masters the segments and constituents, the guide can help the person to integrate them into the wider action whole.

In Chapter 4, Bruner's (1983) analysis of a mother and son playing peek-a-boo was presented as an example of action during Period 3 (Joint Attention: Common Topics and Routines) in the posited sequence of action development during infancy and early childhood in the United States. At one point in the analysis, Bruner comments that Jonathan's mother eventually allowed him "to take possession of the clown whenever he demanded it. To help him manage this, she condensed the surface structure of the game to two essential constituents" (p. 53). That is, she would say "Gone!" when the clown disappeared and "Boo!" upon reappearance (p. 53), thus scaffolding the child's participation in terms of two clearly differentiated segments of the routine.

When adults imitate children, they can be scaffolding children's action, even though it may be commonplace to consider how imitating by the developing person promotes development. Certainly, imitating others can promote development, and imitating was discussed in Chapter 6 as a means through which development occurs in varied cultures. However, as pointed out in Chapter 4, research with American mothers and children indicates that during the first year of life, mothers actually imitate more than children do. According to Užgiris, imitation by the adult can

> contribute to the delineation of action units for the infant. . . . By matching only certain acts, the mother highlights those acts and helps to segregate them into distinct units for the infant. They are lifted out from the flow of experience and can become familiar tokens in their interpersonal exchanges. (Užgiris et al., 1989, p. 120)

In this way, caregivers are imitating to break up the flow of action and are thereby scaffolding it into manageable and distinct chunks. Imitating to make such distinctions can help infants to differentiate among action constituents, which can then also be integrated. In addition, this research shows that mothers typically imitate those aspects of their infants' action that are culturally meaningful, such as hand waving or head nodding. Thus, the social processes that facilitate differentiation and integration are inseparable from cultural processes.

Examples of scaffolding abound around the world. In varied cultures, there are descriptions of scaffolding in the form of "helping children manage scaled-down versions of common chores" (Lancy, 1996, p. 144). As Kwara'ae children learn to engage in verbal repeating routines, their caregivers often "chunk" the routine into smaller segments. Watson-Gegeo and Gegeo (1986/1992) further explain, "If a child consistently fails to be able to reproduce an entire phrase or sentence at a time, the caregiver will break it down into smaller chunks" (p. 43). Such chunking provides a basis for differentiating among and integrating segments of the routine.

Lave and Wenger (1991/2008) describe how Vai and Gola tailors in Liberia develop their abilities while producing garments in reverse. That is,

> apprentices begin by learning the finishing stages of producing a garment, go on to learn to sew it, and only later learn to cut it out. . . . Reversing production steps has the effect of focusing the apprentices' attention first on the broad outlines of garment construction as they handle garments while attaching buttons and hemming cuffs. Next, sewing turns their attention to the logic (order, orientation) by which different pieces are sewn together, which in turn explains why they are cut out as they are. Each step offers the unstated opportunity to consider how the previous step contributes to the present one. (p. 72)

This example nicely illustrates the current approach to how development happens in at least two ways. First, we see the importance of starting with a cultural goal of development, as represented by first working on the almost finished product, which is a wider whole that involves varied skills. Second, we see that as apprentices engage in scaffolded reverse production, they have opportunities to differentiate among and integrate the skills that comprise tailoring as a whole.

Certainly, other forms of guidance that promote development-as-differentiation-and-integration may be involved during scaffolded interactions. For example, the guide may demonstrate, verbally explain, verbally instruct, offer tips or hints, point out what the person is doing correctly or incorrectly, and/or physically guide—all in ways that promote differentiation and integration. Some of the forms of guidance presented in Chapter 6 can promote differentiation and integration. For example, when experts correct or give pointers, they can draw attention to differentiated action constituents as well as to how differentiated constituents function in relation to each other. Guiding by "highlighting" and by "drawing distinctions" during weaving (Paradise & Rogoff, 2009, p.118) also suggest differentiating among task components. As discussed in Chapter 5, research on the development of storytelling in Taipei indicates that caregivers "focus the child's attention" on a misdeed and "point out its consequences" (Miller et al., 2012, p. 78). Focusing attention and pointing out consequences can provide opportunities for children to differentiate misdeeds from other ways of acting, and pointing out consequences can provide opportunities to differentiate self and other, as well as coordinate with others in culturally appropriate ways.

To further think about how differentiation and integration are promoted through guided participation, let us go back to some of the issues discussed in Chapters 5 and 6 pertaining to the different developmental pathways that may be traversed by people of different socioeconomic circumstances in the United States. Research suggests that children of varying socioeconomic circumstances participate in cultural practices that involve some different forms of guidance, thus shaping some different pathways of development for action that may be more or less privileged in school settings. Some differences in guidance are evident with regard to asking questions.

Heath's (1983/1992) classic ethnographic research indicates that children from different racial and socioeconomic circumstances in the United States participate in different cultural ways of telling stories, reading, and using language more generally. And findings regarding socioeconomic differences in language development continue to be a focus of recent research (e.g., Fernald, Marchman, & Weisleder, 2013; Hoff, 2013). When reading to children, middle-class white parents typically engage children in ways that are compatible with the literacy lessons that children encounter in school settings (Heath, 1986/1992). That is, they typically ask "what questions" about different parts of a text. For example, an adult may point to varied parts of a picture and ask, "What's this?" and "What's that?" Middle-class parents also tend to ask questions about the story characters' attributes (e.g., "What does a cat say?"), as well as questions that require a child to explain what is going on in the story (e.g., "Why did the cat do that?"). Parents ask questions about how different story events and/or characters are linked as well as how the story may be linked to the child's own experience (e.g., "Remember when we saw that cat in the street?"). Based on these participation experiences, the middle-class white children go to school knowing how to engage in the kinds of literacy practices that occur in school settings. Part of what is going on when these parents and children read together is that the adults' questions are providing opportunities for differentiating among and integrating the subconstituents of reading. For example, differentiating among parts of the story can be facilitated when adults ask "what questions" and "attribute questions" about events, characters, and pictures. Talking about how story events or characters are linked allows a child to practice integrating ideas about different parts of the story.

In contrast, Heath's (1986/1992) research shows that in working-class white families, there are not simply fewer books, but queries about written texts mostly include "what questions." Moreover, "bookreading time focuses on letters of the alphabet, numbers, names of basic items pictured in books, and simplified retellings of stories in the words of the adult" (p. 107). According to Heath, the children from the lower socioeconomic status white families do well in reading lessons during the first few years of elementary school. However, these children tend not to respond "when the teacher reaches the end of storyreading or the reading circle and asks questions such as 'What did you like about the story?'" (p. 111). They "frequently say, 'I don't know' or shrug their shoulders" (p. 111) in response to questions about what they would do if they were characters in the story. In a poor, rural African-American community, children and adults did not read together, and when these children went to school, they encountered unknown cultural practices, and often "the kinds of questions asked about reading books [were] unfamiliar" (p. 118). However, as described in Chapter 5, the children engaged in oral storytelling practices that required them to be assertive and creative, and they often told stories with complex plots and multiple characters. Thus, the African-American children participated with others in narrative practices that guided their development, but in ways that were not privileged and practiced in formal school settings.

Research with middle-class Americans shows that asking children questions and discussing events in elaborative ways is not exclusive to reading practices (Rogoff, 1990). For example, research on parent–child conversations about past events points to how parental guidance can shape children's autobiographical memories as well as their self-conceptions and perspective-taking abilities (Fivush & Nelson, 2006; Nelson & Fivush, 2004). More specifically, this research shows that parent–child discussions of the past

> vary along a dimension of elaborativeness, with some mothers talking frequently about the past and discussing past events in richly embellished ways. Highly elaborative mothers continue to question their children about the past, giving more and more detail about what occurred with each question even when their children do not recall any information. (Nelson & Fivush, 2004, p. 497)

Such elaborative guidance provides children with opportunities to "construct meaning by weaving the who, when, where, and what of an event into the why" (Fivush & Nelson, 2006, p. 240). In other words, thinking about what happened and where it happened, who was involved, and why the people did what they did involves differentiating the event along varied dimensions and considering how those dimensions are connected or integrated. In addition, when disagreements about past events arise, children have opportunities to differentiate their perspectives from others' perspectives. Through negotiating a common narrative about a past event, the different perspectives may be integrated.

Although characteristic of American middle-class interaction, asking questions is not exclusive to them. In Taipei, children's narrative partners ask questions as a way to help children remember past events and contribute to telling stories about them (Miller et al., 2012). The Kaluli of Papua New Guinea do not believe in talking about what another person might be thinking, and thus all speakers are responsible for expressing themselves clearly. Accordingly, "rather than offering possible interpretations or guessing at the meaning of what a child is saying, caregivers make extensive use of clarification requests such as 'huh?' and 'what?'" (Ochs & Schieffelin, 1984/1988, p. 294). Classic ethnographic research among the Inuit of the Canadian Arctic points to how adults "frequently and repetitively" (Briggs, 1998, p. 5) ask children questions within the context of dramatic routines as a way to get children to think about their own characteristics as well as their roles in relation to others (Briggs, 1998). According to Briggs, the questions posed to children often "present them with emotionally powerful problems that the children could not ignore" (p. 5). Adults ask questions that are

> potentially dangerous for the child being questioned and dramatiz[e] the consequences of various answers: "Why don't you kill your baby brother?" "Why don't you die so I can have your nice new shirt?" "Your mother's going to die—look, she's cut her finger—do you want to come live with me?" In this way, adults created, or raised to consciousness, issues that the children must have seen as having grave consequences for their lives. (p. 5)

Briggs also explains that a child's responses to such questions were often followed by further questions to which the child responded, "and again the adults countered with new problems, and so on" (p. 12). At the same time, the questions were embedded in playful interactions that mitigated the gravity of the issues with which children were confronted. Research is needed to discern if and how cultural ways of asking questions provide opportunities for differentiation and integration.

It is also important to point out that the people being guided are not necessarily the only ones who are developing. During the course of guiding a developing person through some cultural practice, the guide may undergo some development as well. In Chapter 5, we caught glimpses of development for sibling caregivers in their roles as teachers or guides. A guide may become a more expert guide during the course of actually guiding because he or she has opportunities to differentiate and integrate varied forms of guidance. A guide also has opportunities to differentiate and integrate his or her own and others' perspectives, and the guide may be differentiating and integrating the role of being a guide as part of his or her self-conceptions. In these sorts of situations, the developing person may unwittingly serve as a kind of guide to the guide by, for example, asking clarification questions or indicating if he or she does or does not understand what the guide is doing. In some cases, the guide may be guided by yet another guide, pointing to another way in which development for guides may be played out. For example, the heavy focus of research on parent–child interaction emphasizes how children develop through interacting with parents who are taken to be the more competent guides. At the same time, the parents may be undergoing development with the help of guides, such as their own parents or in some cultural circumstances, professionals. The particular guidance circumstances may be played out in varied ways, and the current theoretical approach to basic developmental processes enables us to think systematically about the developmental possibilities for the guide. That is, what the guide does can be understood as a form of cultural action in relation to others that can undergo differentiation and integration while participating with others in cultural practices.

Developing through Peer Interaction

It has long been recognized that peer relationships can contribute much to how development happens (e.g., Piaget, 1932/1950). Throughout the life span, people may interact with varied peers within varied relationships, with potentially varying opportunities for development. Despite differences in the structuring of particular peer relationships, they are typically characterized in terms of egalitarianism and power symmetry. The current theoretical framework provides a conceptual basis for thinking systematically about how engaging with peers in varied cultural practices can provide opportunities for development-as-differentiation-and-integration.

Much developmental research on peer relationships focuses on children and adolescents, and the term *peer culture* connotes modes of action for children and adolescents that can be distinguished from adult modes of action. Momentarily in this section, we will discuss some research that points to some of the ways in which early peer interaction can contribute to how development happens. But first let us briefly address the point that peer relationships are established and maintained throughout the life span. As with other social processes that shape development, there may be both similarities and differences in the ways that interacting with peers promote differentiation and integration at different times during ontogenesis. The life span developmental implications of interacting with peers also depend on the vagaries of particular cultural practices. For example, feedback from peers in a support group may promote different pathways of differentiation and integration than feedback from a close friend over drinks at home, which may promote different developmental pathways than feedback from strangers on social networking sites. There may, of course, be similarities as well. In addition, the developmental implications of interacting with peers may vary as they are played out in different cultures and across particular peer relationships (e.g., casual acquaintances, friends, siblings, life partners, work colleagues). The main point here is that the current theoretical approach provides tools for thinking systematically about how development may happen through peer interaction at any time during a person's life, in any cultural context. That is, we can think about how different ways of interacting with peers promote differentiation and integration for varied modes of action, whatever the particular peer circumstances may be.

A great deal of classic research on the role of peer interaction in development has been directed toward discerning how collaborating with peers promotes cognitive development (e.g., Azmitia & Montgomery, 1993; Doise, Mugny, & Perret-Clermont, 1975; Duveen & Psaltis, 2008; Gauvain, 2001). Many studies have been conducted in schools and involve specialized cognitive tasks, such as Piagetian conservation tasks or scientific reasoning problems. This research shows that development does not simply occur when children are placed together and told to solve problems together. One take-home message from this line of inquiry is, it depends: Peer interaction may or may not facilitate cognitive development, depending on a wide range of factors, including gender, whether one partner knows more or less about the task to be solved, the partners' relationship (e.g., are they friends or acquaintances), the patterning of the children's interaction, and the task itself.

Much research on peer interaction and cognitive development originated with attempts to study Piaget's claim that peer interaction can facilitate cognitive development because the relative power symmetry between peers allows them to express their varied perspectives and to cooperate genuinely. Years ago, studies of the development of children's understanding of conservation (e.g., understanding that the amount of water stays the same when it is poured into a container of a different size) showed that peer collaboration is especially effective when nonconservers are paired with children who do understand the concept of conservation (e.g., Doise et al., 1975). Such findings were corroborated with research using other cognitive tasks (e.g., Azmitia, 1988), and subsequent research suggested that benefits accrue when the more knowledgeable partner explains his or her reasoning to the less knowledgeable one (e.g., Tudge, 1992). Although these studies were not specifically designed to discern issues of differentiation and integration, organismic-developmental theory leads to positing that interacting with peers is conducive to cognitive development in part when it provides opportunities for children's understanding to undergo differentiation and integration. In general, collaborating with someone who expresses a different point of view about a topic can provide opportunities to differentiate among and integrate varied topic components. With regard to conservation, analyses of what children say while collaborating suggest that conservation understanding is promoted by talking about the discrepant height and width of the containers (Psaltis & Duveen, 2007). This finding points to the importance of explicitly differentiating between key features of the containers.

Some research that focuses more specifically on what children say to each other when they interact to solve cognitive problems hints at the possibility that some differentiating and integrating are going on. For example, when collaborating to generate hypotheses about the workings of a computer program, children who talked tended to "refine their hypotheses to include information" and to construct "more elaborated hypotheses" (Teasley, 1995, p. 217). Refining and elaborating hypotheses to include information suggests integrating differentiated information about the task at hand. In addition, children who talk when they work together may be more likely to "coordinate theories with evidence" (p. 218). A study in Finland suggests that collaborative problem solving occurs when the partners interact in ways that enable them to coordinate or integrate their differing perspectives (e.g., Kumpuluainen & Kaartinen, 2003).

It is also important to point out that collaborating to solve a task that is designed to investigate cognitive development is not necessarily a purely cognitive task. According to our current perspective, when children are interacting to solve a task that is supposed to assess their cognitive development, they are acting in relation to others in a cultural practice. As such, the task involves cognition or thinking as well as varied other action constituents, such as interacting, feeling, language, perspective taking, and self-positioning. Thus, it would be interesting to analyze these collaboration sessions to discern if and how they may be facilitating the development of children's cultural action in relation to others. For example, a more knowledgeable peer may not further his or her understanding of a particular cognitive task while interacting with a less knowledgeable peer, but his or her action in relation to others may develop as the person works out ways to explain the task to someone who understands it differently.

Around the world, children play together, and peer play serves as a central arena for development during childhood, even though aspects of play may be understood and structured differently in different cultures. Using a school-based analogy, Lancy (2008/2010) argues that peer play "is the 'classroom' where children try on and practice their culture" (p. 162). Lancy's review of research in varied non-Western cultures indicates that children's pretend play often involves pretending to engage in adult work activities. Such pretend play provides opportunities for differentiation and integration within and across some of the action constituents that comprise modes of action within adult work practices. In addition, "children readily incorporate and rehearse conventional social relationships in make-believe including marriage, kin relations, adultery, birth, and death" (2008/2010, p. 163), which may provide opportunities to differentiate among and integrate cultural practices and the modes of action that are particular to them.

Research with American and British preschoolers shows that during the course of pretend play, children talk a lot about what they and their pretend characters intend, desire, and feel, which can facilitate differentiating among and integrating varied perspectives (e.g., Dunn, 2008). In addition, as we saw in Chapter 4, children are differentiating among and integrating their own and each others' perspectives as they co-construct and negotiate their play. Negotiating play scenarios further provides opportunities for cognitive differentiation and integration as children organize their play thematically and temporally and as they figure out how to solve problems that arise during the course of play.

Preschoolers are also well known for gender segregation. Not only do girls and boys often exclude each other when playing, but they repeatedly comment on each others' shortcomings (e.g., Coplan & Arbeau, 2009; Corsaro, 2003; Nicolopoulou, 1997). Such play suggests that gender is being differentiated as a salient dimension of action. In addition, gender differentiation provides a way to view oneself in contrast to some, but as similar to others, thus facilitating identity differentiation and integration along gender lines. However, sometimes girls and boys do play together. Thus, sex-segregated play and mixed-sex play provide children with different opportunities for developing different modes of action in relation to varied others.

Peer play also includes playing games with rules, which Mead (1934/1962) viewed as critical to how development happens. According to Mead, games with rules are structured in terms of roles that have "a definite relationship to each other" (Mead, 1934/1962, p. 151). Thus, each person "must be ready to take the attitude of everyone else involved in that game" (Mead, 1934/1962, p. 151). Using baseball as an example, Mead argues that a player's action

> is determined by his assumption of the action of the others who are playing the game. What he does is controlled by his being everyone else on that team, at least in so far as those attitudes affect his own particular response. (p. 154)

While playing organized games, action may develop as each player differentiates his or her own role and perspective from all of the other roles and individual perspectives. At the same time, insofar as social roles are defined in relation to each other (e.g., how the pitcher, batter, catcher, outfielder, infielder, and first, second, and third basemen are defined in relation to each other, or teacher–student and parent–child roles), playing games with rules also requires integrating one's own role and perspective with other reciprocal or complementary roles and perspectives.

These varied examples of how development can happen through interacting with peers emphasize how peer interactions provide opportunities for individuals to undergo differentiation and integration. In addition, some examples illuminate some of the ways in which social processes do not necessarily have to involve explicit guidance. Nevertheless, interacting with peers does not preclude explicit guidance, and some of the guidance processes discussed in the previous section can occur among peers throughout the life span. For example, peers can direct attention and ask questions in ways that provide opportunities for differentiation and integration. Peers can also instruct, explain, and offer feedback in ways that may promote differentiation and integration.

Developing through Interpersonal Conflict

Even though some individuals and groups around the world seem unable to settle their conflicts, people the world over often work hard to avoid conflict and to resolve conflicts when they do occur. Despite the obvious negative implications of conflict, it can sometimes contribute positively to development (Shantz & Hartup, 1992). It is readily recognized that conflict is complex and can be structured in varied ways. Within the current discussion of how development happens through social processes, relatively mild conflict is at issue, involving mild opposition or disagreement among people, as well as the mild conflict that can occur when people encounter differing perspectives. We are not talking here about interactions characterized by aggression, coercion, violence, dominance, and/or abuse.

Conflict can provide opportunities to differentiate among individual perspectives, as well as to work out ways of coordinating or integrating different perspectives effectively (Dunn, 2008). For example, in a Japanese preschool, a teacher explains that "bumping up against others is important. Children must learn both to form their own ideas and to understand the ideas of others" (Lewis, 1995/1999, p. 85). The following example of an observation by Corsaro (2003) of two American preschoolers illustrates how the children repeatedly assert their respective points of view, providing opportunities for differentiating among perspectives.

> Richard picks up a block near Barbara and Barbara tries to grab it from him.
> "No. No!" says Barbara, struggling with Richard for the block.
> "No," says Richard.
> "I had it first!" counters Barbara.
> "I want one."
> "But I had it first!"
> "I want one, Barbara."
> "I had that first."
> "I want it."
> "I had it first!" Barbara shouts. (p. 164)

As children participate in resolving conflicts, they may have opportunities to go beyond repeatedly and rigidly asserting their individual claims, as Barbara and Richard do in this example. They can construct ways of integrating their own and others' perspectives as well as differentiate among and integrate different emotions. They may also be differentiating among and integrating varied means for cooperating with each other, as suggested by research with older children who are increasingly likely to resolve conflicts (especially with friends) by negotiating (Bukowski, Motzoi, & Meyer, 2009; Laursen, & Pursell, 2009; Rubin, Bukowski, & Parker, 2006).

Beyond childhood peer interactions, mild conflict and resolving conflicts may promote development at any time during the life span. For example, conflict between adolescents and parents may serve as an arena for adolescent identity development. Parent–adolescent conflict and conflict resolution may provide opportunities for adolescents to differentiate among and integrate their own and others' emotions, as well as to develop cognitive aspects of arguing and defending their own positions. With regard to continued life span development, parents may have opportunities to further differentiate among and integrate their own and others' perspectives through such conflict as well. The same may be the case for any kind of mild conflict that occurs between adults at any time during adulthood.

Throughout the discussion thus far of how development happens through cultural and social processes, I have repeatedly noted that interacting with others provides people with *opportunities* for differentiation and integration. However, just as leading a horse to water does not guarantee that it will drink, guiding a person's action does not guarantee that he or she will develop. Indeed, sometimes interacting with others does not seem to promote a person's development. In order for a person to benefit developmentally from interacting with others in cultural practices, it is often argued that the interaction has to be sensitive to that person's individual abilities and current modes of functioning. Thus, guides ideally adjust their guidance in relation to what the developing person is doing. Moreover, developing people are not passive receptacles for social and cultural processes. Indeed, research has long shown that even infants contribute actively to the structuring of social interaction (Bell & Harper, 1977; Stern, 1977; Užgiris, 1989). Moreover, at any time during the life span, individuals are not the passive pawns of cultural processes because they actively appropriate or construe cultural meanings from their own perspectives and use cultural tools in their own ways (Corsaro & Johannesen, 2007; Gjerde, 2004; Lawrence & Valsiner, 2003; Rogoff, 2003; Turiel, 2008; Valsiner, 1998; Wertsch, 1998). In other words, individual processes are also fully implicated in how development happens.

Individual Processes

In this section, we first consider some of the ways in which development happens through individual processes as a person participates with others in cultural practices. Then we consider how individual processes may shape development-as-differentiation-and-integration when a person is alone.

Participating in Cultural Practices

Individual processes generally refer to what a developing individual does that contributes to his or her own development. Most generally, in order for a person's ways of acting to develop, that person has to act. Let us go back to the basic claim of sociocultural theory that development happens as an individual participates with others in cultural practices. What is a person doing as he or she participates with others in cultural practices? According to our theoretical perspective, much of the time a person is acting in some way, and therefore to participate is to act. As a person acts in relation to others in cultural practices, current modes of action provide a basis for the development of new modes of action, which will then contribute to how further development happens. For example, by engaging with others in play, a child's ways of playing may develop to become new current modes of playing, which can be a basis for the continued development of playing. The same can be said for storytelling. By telling stories with others, a person's ways of storytelling can develop and can then become a basis for the continued development of telling stories. This iterative process means that individual action can be understood as the product of development, as well as part of the process of how development happens. Although action as developmental product and action as part of the process of how development happens are utterly interrelated, they are also being conceptualized as distinct phenomena. As such, one can think about their unique dimensions as well as how they are linked. For example, with regard to action as developmental product, one can think about the organization and meaning of an individual's current modes of action in terms of individual, social, and cultural processes. With regard to action as part of the process of how development happens, one can think about how particular aspects of an individual's ways of acting promote differentiation and integration and also interact with social and cultural processes to make further development happen.

Figure 7.1 provides a view of the ongoing interplay between action as part of the process of how development happens and action as developmental product. It begins with a person's current ways of acting at some time in his or her life. Playing, telling stories, and calming a distressed child are examples of ways of acting that may be typical for someone. A person's current ways of acting provide a basis for the person to participate with others, or act in varied specific contexts that involve playing, telling stories, or calming a distressed child. In these contexts, the process of developing new ways of acting happens as the person participates or acts in ways that promote differentiation and integration within and among action constituents. Those new ways of acting are the products of development that then provide a new basis for the process of development to occur as

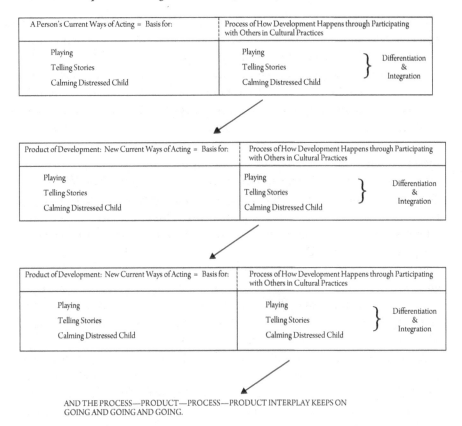

Figure 7.1 The ongoing interplay between action as part of the process of how development happens and action as developmental product.

the person participates with or acts in relation to others in cultural practices in specific contexts. The product of that process would be new ways of acting which provide a new basis for continued development-as-process to occur. And so on and so on.

Within our current theoretical approach, the developing person is viewed as active because he or she is a feeling, meaning-making, goal-setting, and valuing person (Brandtstädter, 2006; Bronfenbrenner, 1979; Budwig, 2003; Edwards, de Guzman, Brown, & Kumru, 2006; Lewis, 1997; Nelson, 2007; Oyama, 2000; Piaget, 1953, 1954/1986; Rogoff, 2003; Užgiris, 1977; Valsiner, 1997; Vygotsky, 1986/1987). As pointed out in Chapters 2 and 4, newborns come to the world able to engage in some individually self-generated sensorimotor action, and increasingly during development, individuals can set goals for their own development that reflect beliefs and values. Although a person can set out to develop in some way, individuals do not necessarily always do the work of differentiation and integration consciously. It can be partly conscious, but it does not have to be. Either way, our current theoretical approach leads to thinking about what a person does that facilitates differentiation and integration within and across action constituents while participating with others in cultural practices.

As a person participates actively in cultural practices with others, it is assumed that the person is doing some of the work of differentiation and integration. Any of the examples of developmental change discussed in Chapters 4 and 5 can be used to illustrate this point. For example, as discussed in Chapter 4, when participating in interaction routines that involve enacting different roles (e.g., hider/seeker), children can be actively differentiating between the roles, as well as integrating them by practicing the modes of action that comprise the different roles. When a child shifts his or her attention from something to follow another person's pointing, the child can be actively making sense of his or her own and the other's interests, which involves differentiating between them and integrating them. The Chapter 4 discussion of Debbie carefully studying Betty and Jenny in the sandbox suggests that Debbie was actively figuring out how to coordinate or integrate her goals with Betty's and Jenny's play. When older siblings take care of younger siblings (discussed in Chapter 5), they are doing the work of differentiating among and integrating their own and their charges' perspectives, as well as figuring out what means to use in varied caretaking situations.

In part because individuals pursue different interests, they also actively contribute to their own development by choosing some of the cultural practices in which they participate. It is argued that already during infancy "the structure of schemes at some given time is the basis for generating selective interest in activities" (Užgiris, 1996, p. 30). Selective interest provides a way to focus attention on some activities rather than others, thereby promoting differentiation among activities. In cultures where children participate in ongoing community practices, they show interest in and "take initiative in finding and creating activities from which to learn" (Paradise & Rogoff, 2009, p. 112). In varied cultures, people are expected to make some of their own choices about cultural practices, based on individual inclinations. Choosing to engage in certain cultural practices rather than others involves differentiating among practices as well as clarifying one's own inclinations. In addition, such choices shape the pathways of differentiation and integration that individuals experience as they develop modes of action within their chosen practices.

Individual processes also contribute to development as individuals seek out some of the social partners who shape their development. For example, in middle-class Western cultures, adults are typically young children's primary play partners. However, by the time children are 3½ and 4 years old, "it is other children who are far more sought out as companions than boring old parents, as long as these other children are individuals whom they know and like" (Dunn, 2004, p. 25). Dunn explains that adults typically structure play rather conventionally and realistically, whereas play with other children takes off in all kinds of exciting directions.

In addition, an individual's ways of acting contribute to how guidance is structured insofar as social partners structure guidance in relation to individual competencies. When interacting with others, individuals may contribute to their own development by shaping guidance in other ways as well. For example, developing individuals can direct their own and others' attention to certain aspects of a situation, which may prompt the others to adjust their guidance to those aspects of the situation. Developing individuals may also ask questions that provide a basis for differentiating and integrating action constituents within a given cultural practice, at least in cultures where asking questions is encouraged. Although we have mostly considered some distinct aspects of how individual, social, and cultural processes contribute to development, these examples show that they are fundamentally interrelated during development.

On One's Own

Although the theoretical approach presented here focuses on how development occurs as individuals participate with others in cultural practices, it is important to recognize that developing individuals are sometimes alone. When alone, individual processes can shape development-as-differentiation-and-integration in varied ways. For example, people can and often do develop their incipient competencies by practicing on their own, sometimes for hours on end. In any culture, and throughout the life span, practice makes perfect or at least has the potential to make perfect because differentiation and integration within and across action constituents can occur. As Užgiris (1996) explains:

> Many have observed children to repeat a fortuitously obtained result numerous times in an apparent attempt to understand it. . . . In everyday language, we would call this practice, but it is not necessarily the simple practice of a skill. It is the practice of running through patterns of schemes with variation. (p. 34)

Practicing variations on modes of action provides opportunities for action constituents to be differentiated and integrated in flexible ways.

In addition, when alone, people may think about their lives and action in relation to others. Classic analyses of a young child's monologues before falling asleep (Nelson, 1989) point to how she used language to make sense of her world on her own (e.g., Bruner & Lucariello, 1989; Feldman, 1989). Little Emily went over the events of the day and also anticipated future events. As she constructed accounts of these events and how she felt about them, she actively worked to make sense of her action in relation to others. She seems to have been working on differentiating among aspects of varied events as well as among people. Her pondering also involved constructing connections within and among events as well as connections among people, including herself and others (e.g., her parents, babysitter, and newborn sibling). Clearly, mulling over the day's events occurs throughout the life span and can be a basis for differentiation and integration at any time.

Also when alone, a developing person can utilize some of the guidance strategies that the person has experienced during social interaction in ways that promote development. For example, a developing person can scaffold his or her own action in ways that promote differentiation and integration. Or a person may be alone watching a demonstration on television, or actively searching for and watching demonstrations on YouTube. The demonstrating may be indirect in these cases, and the guidance cannot be dynamically tailored to what an individual is doing. Nevertheless, the person may benefit developmentally from the demonstration. This example also points to how electronic technologies enable interrelations among individual, social, and cultural processes to shape development in new and varied ways.

Some Final Remarks

To reiterate, development happens through interrelated individual, social, and cultural processes as a developing individual participates with others in cultural practices. This theoretical approach emphasizes thinking about how people's participation experiences promote development-as-differentiation-and-integration. In a nutshell, it is all about what people *do*. Thus, we are led to thinking about the individual, social, and cultural processes that comprise what people do and how they shape the development of what people do.

More specifically, we are led to thinking about cultural meanings and the structuring of action within the cultural practices that a person is participating in, what the developing person is doing while participating that can promote differentiation and integration, and what the people with whom he or she is interacting are doing that can promote differentiation and integration. Of course, we cannot analyze everything about everything that people do all at once, and analyzing what people do does not preclude picking and choosing certain aspects of their action to focus on more specifically. For example, say you are interested in the developmental effects of number of siblings and birth order. Our current theoretical approach to how development happens leads to discerning the meaning of sibling relationships within a cultural community as well as cultural expectations for acting in relation to siblings. In addition, we are led to discerning what a person with this or that number of siblings does with those siblings, and with others, that is promoting differentiation and integration. Or if you are interested in how socioeconomic status affects development, you would focus on what people of varying socioeconomic circumstances do as they participate with others in cultural practices that can promote development-as-differentiation-and-integration in relation to cultural meanings and developmental goals. As discussed in previous chapters and in this chapter, Heath, Lareau, and Miller focused on what people of varying socioeconomic circumstances do together in cultural practices, and we connected their research to organismic-developmental theory's conceptualization of development in terms of differentiation and integration. By emphasizing what people do, we are organizing our thinking about how development happens from the perspective of the forest. Rather than getting lost among the trees by going from one possible causal factor to another, we are led to thinking about how those factors encompass individual, social, and cultural processes and about the varied ways in which individual, social, and cultural processes can be played out and interrelated to shape development-as-differentiation-and-integration.

8

Hot Topics

Implications and Future Directions

[P]sychology . . . must venture beyond the conventional aims of posi-
tivist science with its ideals of reductionism, causal explanation and
prediction. The three need not be treated like the Trinity.

—Jerome Bruner (1990, p. xiii)

The goals of this chapter are to bring together varied points from the previous
chapters in order to think systematically about some of developmental psychology's most vexing issues and to suggest directions for further theory and research.
The chapter is organized around the basic developmental questions and processes
and begins with a discussion of the current theoretical framework's implications
for thinking about and conducting research on what happens during development. The second section of the chapter addresses some implications for thinking about and investigating how development happens. The book ends by coming
back to the wider forest of what develops during development. The present systems conceptualization of action and development is also connected to the wider
whole of human functioning as well as to psychology more generally.

What Happens during Development?

The theoretical approach presented in this book has varied implications for thinking systematically about some of developmental psychology's most vexing issues
regarding what happens during development. This section takes up some implications of organismic-developmental theory for thinking about the following five
issues: 1) criteria for developmental change, 2) varied kinds of change, 3) interindividual and intraindividual developmental variability and similarity, 4) the
ways in which action and development are generalizable and also context specific,
and 5) continuity and discontinuity during development. Implications for new
research directions will be taken up at the end of the section.

Some Vexing Issues

Criteria for Developmental Change

One of my central goals for this book is to offer ways of thinking systematically about action and development without getting bogged down in minutiae. Contemporary developmental psychology is a daunting discipline, and the endless supply of data about change over time and age-based change can be overwhelming. To bring some discipline to the discipline, it is useful to start with a more specific definition of development than change over time or age-based change. From the perspective of organismic-developmental theory, development involves differentiating and integrating action constituents in relation to cultural expectations for development. A major advantage of this conceptualization of development is that it provides systematic criteria for discerning developmental change, thereby making it less likely to get lost among the trees in the myriad of possible changes that people may undergo during their lives. Indeed, synthesizing the conceptualization of cultural action in relation to others with this conceptualization of development enabled us in Chapters 4 and 5 to think systematically about a wide range of research on what happens during development.

At the same time that the orthogenetic principle provides more specific ways of thinking about developmental sequences, it is not overly specific. By not being overly specific, the criteria of differentiation and integration can be applied across individuals, across action contexts, and across cultures. Accordingly, a wide range of research and modes of action were brought together in an orderly way in Chapters 4 and 5. In addition, as illustrated in Chapter 5, differentiation and integration can be played out in varied cultural ways and can potentially illuminate understanding of anyone, anywhere in the world. As such, differentiation and integration are highly generalizable and provide a common language for thinking about development throughout the life span as people go about their lives in all corners of the world.

Yet at the same time, danger lurks when we do not define our terms precisely. If differentiation and integration remain too vague, they may end up being applied haphazardly and inconsistently (Raeff, 2011). As discussed at the end of Chapter 4, Fischer offers a more specific way of analyzing differentiation and integration that proceeds from differentiating single sets to integrating single sets into mappings. As mappings are further differentiated, they can be integrated to form systems, which can be integrated into systems of systems. This analytic framework is particularly well suited for cognitive constituents of action and may provide a basis for specifying differentiation and integration for other constituents of action as well as for action in relation to others as a whole. Wapner posits a developmental ordering of person–world relations in terms of differentiation and integration that has been applied to changing modes of functioning during critical life transitions, including adapting to nursery school, immigration, and retirement, as well as coping with natural disasters (Wapner, 2000; Wapner & Demick, 1998, 2005). The least developed mode is characterized by dedifferentiated person–world relations, whereby there is "passive accommodation" to "environmental demands" (Wapner & Demick, 2005, p. 292). In differentiated and isolated person-in-environment relations, a person disengages from the environment, and non-constructive ventilation relations occur when "the person maintains conflicted relations with aspects of the environment" (Wapner & Demick, 2005, p. 292). The most developed mode of person–world relations is taken to involve "a differentiated and hierarchically integrated person-in-environment system with flexibility, freedom, self-mastery, and the capacity to shift from one mode of person-in-environment relationship to another as required by goals, by demands of the situation, and by the instrumentalities available" (Wapner & Demick, 1998, p. 775). Both Fischer's and Wapner's approaches provide entries into thinking about differentiation and integration more specifically. However, further theorizing and research are necessary for identifying some of the more specific ways in which differentiation and integration play out for the development of varied modes of action in relation to others.

Although my goal for this book is to articulate an overarching theoretical framework for thinking systematically about basic developmental processes, this goal was challenged particularly in Chapter 4, by the vast amount of research on infancy and early childhood. Only some of this research is included in Chapter 4, but the current approach in no way precludes delving into further details about the development of action constituents. On the contrary, this theoretical framework invites further consideration of the details of action, because it can be used to think systematically about any action constituents and it enables us to synthesize a range of findings into an overall understanding of what happens during development throughout the life span. As summarized in Box 8.1, we can use this integrative theoretical framework for thinking systematically about what

---

Box 8.1 **How to Use the Current Theoretical Framework to Think Systematically about What Happens during Development**

When you are trying to understand some research about development and/or when you are trying to understand someone's development,

THINK ABOUT

- How development for any action constituent(s) may be linked to the development of action in relation to others.
- The ways in which differentiation and integration are occurring.
- How development for one action constituent may be linked to development for other action constituents.
- The ways in which individual, social, and cultural processes are involved.

happens during development so that we do not get lost among the trees. That is, one can think about the implications of some findings about distinct action domains for the development of action in relation to others as a wider whole. One can think about the ways in which differentiation and integration occur, even if they are not the focus of a research report. One can think about how studies of development for one action constituent may be linked to findings about development for other constituents, even if such links are not discussed in the research reports themselves. One can think about how any details regarding what happens during development involve individual, social, and cultural processes as a person participates with others in cultural practices. The bottom line here is that there is a forest, or a Big Picture, within which to view any particular details and findings about development.

As discussed in Chapter 3, a major advantage of conceptualizing development in terms of differentiation and integration is that we have ways to think about developmental processes. There are several definitions of *process* in my trusty *Webster's New Collegiate Dictionary*, including:

- A series of actions or operations conducing to an end
- A continuous operation or treatment

According to the online *Free Dictionary*, definitions of process include:

- A series of actions, changes, or functions bringing about a result
- The condition of being carried on
- A systematic series of actions directed to some end

Defining development in terms of differentiation and integration is in keeping with these characterizations of a process as dynamic, ongoing, and systematic. In contrast, identifying what a person can do at Age 1 and then at Age 2 and then at Age 3 tells us about the relatively static products of a process that occurred, but it does not tell us about the systematic, dynamic, and ongoing series of functions or processes that occurred along the way.

Thinking about development in terms of differentiation and integration not only enables us to think about developmental processes; it enables us to disentangle development and age altogether. Insofar as increasing age or getting older does not guarantee development, it is useful to define development independently of age. Nevertheless, I readily recognize that it can be useful to know what people of this or that age, in this or that culture, typically do, or to know about what is considered normative for people of this or that age, in this or that culture. I myself want to know how old a person is when getting to know someone or when I hear about someone whom I do not know personally. I also included information about age ranges and life-phases in the discussion of what happens during the development of action in Chapters 4 and 5. However, it is important not to lose sight of the point that what people of a certain age do *develops*. A person's age can be viewed as a correlate of action that we can use to get a general sense of his or her ways of acting, but it does not offer much insight into the person's individual developmental experiences or the developmental processes that his or her ways of acting underwent and are undergoing. Moreover, some people develop ways of acting that are not normative in their cultures or at ages that are not normative in their cultures. For example, most people may not become leaders, yet leading can be viewed as action that develops, and leading can potentially develop at different ages. There may be a normative age for the development of reading, but people can learn to read at non-normative ages. Varied constituents and modes of action still undergo development regardless of whether or not they are tied to particular ages, and the criteria of differentiation and integration provide us with ways to think systematically about developmental processes independently of age.

Of course, human development (indeed all of human functioning) always occurs over time, making it necessary to think about development in relation to time. The point here is that time frames for thinking about development do not have to be age based. Accordingly, we can consider development as it occurs between Time 1, Time 2, Time 3, and so on, rather than between Age 1, Age 2, and Age 3. However, trading age for time does not release us from the difficult task of thinking about development over different time intervals. We can think about microdevelopment, which occurs in the short term within a particular context, perhaps over the course of a few minutes, hours, or days. We can also think about macrodevelopment, which refers to action that develops across contexts and occurs over longer periods of time, such as months and years. For example, the four stages of Piaget's theory (sensorimotor, pre-operational, concrete operational, and formal operational) represent macrodevelopmental changes that occur over years. However, as the analysis of object permanence in Chapter 3 indicates, Piaget himself paid painstaking attention to microdevelopmental changes. There will be more to say about microdevelopment and macrodevelopment as this chapter proceeds.

Thinking Systematically about Varied Kinds of Change

As pointed out in Chapter 3, organismic-developmental theory recognizes that people may undergo varied kinds of change, and thus differentiation and integration are not taken to be inevitable. Defining development in terms of differentiation and integration also does not mean that other types of change are not significant in a person's experience. More than not denying that other kinds of change occur, we can use the differentiation and integration constructs to identify and think systematically about different kinds of change. For example, regression in a person's functioning is a form of change that implies engaging in some previous and comparatively less developed form of action. In what way is it less developed? It is less developed not simply because it occurred previously, but insofar as it can be characterized by comparatively less differentiation and integration. Or one may say that a person's action is deteriorating, implying that the person's action is less developed, but there is not necessarily a return to previously occurring modes of action. Again, the person's deteriorated action can be understood in terms of the ways in which some action constituents have become less differentiated and integrated. Moreover, both regression and deterioration imply a negative change, or movement away from a developmental goal or normative standards of behavior.

By identifying different kinds of change in terms of consistent criteria, it becomes possible to discern how they are related to each other, including to developmental change. As noted in Chapter 3, systems theory and organismic-developmental theory posit that there can be (and often is) regression before development, as current modes of functioning are dismantled before more developed modes of functioning can be constructed. At one point, Werner even argues for the necessity of regression before development: "One has to regress in order to progress" (Werner, 1957, p. 139). Regression or any kind of deterioration in functioning sometimes serves a very useful purpose, such as when someone is "trying to construct new skills" by "breaking a problem down into its simplest units and starting again from the beginning" (Fischer, Yan, & Stewart, 2003, p. 508). Throughout the life span, engaging in less developed modes of functioning enables people to "perform flexibly and to devise ways of solving complex tasks that are initially beyond them" (Fischer et al., 2003, p. 508). As such, regression and deterioration are not necessarily problematic if they facilitate subsequent developmental change.

Some research shows further that the connections among regression, deterioration, and development are not simply a matter of engaging in a less developed form of action and then moving directly to engaging in a more developed form (Fischer & Bidell, 2006; Fischer et al., 2003; Yan & Fischer, 2002, 2007). Rather, people's action may fluctuate among more and less developed ways of acting before a more developed way of acting is stabilized (Fogel, 2006; Thelen & Smith, 1994/1996; van Geert & van Dijk, 2002). Using Wernerian terms, action can be characterized along the labile–stable dimension. Fluctuation or lability may provide a basis for development to occur because it enables a person to try out different constellations of action constituents or variations of an overall pattern of action (Užgiris, 1996). Also, part of what happens when action is reorganized is that less developed modes of action are integrated with the more developed modes that are emerging. Thus, fluctuation or lability is likely, because integrating the less developed modes with the more developed mode does not happen in one fell swoop. Sometimes a person may engage in a less developed mode of action on its own before being able to integrate it with a new mode of action that is emerging.

Thinking Systematically about Developmental Variability and Similarity

Defining development in terms of differentiation and integration in relation to cultural meanings, including expectations for development, also provides consistent criteria for thinking systematically about developmental variability and similarity. In this section, we first consider developmental variability and similarity between people, both within and across cultures. We then raise the issue of intraindividual developmental variability. The developmental variability that can characterize a single person's action is expanded in the next subsection, on the ways in which action is both generalizable and context specific.

Within cultural communities, there clearly can be similarities in action and development between people as they participate in some of the same cultural practices and develop in relation to some of the same cultural goals of development. At the same time, however, there can be developmental variability between individuals within a culture, and such variability can arise from varied sources. For example, as pointed out in Chapter 7, there can be developmental variability between individuals within an identified cultural community when they participate in some different cultural practices and in relation to some different developmental goals. In addition, individuals may experience different pathways of development toward some common cultural expectations. We can think systematically about varied manifestations of interindividual similarity and variability within a culture through the common language of differentiation and integration. That is, we can analyze the organization of action for particular individuals, and we can discern patterns of differentiation and integration for each individual. In doing so, we are thinking about each person's action and we are applying the same criteria to understanding each person's development—all of which permit comparisons between and among them while simultaneously preserving their individuality. Taken together, we have tools for discerning and thinking about both similarities and differences in people's developmental experiences.

In this way, our current approach to what happens during development provides an alternative to the conventional practice in psychology of generalizing from samples to populations. As van Geert (2011) points out, generalizing from samples to populations is but one way of defining generalization. He argues that "a truly general theory of developmental processes is one that can be 'individualized'—it can generate theory-based descriptions of individual trajectories in a nontrivial sense" (p. 276). Organismic-developmental theory is such a theory, because differentiation and integration are potentially highly generalizable to individuals. At the same time, accounting for individual developmental trajectories does not inevitably or necessarily lead to "irreducible incommensurability" (Salvatore & Valsiner, 2010, p. 829). On the contrary, thinking about development in terms of differentiation and integration provides a common language for considering similarities as well as differences across individuals. In addition, we can work to discern clusters or patterns of differentiation and integration that may be common among people. In doing so, we can think about the development of people as unique individuals while simultaneously identifying some common pathways of human development.

The current theoretical approach to what happens during development can also be used to think systematically about how there are potentially universal or similar aspects of development across cultures as well as cross-culturally variable pathways of development. In addition to being generalizable across individuals, defining development in terms of differentiation and integration is generalizable across cultures because differentiation and integration refer to processes that can potentially happen to any form of action, to any person, anywhere in the world, at any time, and even as cultures change. We can remain culturally sensitive because this theoretical approach starts with the premise that development occurs in relation to cultural meanings and conceptions of development. Then, we can proceed to using the constructs of differentiation and integration to think about the development of culturally particular forms of action. Taken together, our theoretical approach to what happens during development does not stipulate any specific modes of action that undergo development, but it can be applied to any cultural modes of action as people go about their lives in all corners of the world. This approach also does not stipulate any specific pathways of differentiation and integration, but it can be used to discern multiple pathways of development across cultures. Analyses from an organismic-developmental perspective would involve discerning cross-cultural similarities and differences in goals of development as well as identifying ways in which pathways of differentiation and integration are both similar and different around the world.

As mentioned in Chapter 3 and illustrated in Chapter 4, according to the genetic principle of spirality, there can also be intraindividual variability in action and development. That is, a person may act in more or less developed ways for varied reasons, such as stress or fatigue, or in relation to different people. By conceptualizing development in terms of differentiation and integration, we can think systematically about how a person's action involves coexisting patterns of differentiation and integration (Bibace, 2005). In addition, as just discussed with regard to regression and deterioration, intraindividual developmental variability also includes the fluctuation that occurs as a person is in the midst of developing new forms of action. Another form of intraindividual developmental variability may be apparent when a person acts differently across contexts, thus taking us to the very vexing issue of the ways in which action is generalizable across contexts as well as context specific.

Generalizing across Contexts and Context Specificity

Intraindividual developmental variability includes variability in a person's action across contexts, as pointed out theoretically in Chapter 3. This point was illustrated empirically in Chapter 4, with a discussion of the development of different modes of acting in relation to parents and peers during infancy and early childhood. According to organismic-developmental theory's principle of spirality and in accord with contemporary systems approaches to development, a person's action can be variable across contexts, and people may act in more or less developed ways across contexts. For example, a student might write a well-organized and insightful essay in one class, offering developed claims about the issue at hand. However, he or she might struggle to put together a few sentences for an essay in another class. It is not always straightforward for a person to generalize abilities across action circumstances, no matter how similar they may appear to be (especially to someone who already knows how to generalize). A goal of formal schooling is for students to be able to generalize abilities across subjects and ultimately to generalize from school activities to action in contexts beyond school, especially jobs. However, such generalization is not straightforward, and thus anyone's inability to generalize across contexts is not surprising. We cannot assume that generalizing across contexts occurs automatically, because when developing individuals

> encounter some change in the narrow context, their skill collapses and they regress back to a low level and then rebuild the skill again in this new context . . . they build and rebuild each skill again and again with each small change in task and context until they consolidate their performance to form a skill of some generality. (Fischer & Bidell, 2006, pp. 365–370)

Perhaps another way of putting it is to say that being able to generalize modes of action develops. To find out if being able to generalize develops, organismic-developmental theory leads to conducting research to discern if and in what ways differentiation and integration occur during the process of generalizing varied modes of action across contexts.

In developmental psychology, much research is directed toward identifying sequences of development for functioning that is generalizable across contexts or action circumstances. For example, Piaget's stages of cognitive development refer to generalizable cognitive schemes or structures that can be used in different specific situations. At the same time that there may be generalizable aspects of action, research from a systems perspective also focuses on the development of action within particular contexts. For example, Thelen argues that a child's performance on Piagetian assessments of cognition depends on the specifics of how the task is set up and on a child's immediate experience (Gershkoff-Stowe & Thelen, 2004; Thelen & Smith, 1994/1996, 2006).

The concepts of microdevelopment and macrodevelopment can be used as one way to reconcile and synthesize these different perspectives and thereby move beyond thinking dichotomously about generalization and context specificity. As pointed out earlier, microdevelopment and macrodevelopment refer, respectively, to development within contexts over relatively short periods of time and to development across contexts over longer periods of time. We can now add the point that microdevelopment and macrodevelopment occur in relation to each other. More specifically, insofar as all action takes place within some particular action context, people have to develop ways of acting that are appropriate to those particular contexts. Microdevelopment occurs in those particular contexts, and macrodevelopment involves abstracting or generalizing principles of action from those particular contexts.

In this way, macrodevelopment is derived from microdevelopment, because short-term and context-specific microdevelopmental changes consolidate in the formation of generalized macrodevelopmental changes over longer periods of time. As Fischer and Bidell (2006) explain, during microdevelopment

> people construct new skills for participation in specific contexts. . . . Macrodevelopment describes the larger-scale processes in which many local constructive activities in different contexts and domains are gradually consolidated, generalized, and related to form the big, slow changes of development over long periods. (p. 363)

Yet at the same time that macrodevelopment is derived from microdevelopment, macrodevelopment informs further microdevelopment, because the generalized action of macrodevelopment provides an overall organization or basis for a person to act in particular contexts. As a person acts in particular contexts, microdevelopment may occur, which in turn provides a basis for further macrodevelopment to occur, which then can lead to further microdevelopment. This process continues, making for ongoing interrelations between microdevelopment and macrodevelopment, as well as between context-specific and generalizable aspects of action. Once again, differentiation and integration can be used for thinking systematically about what happens during development, and in this case during both microdevelopment and macrodevelopment.

In the interplay between microdevelopment and macrodevelopment, the generalized ways of acting that develop can also be understood as "the context-general, organizational characterization of the organism" (Witherington, 2011, p. 86), or a person's relatively stable and generalized ways of structuring action across contexts. Yet at the same time, the particulars of how those modes of action are instantiated may be different within specific contexts and practices. We may recall the systems theory premise of soft assembly, whereby functioning in any context emerges on the spot and thus is never exactly the same in all of its details. In other words, you cannot step into the same river twice. Thus, there can be stable overall organization to a person's action, as well as variability in the specifics of how his or her action is assembled across contexts. The overall organization, or macrodevelopmental structuring, of a person's action can further be understood as the typical or stable ways in which a person acts in his or her "characteristic multitude of contexts" (van Geert & Fischer, 2009, p. 327). However, in any "specific temporary context" (p. 328), a person's action can be organized differently, especially if a temporary context is not typical for someone. In keeping with this claim, Werner (1957) points out that "adaptive behavior" requires both "stability" and "pliability," or "a paradoxical 'stable flexibility'" (p. 140). Thelen and Smith (1994/1996) refer to the "global regularities" and "local variability" of action (p. xviii), and Fogel (2006) points out that action is characterized by "dynamic stability" (p. 9).

For example, people in varied life-phases may cooperate with others in their characteristic multitude of contexts. Although cooperating may be a mode of action that occurs in many contexts, it may be organized differently across specific action contexts or across different cultural practices. Thus, even as a particular person develops some typical or generalized ways of cooperating with others, the specific structuring of how that person cooperates in a particular situation can vary in relation to the particular subject of cooperation and the particular other people in the situation. As such, the development of cooperating with others can be characterized by dynamic stability or stable flexibility when a person generally strives to cooperate with others yet also cooperates in context-specific ways. Thinking about action and development in terms of dynamic stability or stable flexibility may also inform considerations of personality, a messy and intractable construct if ever there was one in psychology. That is, personality can be used to refer to generalizable aspects of a person's action, with the recognition that action can be assembled in varied specific ways within particular contexts. Personality represents the macrodevelopment of a person's overall functioning that can be played out in different specific ways in specific contexts. As such, personality is neither totally fixed, nor totally nonexistent.

Figure 8.1 offers a schematic of the ongoing interplay between macrodevelopment and microdevelopment. It begins with the overall organization of a person's action, which encompasses generalizable ways of acting and his or her typical ways of acting—say at home, or at work, or in the neighborhood. This overall macrodevelopmental organization of action provides a basis for acting in varied specific contexts where microdevelopment can occur. Some of those specific contexts may be new or somewhat unfamiliar, such as when work involves starting a new job. As microdevelopment occurs through participating in those specific contexts, a person can then undergo macrodevelopment by consolidating and generalizing context-specific ways of acting. The new overall macrodevelopmental organization of a person's action then provides a basis for

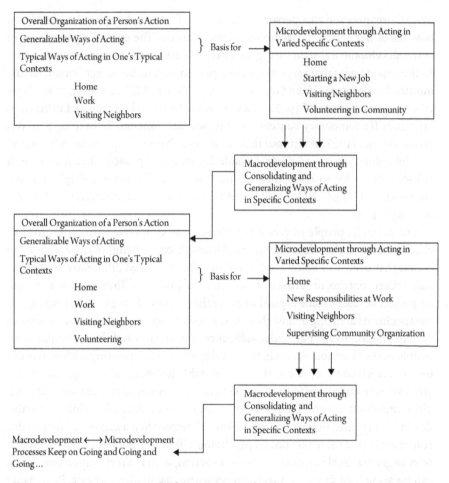

Figure 8.1 The ongoing interplay between macrodevelopment and microdevelopment.

acting in specific contexts where microdevelopment can occur. This interplay between macrodevelopment and microdevelopment can continue, potentially indefinitely.

To further muddy these already murky waters, it is also important to point out that generalizing across contexts is not always considered desirable. For example, in her detailed observations of her grandson's early development, Shatz (1994) describes the following scene:

> One day as we were leaving a restaurant, he stopped at each booth on the way out, smiled, waved, and said, "Bye-bye." Although greeting the other patrons may be conventional practice in some parts of the world, it is not in the United States. Ricky could not have observed such behavior by others in restaurants, yet it must have seemed to him to be an appropriate

extension of leave-taking behavior within the family. Needless to say, there was considerable mirth in the restaurant by the time he reached the door. (p. 36)

In this case, Ricky has to learn when NOT to generalize certain ways of acting by differentiating among action circumstances. In Chapter 5, this point was illustrated with research on the Japanese distinction between inner/private and outer/public contexts. The issue is further complicated because it is not always a matter of simply distinguishing or differentiating between formal and informal contexts or public and private contexts. In Chapter 5, we also saw that in Japan, people integrate inner/private and outer/public modes of action in the same context. Taken together, it is not simply a matter of either generalizing across contexts or not generalizing across contexts. As Rogoff points out, it is a matter of "appropriate generalization" across contexts (2003, p. 253), and thus the ways in which action is both generalizable and context specific are inextricably linked to cultural meanings insofar as what counts as appropriate generalization is partly culturally stipulated.

Cultural processes are further implicated when generalizing modes of action across contexts, because cultural meanings are part of what constitute modes of action. Thus, cultural meanings are part of what is generalized across contexts. From a Piagetian perspective, Užgiris posits that schemes for acting in terms of values and standards, or the "manner of carrying out actions" (Užgiris, 1996, p. 28), are part of development even during infancy, because infants are interacting with others whose action reflects cultural values and standards. As we saw in Chapter 4, young children increasingly regulate their own action in relation to cultural values and standards, including when their caregivers are not immediately present. As a person encounters varied situations throughout the life span, he or she may not always generalize the particulars of action from one situation to another. However, that person might approach varied situations by generalizing values and standards, such as being considerate of others, working hard, deferring to authority, or taking initiative.

Continuity and Discontinuity

Much ink and toner have been used up in discussions about the extent to which development is continuous or discontinuous. However, continuity and discontinuity do not have to be treated dichotomously, and the orthogenetic principle provides ways of thinking about how both continuity and discontinuity characterize development (Werner, 1957). Throughout this book, the continuity of development has been encapsulated by pointing out that nothing comes from nothing. At the same time, our current conceptualization acknowledges discontinuity in development by positing that development involves the emergence of new forms of action that build on, but cannot be reduced to, earlier forms. Development-as-differentiation-and-integration involves continuity insofar as a person's current modes of action provide a basis for differentiation and integration to occur. Thus, differentiation and integration build on what is already there. Development is also discontinuous, because differentiation and integration lead to new forms of action. In Chapter 4, the periods of action development were described in terms of both continuity and discontinuity, as each period provided a continuous basis from which differentiation and integration occurred, which also enabled new modes of action to emerge. In addition, in Chapter 3 we considered Werner's claim that earlier modes of functioning do not necessarily disappear when new modes of functioning develop. Rather, there is continuity insofar as earlier ways of acting are integrated with the new ways of acting. At the same time, there is discontinuity in this process, because the earlier ways of acting take on different functions within the new whole.

Whether one discerns continuity or discontinuity or both during development depends partly on the time frame during which one is analyzing development, because development may appear more continuous over shorter periods of time than over longer periods of time. For example, when you see the same people every day or every week, their looks seem to change gradually, and you see continuity in their looks from one day and week to the next, one month to the next, and one year to the next. But perhaps you do not recognize a fifth-grade classmate from 40 years ago. The person's appearance seems utterly discontinuous, and a different person seems to have replaced the one you remember. Again, we find ourselves confronting issues of microdevelopment and macrodevelopment. It is during the shorter time spans of microdevelopment that we can discern the ongoing or continuous processes of differentiation and integration as they are occurring. Over longer time periods we can discern macrodevelopment, or the discontinuous emergence of new modes of action that are characterized by more differentiation and integration.

Perhaps in part because there is continuity in development, and because it is conventional practice in psychology more generally, many developmentalists try to predict development. However, the discontinuity of development suggests that what happens during development cannot be easily predicted. Trying to predict future action and development represents one way of doing psychology, but as pointed out in Chapter 3, it is not the only way. Within developmental psychology, trying to predict behavior includes trying to predict developmental outcomes based on knowledge of earlier behavior and/or experience. These efforts have yielded mixed results. For example, for years, and with "almost Messianic fervor about the capability of infant–caregiver attachment security to account for a wide range of psychosocial outcomes" (Levitt, 2005, p. 31), a major focus of attachment research was directed toward discerning the links between early attachment patterns and later functioning (Thompson, 1999). This research failed to reveal consistent links, and one overall conclusion is that "sometimes attachment in infancy predicts later psychosocial functioning, and sometimes it does not" (Thompson, 1999, p. 274). This conclusion makes sense from a systems perspective, which posits that development can sometimes be highly unpredictable because development depends on interrelations among multiple processes that can be played out in varied ways. For example, we do not know at birth exactly what conditions a person will experience, with whom the person will interact, and in which cultural practices he or she will participate. Therefore, Gottlieb characterizes development as a process of probabilistic epigenesis, whereby individual development cannot be predicted exactly, given the varied possible ways in which system processes may be played out and interrelated (Gottlieb, 1991, 2007; Gottlieb, Wahlsten, & Lickliter, 1998). Along similar lines, Lewis (1997) argues that people generally "realize that life is dangerous and capricious. A potentially huge number of people and events can intervene in our lives" (p. 4), making it problematic to expect straightforward predictability from some earlier experience to later ways of acting. Moreover, it is not simply the number of people and events that are at issue but the ways in which interacting with others and participating in events are structured that may or may not promote development.

At the same time, however, a lack of predictability does not mean that development is arbitrary, random, or unsystematic. Development is at once "spontaneous although constrained" (van Geert, 2011, p. 274), "indeterminate as well as principled" (Lewis, 2000, p. 38). Insofar as development occurs in relation to cultural meanings, one may be able to anticipate the broad contours of developmental achievements while simultaneously leaving room for the vicissitudes of varied individual developmental pathways. For example, in a Western middle-class setting, one can posit that a person's development may lead to pursuing a profession, without being able to predict the person's specific professional achievements. In addition, development is not arbitrary, because a person's current and individual ways of acting provide a basis for further development, and thus some developmental pathways may be more or less likely than others. Accordingly, Valsiner (1997) conceptualizes development as a process of bounded indeterminism, whereby development is "oriented toward (in contrast to determined by) a future state [but] . . . the actual courses of individual development are unique, and mostly unpredictable, except for their general direction" (p. 146).

Moreover, Werner states explicitly that the orthogenetic principle, "being a formal regulative principle, is not designed to predict developmental courses in their specificity" (1957, p. 130). The continuity of development may make some future modes of action more likely than others, but the discontinuity of development makes it impossible to know for sure. We can also predict that around the world, most people will develop with regard to varied domains of functioning—from walking to talking, to feeling, to thinking, to interacting with others, to constructing values, to self-construction. We can also generally predict that people will develop culturally particular ways of acting. But predicting the specifics of a person's ways of acting in varied contexts and the particular sequences of differentiation and integration that the person will go through are not so straightforward, because action and development are always emerging through dynamic individual, social, and cultural processes.

Although we may not be able to predict development, the current conceptualization does not deny continuity between earlier and later functioning because later modes of action necessarily build on earlier ones. The point here is that earlier experiences can influence later ones without determining them unilaterally or linearly. To the extent that earlier modes of functioning are part of what shapes development, we can discern continuity between earlier and later experiences by thinking about how earlier ways of acting provide a basis from which differentiation and integration can proceed. One can also look back from the vantage point of a person's current modes of action to discern the differentiation and integration that occurred. In addition, understanding systems functioning and understanding what happens during development can help us to imagine possible futures. And such understanding, along with understanding of how development happens, provides conceptual tools for working to actualize those imagined possibilities.

Implications for Conducting Research on What Happens during Development

Conceptualizing development in terms of differentiation and integration has varied implications for conducting research about what happens during the development of action. By starting from the position that development involves differentiation and integration in relation to cultural expectations for development, our empirical attention is focused on developmental processes as they occur. Thus, a goal for Chapter 4 was to posit the ongoing differentiation and integration that occur within and across action constituents during infancy and early childhood. Similarly, for Chapter 5, a goal was to draw attention to the processes of differentiation and integration as they may occur around the world and throughout the life span. In both chapters I drew on a wide range of research, but none of that research is specifically based on organismic-developmental theory, thus leaving much room for conducting research that is specifically designed to discern differentiation and integration as they occur.

It is very difficult to capture the processes of differentiation and integration as they occur, because a process is, by definition, ongoing and does not stop in time. Any attempt to capture a process runs the risk of stopping it in its tracks, thereby rendering it static and depriving it of what makes it a process. Developmentalists are thus faced with the problem of trying to analyze an elusive phenomenon because development occurs "in the fuzzy 'zone' in which A no longer is clearly observable and B is not yet equally clearly observable" (Valsiner, 2011, p. 213). In addition, any particular analysis of differentiation and integration for some mode of action is likely to be incomplete, because it is impossible for any researcher to analyze all possible action constituents and subconstituents simultaneously. However, researchers make choices about how to conduct research all the time, and the current theoretical approach to what happens during development provides a theoretical basis for making such choices.

Rather than starting with a particular method, research design best begins by conceptualizing a particular research issue or question. The choice of method then depends on how the research issue is conceptualized. The general research issue or question we are addressing now is: What happens during the development of action? Within our current theoretical framework, addressing this issue begins by conceptualizing action in terms of interrelations among multiple action constituents. In addition, this issue is conceptualized in terms of differentiation and integration within and across action constituents in relation to cultural expectations for development. From this theoretical perspective, research on what happens during the development of action involves tracking pathways of differentiation and integration for constituents and modes of action for individuals over time. This conceptualization of action and of what happens during development leads to research that builds on and also departs somewhat from conventional practices in psychology and developmental psychology. In particular, this approach builds on cross-sectional and longitudinal analyses of development, and it departs from psychology's overall emphasis on group-level analyses.

In many developmental studies, individuals are typically grouped by age, and analyses involve discerning differences in the behavior of different age groups. Research in developmental psychology is also replete with other groups. For example, studies may be designed to discern if there are different developmental outcomes for groups defined in terms of different characteristics, from attachment classification, to personality traits, to socioeconomic status. This research has yielded a wealth of information (some of which I have drawn on throughout this book) about new modes of functioning that emerge over time and how different age-based modes of functioning are linked to varied characteristics. However, these methods do not readily permit analyses and descriptions of ongoing developmental processes (Adolph & Robinson, 2008). I believe the time is ripe to build on this work, with studies of the ongoing differentiation and integration that occur as new forms of behavior emerge and that occur in between the time of the initial classification and later outcome.

In addition, a useful direction for future research will be to pay more attention to the individuals whose action is developing. When people's data are aggregated within a group, each individual basically becomes an interchangeable, random cog in a sample, and analyses do not typically illuminate any particular person's action or development (Billig, 2013; Boker, Molenaar, & Nesselroade, 2009;

Danziger, 1990/1998; Lamiell, 2003; Molenaar, 2008; Molenaar & Valsiner, 2008; Nesselroade & Molenaar, 2010; Salvatore & Valsiner, 2010; van Geert, 2011; van Geert & Steenbeek, 2005). Sometimes individuals within an identified group may not behave in accord with the group's average behavior. In addition, I start from the premise that when it comes to action and the development of action, individuals are neither interchangeable nor exchangeable, because a person's ways of acting are part of what makes that person unique. At the same time, let us recall that uniqueness is not equivalent to "irreducible incommensurability" (Salvatore & Valsiner, 2010, p. 829), and it is precisely by studying the development of individuals that we can discern common and individual pathways of development.

Analyses of individuals can also illuminate aspects of the variability that characterizes action and development. That is, if individual data are kept intact, it is possible to discern developmental differences between individuals, both within and between groups. Moreover, analyses of individuals permit us to discern fluctuations between more and less developed modes of individual action, as well as to discern intraindividual developmental variability across contexts. Finally, by analyzing individuals (or individual data), there is a way to discern if a theory is general enough to be individualized.

Taken together, the current theoretical approach to what happens during development leads to studying individuals as they act in relation to others in cultural practices over time (Fogel, 2006; Molenaar, 2004; Molenaar & Campbell, 2009; Nesselroade & Molenaar, 2010; van Geert, 1998). Analyses would be directed toward discerning if a person moves toward cultural goals for the development of action, as well as if and in what ways differentiation and integration occur during the course of such progress. In some cases, it might be possible to predict some sequences of differentiation and integration, but that depends partly on the particular modes and/or constituents of action. The theoretical approach presented here further leads to positing spirality in functioning, meaning that periods of developmental change will be interspersed with periods of nondevelopmental change.

To conduct research on what happens during development, a researcher must make decisions about what modes and/or constituents of action to study, the time frame for a particular longitudinal study, and the time intervals for the study. Once initial decisions about topic and time have been made, observations of people acting can be conducted. This research can be conducted in naturalistic settings, and it may also involve standardized tasks specifically designed to identify whether and in what ways differentiation and integration occur for some mode or constituent of action. For example, participants could be asked to tell a story about a particular issue in order to investigate the development of storytelling. Or, to analyze the development of cognitive action constituents, participants could be asked to figure out how to solve a particular cognitive problem.

Whether research is naturalistic or standardized or both, our current theoretical framework leads to observing and analyzing development as it occurs. Toward that end, researchers can draw on a rich history in developmental psychology of using systematic observational and interpretive methods, from Piaget's detailed observations of his own three children to contemporary studies of cultural activities around the world (many of which have been cited and discussed throughout this book).

Any modes and constituents of action, within any cultural practices, at any time during the life span could certainly be fruitfully investigated on the basis of our current theoretical approach to action and development. I personally would be excited to see studies of differentiation and integration for any of the modes and constituents of action discussed in this book (perhaps most especially those considered in Chapters 4 and 5). In the following discussion I will focus on observational research. I will first present the basic steps involved in this kind of empirical endeavor; the steps are outlined in Box 8.2. These steps will then be illustrated more concretely by using the development of sibling caregiving as an example.

First, based on the premise that development occurs in relation to cultural meanings, conducting research begins with identifying some cultural expectations or goals for action. For some modes of action, it might be relatively straightforward to identify developmental goals, but sometimes specific expectations or goals are difficult to articulate. It may also be difficult to articulate goals of development in cultures that are undergoing significant cultural change. Nevertheless, as discussed in Chapter 3, a researcher has to use some criteria for what counts as a developed mode of action in order to identify some constituents of action for which differentiation and integration can be analyzed. Cultural

---

Box 8.2 **Outline of Steps for Conducting Research on What Happens during the Development of Action**

1. Identify some cultural expectations for acting in relation to others.
2. a. Define modes of action in terms of particular constituents.
   b. Create coding categories that correspond to those constituents.
3. Code the data and establish inter-rater reliability.
4. a. Analyze individuals' data to identify points of differentiation and integration.
   b. Analyze individuals' data to discern periods of spirality in functioning.
5. Analyze data across individuals to discern if there are multiple sequences of differentiation and integration.

expectations for development can be identified in varied ways depending in part on the cultural practice, the mode of action, and the constituents of action under scrutiny, including interviewing cultural informants, observing people who are considered to be adept cultural participants or actors, as well as reviewing historical records and written accounts of cultural practices. Depending on the mode of action and the people to be studied, one could also identify some individual developmental goals.

Second, using information about cultural expectations for development as well as continued input from cultural informants, the researcher can move on to defining modes of action in terms of particular constituents. This step also involves the usually arduous work of creating and defining coding categories that correspond to those constituents.

The third step is to code the data (live or from video) by recording sequentially what the developing person does in terms of the codes. A coding sheet can be used to record instances of each code as they occur sequentially. In addition, inter-rater reliability for the coding scheme needs to be established.

Fourth, for each participant, the researcher would analyze development by identifying points on the sequential record when differentiation and/or integration occur. Such analyses would include discerning more specific aspects or forms of differentiation and integration for the particular modes or constituents of action under scrutiny. Individual sequential records can also be analyzed to discern if periods of spirality in functioning occurred.

Finally, the fifth step is to analyze the data across individuals in order to discern if there are multiple patterns for sequences of differentiation and integration.

To illustrate how to utilize this general research design more concretely, let us consider a hypothetical example of research on the development of sibling caregiving. Using the general research design just presented, we first identify some cultural expectations for caregiving within a particular cultural context. Varied specific methods could be used, including interviewing adults to find out what they value and expect in a sibling caregiver, and observing some sibling caregivers who are considered by their elders to be highly competent caregivers. Identifying developmental goals for sibling caregivers would enable a researcher to proceed to the second step of identifying some modes of action that comprise sibling caregiving to focus on. For example, interviews with adults may indicate that sibling caregivers are expected to calm a distressed child quickly and flexibly by using varied means depending on why the child is distressed; to keep a child from bothering adults who are working by keeping him or her occupied; and to teach a child to do some household chores. For the purposes of this example, I will focus on calming a distressed child. The upcoming example is purely hypothetical and is meant only to illustrate a way in which research from the current perspective can be conducted.

The next task is to create and define systematic coding categories that correspond to varied constituents of calming a distressed child. There are certainly many ways to calm a distressed child, and specific coding categories can be derived from the interviews, from discussions with cultural informants, as well as from watching a sampling of caregiving situations. A few possible ways of or means for calming a distressed child might include the following: bouncing, singing, verbal soothing ("It's ok, don't cry."), asking a general question ("What's wrong?"), asking a specific question ("Are you hungry? Are you tired?"), and giving general commands ("Stop! Be quiet!"). In this case, what counts as child distress in a particular cultural context also has to be defined more specifically. For example, an episode of child distress may be defined as beginning when a child fusses (e.g., whimpers, squirms) or cries. An episode of child distress may be defined as ending when the child stops fussing or crying, when someone intervenes, or when the sibling caregiver leaves the scene but does not seek help.

The third step would be to code the data for each observation session. Every episode of child distress would be coded on a coding sheet that enables the researcher to keep sequential track of the means that a sibling caregiver uses to calm a distressed child. On the coding sheet, the researcher would indicate the date of observation and provide information about who the sibling caregiver and child charge are. Then, each episode of calming a distressed child would be coded in terms of the coding categories created in step two. In addition, it would be useful to include information about the time and ostensible reason for the onset and ending of each distress episode, as well as the time that the sibling caregiver began trying to calm the distressed child. Such coding would provide a systematic and sequential record of what the sibling caregiver did to calm the distressed child. Once coding is complete and inter-rater reliability is established, data analysis can proceed as outlined in steps four and five.

The data can be analyzed to discern if and when differentiation and integration occurred. Let us consider a hypothetical example. For the first two observation days, a sibling caregiver uses one global means to calm her charge, namely bouncing the child on her lap. On the third day, the sibling caregiver continues with this means, and some differentiation of means begins to occur as she sings to the child during three distress episodes. On the fourth day, five distress episodes are observed, and the sibling caregiver sings to the child during the first three distress episodes. During the fourth distress episode of this fourth observation day, some beginning or intermediate integration is evident as the sibling caregiver sequentially combines singing and bouncing the child during a single distress episode. Subsequently, the sibling caregiver goes back to bouncing only. On the fifth observation day, the sibling caregiver bounces only for two distress episodes and then differentiates verbal soothing as another way of trying to calm her charge. During the final distress episode of day 5, she begins integrating bouncing and verbal soothing by using them sequentially in one distress episode. On the sixth day, the sibling caregiver first sings only, and then proceeds to fully integrate bouncing and singing by bouncing and singing at the same time, and then integrates bouncing and verbal soothing by bouncing and soothing verbally at the same time.

With such data, we can identify an overall sequence of developmental changes that occurred. This sibling caregiver's development occurred in the following sequence: global use of one means; differentiation of second means; sequential use of first and second means; differentiation of third means; sequential use of first and third means; and integration of first and second means and integration of first and third means. These ways of coding and analyzing other individual sibling caregivers' data would permit discerning if there are other sequences of differentiation and integration. Such analyses would then permit identifying patterns or clusters of developmental sequences. For example, the same overall sequence may be followed, even if another sibling caregiver uses some different means (e.g., patting and asking a general question). It would also be possible to determine if a different sequence is followed, using the same or different means.

Once coded, it is possible to plot the sequence of a developing person's action in a way that permits analysis of spirality, or forward and backward movement. For example, in this hypothetical scenario, forward movement in the form of differentiation occurred on day 3, when the sibling caregiver used singing for the first time, after two days of bouncing only. On the fourth observation day, the sibling caregiver progressed from singing only to a kind of intermediate integration by combining singing and bouncing sequentially. This progress was immediately followed by backward movement when she went back to bouncing only. On day 5, forward movement occurred when verbal soothing was differentiated as a new means for calming the distressed child, followed by further forward movement when the sibling caregiver combined bouncing and verbal soothing sequentially. From day 5 to day 6, backward movement occurred as the sibling caregiver used singing only, followed immediately by progressing to or moving forward to integrating bouncing and singing, and then integrating bouncing and verbal soothing.

In addition to being hypothetical and idealized, this example is relatively simple with regard to what happens during the development of calming a distressed child. The entire analysis could be more involved in many ways. For example, studies could include more means to code and analyze. Moreover, a more nuanced coding scheme would permit analyses of differentiation and integration within each means. For example, one could code bouncing in ways that enable one to discern if the sibling caregiver differentiates between bouncing while sitting down and standing up, as well as between bouncing gently and bouncing vigorously. One could also analyze singing in ways that permit analyzing differentiation and integration for perspective taking by, for example, coding if the sibling caregiver initially sings a song that she likes and then comes to sing a song that she knows the child prefers. It would also be interesting to analyze if spirality in functioning occurs when the sibling caregiver is tired, or if there is conflict between taking care of a sibling and attending to another task. Such analyses could also shed light on connections among different kinds of change, such as regression, deterioration, and development. As pointed out in Chapter 5, sibling caregiving involves varied constituents of action, including emotion regulation and identity construction. Research on the development of caregiving identities could involve interviewing caregivers and/or asking them to tell narratives about their caregiving experiences. These identity constructions could then be analyzed in terms of the differentiation and integration of identity constituents along the lines outlined here. Insofar as sibling caregiving occurs in varied cultural communities, cross-cultural research could illuminate cultural similarities and differences in the development of sibling caregiving. For example, the research design just presented would permit analyzing cultural similarities and differences in the means that sibling caregivers use to calm a distressed child, as well as cultural similarities and differences in sequences of development. Analyses could also be directed toward discerning the ways in which caregivers generalize some aspects of caregiving across situations, and also construct or assemble caregiving on the spot in particular situations. For example, now that our hypothetical sibling caregiver can integrate bouncing and singing as well as bouncing and verbal soothing, what does she do when she has to take care of an additional child? Does she generalize her integrative skills, or does she go back to using one global means to calm the second child? Clearly, the process of what happens during the development of sibling caregiving is complex, and analyses of this process could be conducted in different ways depending on a researcher's focus. Sibling caregiving also involves other developing modes of action besides calming a distressed child that could be studied as well. Nevertheless, the basic research design outlined here provides a systematic and consistent basis for conducting research on varied aspects of what happens during development, and not only during the development of sibling caregiving.

Although sibling caregiving is typically associated with traditional and non-Western cultures, it occurs in industrialized and Western settings in the form of babysitting for younger siblings, as well as for younger children who are not necessarily related in any way. Research could also be conducted on the development of babysitting along the lines outlined earlier. Taking care of others is an interesting cultural practice to study, because it occurs throughout the world and throughout the life span as people care for varied others, such as their own children, a sick spouse, a friend, an adult sibling, or aging parents. Some people may volunteer in different kinds of caregiving settings. Doctors, nurses, and a wide range of health-care professionals take care of others. Whatever the specific circumstances may be, caregiving practices can be characterized in terms of varied modes of action that are structured in culturally particular ways. Analyses could be directed toward discerning similarities and differences in the structuring or organization of caregiving across cultures. Moreover, taking care of others involves modes of action that develop, and thus what happens during the development of anyone's ways of caregiving can be analyzed in terms of differentiation and integration within and across action constituents, as well as in terms of movement along the continuous dimensions.

Also with regard to future research on what happens during development, varied issues from Chapters 4 and 5 remain open for further investigation and can be studied using the basic research design just presented. The research used in Chapter 4 to posit a sequence of development for action in relation to others during infancy and early childhood is not specifically based on the current theoretical approach to action and development, and thus the posited sequence is open to research for empirical confirmation and elaboration. In Chapter 4, I posited a relatively macrodevelopmental sequence for the early development of action, and I assume that it is representative of typical development for middle-class American infants and young children in general. However, as pointed out earlier in this chapter, development is an ongoing and cumulative process that requires microdevelopmental as well as macrodevelopmental analysis. Thus, one could conduct at least weekly observations of parent–child interactions over the course of the first years of life to discern some of the ongoing microdevelopmental dynamics of differentiation and integration as well as movement along the continuous dimensions. In addition, the development of action for any particular child is played out in particular ways, making it important to also analyze individual pathways of differentiation and integration for the early development of action. One could then go on to analyze intraindividual and interindividual developmental variability, as well as identify common patterns of differentiation and integration. The research used for Chapter 5 is also not specifically based on the current approach to action and development, and there is much room for studying the development of action around the world.

How Does Development Happen?

The current theoretical approach to how development happens provides ways to think systematically about the myriad of possible causes of development that have been identified and investigated over the years (Box 8.3). It enables us to think about how they involve individual, social, and cultural processes, and how they may be particularized as a person participates with others in cultural practices. In addition, we are led to thinking about how such participation with others in cultural practices is linked to development-as-differentiation-and-integration. In this section, I discuss some implications of this theoretical approach for thinking about some issues that inform many contemporary discussions of how development happens, namely patterns of childrearing and socialization. I further

---

Box 8.3 **How to Use the Current Theoretical Framework to Think Systematically about How Development Happens**

When you are trying to understand some research about the causes of development and/or you are trying to understand how someone developed or is developing,

THINK ABOUT

- How an identified cause of development involves individual, social, and/or cultural processes.
- What cultural practice the person is participating in.
- Some cultural expectations for development.
- With whom the person is engaged.
- What the person is doing to promote differentiation and integration.
- What the other(s) is doing to promote differentiation and integration.

---

consider some implications of this theoretical approach for addressing the vexing issue of how qualitatively different modes of action sometimes seem to mysteriously develop out of nothing. This section ends with a discussion of future directions for research about how development happens.

Patterns of Childrearing and Socialization

In Chapters 6 and 7, some readers may have missed a discussion of issues that developmentalists typically pay much attention to in research on how development happens, such as discipline and patterns or styles of childrearing. Much research on these issues has been and continues to be conducted on the patterns of childrearing originally identified by Diana Baumrind in the late 1960s (Baumrind, 1967, 1989). Based on interviewing parents and observing parent–child interactions, Baumrind identified four patterns of childrearing, whereby parents are rated as high or low on the dimensions of demandingness and responsiveness. According to Baumrind (1996), "responsiveness refers to the extent to which parents intentionally foster individuality and self-assertion by being attuned, supportive, and acquiescent to children's needs and demands" (p. 410). Responsiveness further "includes warmth, autonomy support, and reasoned communication" (Baumrind, 2005, pp. 61–62). Demandingness "includes direct confrontations, monitoring, and consistent, contingent discipline. Demandingness refers to the claims that parents make on children to become integrated into the family and community by their maturity expectations, supervision, disciplinary efforts, and willingness to confront a disputative child" (1996, p. 411). The authoritative pattern is characterized by high responsiveness and high demandingness; the authoritarian pattern is characterized by low responsiveness and high demandingness; the permissive pattern is characterized by high responsiveness and low demandingness; the uninvolved pattern is characterized by low responsiveness and low demandingness.

These patterns provide cultural descriptions of how parents act in relation to children (Chao, 1994) as well as descriptions of children's participation with others in cultural practices. For example, within the authoritative pattern, which is most common among middle-class European-Americans, parents typically interact with children by being

> receptive to the child's views but take responsibility for firmly guiding the child's actions, emphasizing reasoning, communication, and rational discussion in interactions that are friendly as well as tutorial and disciplinary. The balanced perspective of authoritative parents is neither exclusively child-centered nor exclusively parent-centered but, instead, seeks to integrate the needs of the child with other family members, treating the rights and responsibilities of children and those of parents as complementary rather than as identical. (Baumrind, 1996, p. 412)

This description of parent–child interaction suggests that within authoritatively structured interactions, children have opportunities to voice their perspectives, reason through issues, and discuss issues. In doing so, there is much opportunity for differentiation and integration within and across action constituents. For example, a child can differentiate his or her perspective by explaining it, and the child also has opportunities to differentiate his or her perspective from and integrate it with others' perspectives. By reasoning through and discussing issues, there are opportunities for differentiation and integration within and across cognitive and linguistic action constituents.

Within this context, it is not surprising that the children of parents who are classified as authoritative generally control themselves, interact sociably with peers, explore, and assert themselves (Baumrind, 1967). The point here is that children develop these ways of acting in relation to others because they practice doing so and because they are guided in doing so. Accordingly, if one is concerned with how parents affect children's development, it is necessary to discern what the parents *do* that can promote children's differentiation and integration, as they engage with children in culturally particular ways.

Parents and others may interact with children in varied ways, and many others may engage with developing people in varied ways throughout the life span. In developmental psychology, the wider construct of "socialization" is often used to understand and investigate how interacting with others promotes development. According to Maccoby, socialization "refers to processes whereby naïve individuals are taught the skills, behavior patterns, values, and motivations needed for competent functioning in the culture in which [they are] growing up" (2007, p. 13). Although socialization research focuses on child development, people may be taught to function in culturally particular ways at any time during the life span. A great deal of socialization research is devoted to investigating whether and how varied aspects of social interaction facilitate culturally competent functioning.

As I have argued elsewhere, in some treatments of socialization, it is not always clear why and how varied ways of interacting with others enable naïve individuals to become competent cultural participants (Raeff, 2014). Thus, we can ask: What happens during socialization? Socialization research implies that the development of culturally competent behavior happens during socialization and, therefore, to be socialized means to develop cultural ways of behaving. A clear conceptualization of what happens during development would permit discerning if different forms of socialization (i.e., different ways of interacting with and teaching cultural novices) are more or less effective in promoting the development of culturally competent functioning. The theoretical framework offered here provides a systematic theoretical basis for linking how development-as-differentiation-and-integration happens through social interaction. Conceptualizing development in terms of differentiation and integration leads to positing that socialization "works" insofar as interactions with others enable a person's action to undergo differentiation and integration. Some of the ways in which interacting with others can promote differentiation and integration were discussed in Chapter 7.

In addition, socialization occurs in relation to cultural processes because developing individuals are being guided to engage in culturally particular modes of competent functioning. Moreover, as socialization researchers acknowledge, individuals contribute to their own socialization by actively construing experience and by shaping the patterning of interactions with others. This book's conceptualization of development leads to thinking systematically about how development-as-differentiation-and-integration occurs during socialization and about how socialization ultimately involves developing through interrelated individual, social, and cultural processes.

The Mystery of Development

Although conceptualizing how development happens in terms of individual, social, and cultural processes is incredibly useful for thinking systematically about how development happens, I am plagued by a nagging sense of mystery. How can something qualitatively different arise or emerge if it was not there to begin with or if the instructions for it were not there before? How can more complex action emerge from simpler action? It sometimes appears as if something actually does come from nothing. However, appearances can be deceptive.

One way of making progress toward answering these questions lies in starting from the premise that a person's action can be understood as a system that always includes individual, social, and cultural processes. When a person participates in cultural practices with others who guide him or her in some way, those others are doing some of the action that makes up the practice. Thus, the developing person is experiencing, or participating in, a more developed form of the action, even if that person cannot yet engage in that form of acting on his or her own. In other words, the to-be-developed form of action is indeed there, as it were. It is part of the person's *systemic functioning*, and thus can be experienced and constructed by the developing person (Užgiris, 1989, 1996). In addition, as pointed out in Chapter 7, a person may envision or articulate a goal of development and work (alone and/or with others) to achieve that goal. Insofar as a person can construct how he or she wants to act, the action goal is "there" in symbolic form, and the person can work to actualize it in concrete action.

The development of qualitatively new forms of action may seem particularly mysterious when one focuses on the discontinuous aspects of development. However, as pointed out earlier, development can be understood as both discontinuous and continuous, and the continuity of development is most apparent over relatively short time intervals. Thus, by analyzing differentiation and integration over relatively short time intervals, one can discern the ongoing processes through which a new mode of action develops from the foundation of a qualitatively different mode of action. In addition, development is continuous insofar as the development of new modes of functioning involves integrating earlier modes into the new mode. Therefore, the new mode of functioning may be qualitatively different, but to the extent that it involves the reorganization of what went before, it is linked to and incorporates what went before. In this way, the new form of functioning was not preset or predetermined, yet at the same time it did not emerge mysteriously out of nothing.

Implications for Conducting Research on How Development Happens

Based on the theoretical premise that development happens as individuals participate with others in cultural practices, research on how development happens ideally would involve analyzing individuals as they actually engage with others in cultural practices. Specific analyses would be focused on discerning ways in which varied individual, social, and cultural processes promote development-as-differentiation-and-integration. Particular analyses of individual, social, and cultural processes would further depend on the particular cultural practices and modes of action under scrutiny. Research could certainly be conducted on how development happens for any of the modes and constituents of action discussed in this book, and then some.

With regard to how development happens through cultural processes, let us go back to the development of caregiving. As was the case for research on what happens during development, research could be conducted to discern what caregiving means within and across different cultures as well as to identify some cultural goals and expectations for different kinds of caregiving, such as sibling caregiving in the traditional sense; babysitting; caregiving as a doctor or hospice volunteer; or caring for a life partner, friend, or parent. In addition, research could be directed toward discerning what kinds of opportunities there are for people to participate in caregiving practices, who has access to such practices, and how those practices reflect cultural ways of structuring power and authority. For example, medical school is a cultural institution for training doctors, but not everyone has equal access to medical school. In addition, doctors may enjoy great prestige and high incomes in many cultural settings, but home healthcare workers and hospital aides, who do a great deal of the arduous work of caregiving, may not make much money and may be rather minimally trained.

The current theoretical approach also has implications for conducting research on how life span development happens through social processes. As discussed in Chapters 6 and 7, much research has focused on identifying the varied ways in which others guide developing individuals as they engage together in cultural practices. The theoretical approach presented here builds on this previous research by focusing attention on how varied forms of guidance provide opportunities for differentiation and integration. That is, many guidance strategies can be further characterized as global, specific, or integrative. For example, a guide might try to direct a person's attention toward aspects of a task or situation. The directing would be considered global if the guide points in a general direction or says, "Look," but does not specify what the person should look at in either case. The directing would be considered specific if the guide points to some object or activity in particular for the developing person to focus on and/or if the guide verbally indicates what specifically should be looked at. Such specific directing could provide opportunities for the developing person to make distinctions among, or differentiate, aspects of the activity. Integrative directing might involve pointing to or labeling at least two specific aspects of an object or activity that go together. Integrative directing could also involve pointing to a part of an activity while a developing person is focused on another part to suggest that the parts go together. A guide might use questions to guide a developing person's activity. For example, someone might ask questions while a child is telling a story. Consider the following hypothetical scenario.

CHILD: Sebastian went to the store.
OTHER: What does Sebastian look like?
CHILD: I don't know.
OTHER: Is he tall or short?
CHILD: Sebastian is very tall.

In this case, the Other's first question is global, whereas the second question is specific and seems to provide a basis for the child to describe Sebastian's looks in terms of one differentiated feature, namely height.

The current theoretical approach leads to studying developing individuals as they interact with others to discern if those others guide them in ways that foster differentiation and integration. The basic steps for conducting such research are similar to those presented for conducting research on what happens during development. Insofar as guided participation involves guiding developing individuals in relation to cultural meanings, conducting research begins with identifying some cultural expectations or goals for action and, if applicable, some individual developmental goals. The second step involves identifying some modes of action that may develop through guidance. With regard to sibling caregiving, for example, observations could be focused on a sibling caregiver who is trying to calm a distressed child with the aid of a more competent caregiver. Next, coding categories could be created by identifying and defining forms of guidance or guidance strategies. The guidance strategies identified in previous research provide a rich set of coding categories that can be used to study how social processes shape the development of varied modes and constituents of action (e.g., Mascolo, 2005, 2013; Rogoff, 2003; Rogoff, Mistry, Göncü, & Mosier, 1993). According to our theoretical framework, those coding categories would be further defined in terms of globality, specificity/differentiation, and integration. A third step would be to code the data and establish inter-rater reliability.

The data could then be analyzed to discern if and in what ways someone guides a developing person. The current theoretical framework also leads to asking when or under what circumstances does a guide use strategies that promote differentiation and integration? This empirical question can be analyzed in at least two ways, with one focusing on the guide, and the other focusing on the joint activity occurring between the guide and the developing person. With regard to the former, one can investigate how varied processes, such as fatigue, stress, or preoccupation with another task, affect a guide's guidance. Analyses could also be directed toward discerning how familiarity with a cultural practice is linked to different modes of guidance.

Of course, insofar as the guide and developing person are acting in relation to each other, what the guide does depends in part on what the developing person is doing. Thus, it is necessary to analyze the guide's and developing person's joint action. For example, the guide may guide globally if the developing person is acting relatively competently, but may use more specific and more integrative strategies when the developing person is struggling. The guide may also be more likely to use strategies that provide opportunities for differentiation and integration if the developing person asks a question about a particular aspect of the activity or situation. Taken together, such analyses would shed light on some of the ways in which social and individual processes mutually contribute to how development happens. In addition, analyses could be directed toward discerning if and how other social processes function in relation to guidance that fosters differentiation and integration. For example, in what ways do encouraging and/or warmly supporting the developing person contribute to the effectiveness of guidance strategies that foster differentiation and integration?

Much could also be learned about how development happens when people interact with others who are not necessarily more competent guides. In addition, depending on how one defines guidance, interacting with people who happen to be more competent does not always involve guidance. Research is needed in both of these cases to discern how varied social processes may provide opportunities for development-as-differentiation-and-integration. In addition, research could be directed toward discerning how resolving interpersonal conflicts provides opportunities for development, such as differentiating between and integrating one's own and another person's perspectives. The possibilities for empirical work seem vast, and there is much room for constructing appropriate research methods and analytic techniques. The main point here is that investigating how life span development happens through interacting with others involves analyzing what people do to enable a developing person's action to undergo differentiation and integration.

In Chapter 6 we considered some research which suggests that in some cultures, people, especially children, are expected to learn and develop largely through their own initiatives by observing and imitating. Based on sociocultural theory and research, we concluded that varied forms of guidance shape development, even in cultures where observing and imitating are emphasized. I also argued that both observing and imitating can be viewed as modes of action that develop, and that some research suggests children may be guided to observe and imitate. The ways in which observing and imitating develop through social processes and then become constituents of the individual processes that enable further development to occur are issues in need of much research. Such research could also shed light on some of the ways in which social and individual processes are interrelated during development.

The current theoretical approach additionally leads to asking about and investigating a wide range of individual processes to discern what developing people themselves do to facilitate their own development, knowingly or unknowingly. To that end, one can observe developing individuals as they practice an activity to discern how their own activity provides opportunities for development-as-differentiation-and-integration. For example, a developing person may practice a specific or differentiated part of an activity. Research on the developmental roles of asking questions could involve analyzing a developing person's questions in terms of how they address specific or differentiated aspects of an issue, or the ways in which they reflect a developing person's attempts to integrate different aspects of an issue. Insofar as questions are posed to other people, question asking is also obviously inseparable from social processes, which leads to analyzing others' responses to a developing person's questions. Asking questions is also inextricably linked to cultural processes, because question asking on the part of developing individuals may be differentially encouraged in different cultures (Rogoff, 1990, 2003).

The research implications discussed thus far focus on what developing individuals and others do to "provide opportunities for," or "foster," or "enable" development-as-differentiation-and-integration to occur. Ultimately, it is also necessary to conduct studies to discern if and in what ways these opportunities actually shape a person's development. In other words, in what ways do individual, social, and cultural processes influence or affect a person's development? There are varied ways to go about conducting research to answer this question. With regard to social processes, analyses could be conducted to see if a developing person appropriates or in some way incorporates varied forms of guidance into action at a later time. With regard to individual processes, analyses could be conducted to discern if and how practicing with variations facilitates development and is reflected in flexible action at a later time. In both cases, "later" could be relatively short term or long term, depending on a researcher's specific concerns. For example, a guide might give some instructions about a specific part of an activity, and one could analyze whether the developing person follows the instructions immediately after they are uttered and/or if the developing person follows the instructions on a different occasion. In addition, analyses would involve discerning whether differentiation and/or integration occur when the developing person follows the instructions. Depending on the developing person, the guide, and the mode or constituent of action under scrutiny, development may or may not be evident immediately after guidance.

According to our current theoretical approach, development is not primarily the subsequent effect of antecedent and independent causes. Rather, this approach holds that development occurs *while* a person participates with others in cultural practices. As such, it is not only about what the developing person and the guide do independently, nor is it only about what the developing person does after interacting with someone. It is primarily about how development emerges through their joint action, or through their action in relation to each other. Thus, we would want to discern if a developing person follows another's instructions while they are being uttered, and if the other adjusts his or her instructing in relation to what the developing person is doing. Analyzing how development happens during joint action involves integrating analyses of how development happens through individual, social, and cultural processes with the research outline discussed earlier for what happens during development. The specifics of conducting such research depend on the particular mode and/or constituents of action under scrutiny, but we can outline the basic process. We again begin by identifying cultural expectations for acting in relation to others, as well as by identifying modes of action that develop. The researcher can then define modes of action in terms of particular constituents and create coding categories that correspond to those constituents.

In addition, coding schemes for social and individual processes that foster development need to be created (along the lines presented a few paragraphs ago). Coding the data involves identifying what the developing person and the other(s) are doing simultaneously to contribute to the joint action under scrutiny as well as to the developing person's development. Once the data are coded and inter-rater reliability is established, the data can be analyzed to track differentiation and integration as they occur during joint action and to identify the individual and/ or social processes that support development-as-differentiation-and-integration.

For example, let us say that a researcher is observing a sibling caregiver and an adult calming a distressed baby. The adult is bouncing the crying baby on her lap while sitting, and both are facing the sibling caregiver who is standing in front of them. The sibling caregiver is looking intently at the whole scene. After a minute, she looks at the baby directly, takes hold of the baby's finger, and lifts it up and down in synchrony with the bouncing. While the sibling caregiver is looking at the baby and still lifting the baby's finger up and down, the adult starts to sing while continuing to bounce the baby. The baby's crying tapers off to whimpering, and the sibling caregiver looks at the adult while still lifting the baby's finger up and down. During this time, the baby is still whimpering, the adult is looking and smiling at the sibling caregiver and exaggerating her singing to emphasize the efficacy of the singing. The sibling caregiver drops the baby's finger and starts to sing as well.

In this case, calming the distressed baby is the joint action under scrutiny. Some constituents of this mode of action were identified in the earlier example of research on what happens during development. Coding such data would involve coding the adult's and sibling caregiver's action in terms of the coding categories for the constituents of calming a distressed child (e.g., bouncing, singing, soothing words). The adult's action would also be coded in terms of coding categories for social processes that promote development, and the sibling caregiver's action would also be coded in terms of coding categories for individual processes that promote development. The codes for each participant could be recorded side-by-side on a coding sheet to enable discerning what the adult and sibling caregiver are doing simultaneously. Analyzing the data would involve identifying points of differentiation and integration for the developing person's action. For example, in the hypothetical case of the adult and sibling caregiver who are jointly calming a distressed baby, the scenario begins with the sibling caregiver looking at the adult and baby globally. When the sibling caregiver lifts the baby's finger in synchrony with the adult's bouncing, she is starting to differentiate bouncing as a means for calming the distressed baby. When the sibling caregiver drops the baby's finger and sings, she is differentiating another means for calming the distressed baby. It is also important to note that throughout the entire session, the sibling caregiver is participating in the wider joint action of calming the distressed baby by integrating bouncing and singing, even though she is not fully responsible for calming the baby in this way. Additional analyses would involve identifying the individual and social processes that support the sibling caregiver's development. For example, an individual process contribution occurs when the sibling caregiver shifts her attention from the baby to the adult who has started to sing. In this case, she is directing her own attention to a specific or differentiated part of the action. When the adult exaggerates her singing, she is directing the sibling caregiver's attention to a specific or differentiated part of the action. In addition to analyses of joint action, researchers could observe the developing person's action without guidance to discern connections between development during guided joint action and subsequent action.

The examples of directions for research on how development happens, in conjunction with directions for research on what happens during development discussed in the previous section of this chapter, provide a general overview of the current theoretical framework's empirical implications. Methodological details have to be worked out in relation to specific studies, and analytic techniques can certainly be refined. A main point here is that longitudinal observations and analyses of varied constituents and modes of action can be conducted to advance our understanding of what happens during development as it happens. The research directions outlined here can also provide a basis for understanding and explaining how development-as-differentiation-and-integration happens through participating with others in cultural practices.

In Chapter 6, I argued against some currently popular ways of thinking about genetic and neurological processes. However, I am in no way trying to suggest that genetic and neurological processes are insignificant to the development of action. The current theoretical framework leads to conducting research on the ways in which genetic and/or neurological processes are linked to individual, social, and cultural processes as co-equal and interrelated causal constituents in the development of action. Some promising research in the field of cultural neuroscience is being conducted on how behavior in different cultures seems to promote different patterns of brain functioning and on how changing patterns of behavior lead to neurological changes (Miller & Kinsbourne, 2012). A book entitled *The Encultured Brain* provides an introduction to the emerging field of neuroanthropology, which is based on the premise that the "brain and nervous systems are our most cultured organs" because the brain functions within and is shaped by a cultural environment (Downey & Lende, 2012, p. 23). At the same time, cultural environments are shaped by people, who of course act using their brains, making for ongoing interactions between cultural and neurological processes.

In Chapter 2, I mentioned that physical aspects of the environment partly constitute action. Although this issue was not explored further, I do not mean to suggest that physical environmental processes are not essential to human action and development. Indeed, the earth is a constituent of the human action system, and life in cultural communities is organized partly in relation to physical environmental conditions, such as terrain and climate. From a systems perspective, physical environmental processes can be viewed as systemic causal constituents of action and development that are inseparable from individual, social, and cultural processes. Research could be directed toward discerning pathways of differentiation and integration for varied modes of action in relation to environmental circumstances. In addition, research is and will be needed to discern interrelations among global climate change, cultural change, social interaction, and the development of action.

What Develops during Development?

One of my main goals for this book is to offer an integrative theoretical framework for thinking systematically about human action and development that encompasses the currently fragmented areas of specialization within developmental psychology as well as within psychology more generally. The first step toward that goal was to identify a way of conceptualizing human functioning in terms of individual, social, and cultural processes. I have been ruminating about individual, social, and cultural processes for many years now, and that ruminating has led me to the current version of conceptualizing cultural action in relation to others as a wider whole, or a system of human functioning that develops during development. Action is taken to emerge through interrelated individual, social, and cultural processes, and action is further taken to involve interrelations among varied domains of functioning, including but not limited to moving physically, perceiving, thinking, feeling, valuing, interacting with others, self/identity construction, using language, and perspective taking. There are many advantages to this conceptualization of what people do, and I believe that it has great potential to further our understanding of human functioning as an integrative whole, in ways that embrace complexity, variability, meaning, and dynamism. The theoretical approach presented here can also further our understanding of human functioning as an integrative whole because it has the potential to lead to productive collaborations among psychologists within different areas of specialization and to productive connections between psychology and other disciplines. I will end this section, and the book, by linking this conceptualization of action to the wider whole, or forest, of human functioning. But first it is important to consider some vexing issues and some directions for further theory and research on cultural action in relation to others.

Some Vexing Issues

Cultural Practices and Modes of Action

According to the theoretical approach presented in this book, people act in relation to others in cultural practices, and different modes of action are taken to comprise different cultural practices. Modes of action and cultural practices are complex and messy phenomena that can sometimes be difficult to pin down. In Chapter 2, cultural practices were defined as relatively demarcated and repeated action contexts in which modes of action are organized in relatively particular or consistent ways. It is the "relativelys" that are a source of consternation, and articulating what counts as "a" cultural practice or "a" mode of action is not straightforward. Sometimes it is even difficult to distinguish between cultural practices and modes of action, as in the case of storytelling, which was treated as a mode of action in Chapter 5, but it could also be understood as a cultural practice. For example, within the wider cultural practice of taking care of a younger sibling, storytelling is a mode of action, but storytelling could be analyzed as a wider cultural practice when people gather somewhere specifically to tell stories. Human action is very dynamic and fluid.

Cultural practices can vary with regard to being demarcated, and sometimes there are clear boundaries between cultural practices, but sometimes cultural practices seem to blend into one another. If someone asks you what you did today, you might respond with a list of apparently demarcated cultural practices, such as getting up, driving to work, working, exercising, going to a museum with a friend, and eating dinner with your family or some friends. At the same time, however, exercising is also where you meet with some friends, and at work you engage in a variety of practices (depending on your line of work). Dinner with the family or friends is not only about ingesting food but about engaging with people. At the museum, you and your friend look at some paintings, but you also talk about life. Research may be fruitfully directed toward discerning the dimensions by which cultural practices are delineated in different cultures, such as the people who populate them, physical location, and the structuring of modes of action. Another dimension includes the goal or goals that people pursue within cultural practices, which may also be understood systemically in terms of wholes and constituents, or in terms of goals and subgoals.

These examples of cultural practices further indicate that we often engage in multiple cultural practices simultaneously, and a systems perspective provides a useful framework for thinking about how they are structured in relation to each other. That is, as the day proceeds, some practices may serve as the whole within which other practices are subsystemic constituents, and sometimes they are the subsystemic constituents of wider wholes. There is a need to investigate the ways in which cultural practices are linked to each other as constituents and wholes. In addition, research could be conducted on how the varied practices in which a person participates directly are interrelated and how those interrelations influence a person's development. There is also room to conduct research on how the practices in which a person participates directly are connected to ones in which he or she does not participate directly.

Within cultural practices, people may engage in varied modes of action. Theoretical elaboration is needed for a more nuanced conceptualization of modes of action that would enable us to distinguish among them, as well as discern how they are interrelated within and across cultural practices. As with cultural practices, it is also the case that sometimes what a person does is a mode of action as a whole, and sometimes it is a systemic subconstituent of another mode of action. For example, in Chapter 4, imitating was viewed as a form of action in and of itself that develops, and I also discussed research which shows that imitating is a means for establishing and maintaining mutual attention. Imitating is thus being treated as a mode of action and also as a constituent of another mode of action. How can it be both? From a systems perspective, these two ways of characterizing imitation are not necessarily incompatible or inconsistent. That is, sometimes imitating another person may be a mode of action in and of itself, and sometimes it may be a subsystemic constituent of another mode of action. In addition, during development, earlier modes of action may become integrated as subconstituents of new modes of action. Again, human action is dynamic and fluid.

As explained in Chapter 2, modes of action are taken to emerge through individual, social, and cultural processes that can be structured and interrelated in different ways. In addition, modes of action are taken to be made up of varied action constituents, from perceiving, to thinking, to using language, to interacting with others, to feeling, to self/identity construction. There can be varied ways to identify, categorize, and conceptualize these and other action constituents, and I admit to some slippage throughout this book in my own ways of identifying, listing, and referring to them. In fact, I intentionally did not always list them in the same way, in order to indicate that the lists are not exhaustive and that action constituents (or psychology's domains of functioning) can be identified in varied ways. There may also be cultural differences in how people identify and conceptualize domains of functioning. Danziger (1997) points out that mainstream American psychology's ways of identifying domains of functioning are not necessarily commensurate with other cultural ways of categorizing human psychological processes. In addition to theoretical refinement, research is needed to discern more about the ways in which action constituents are structured and interrelated to comprise wider modes of action. It is also important to acknowledge that action in relation to others as defined in this book may not adequately encompass all that people do. Sometimes a person may not be acting in relation to others. Nevertheless, cultural action in relation to others certainly seems to cover a great deal of what people do. As the notion of cultural action in relation to others is refined theoretically, it can be more clearly differentiated from and integrated with conceptualizations of other forms of functioning.

Interrelations among Action System Constituents

Thinking about the varied ways in which action system constituents are interrelated could benefit from theoretical refinement and empirical scrutiny. According to the current theoretical approach, action is a system that is made up of multiple and interrelated constituents. In this book, I have emphasized two main categories of action system constituents, namely individual, social, and cultural processes as "causal constituents," and action constituents as "developmental constituents." As suggested in Chapter 2, I am not completely satisfied with these terms, and it is certainly difficult "to arrive at a vocabulary adequate to the complexities involved" (Wertsch, 1998, p. 175). Part of the complexity we are grappling with here is that these constituents are distinct, yet also utterly interrelated, and it is difficult to arrive at felicitous terms that capture both the distinctions and the interrelations. Nevertheless, we can move forward with these terms as defined and used in this book to consider some issues regarding interrelations among action system constituents.

In this book, only some interrelations within and among action system constituents have been considered. That is, we considered how action and development occur through interrelations among individual, social, and cultural processes. We have also considered some of the ways in which action constituents are interrelated during development to comprise the development of different wider modes of action. However, this analysis of systemic interrelations is hardly exhaustive, and further theory and research are needed. Research is most certainly needed to discern more about how action constituents are interrelated to comprise different wider modes of action and how developing action constituents are interrelated to comprise the development of wider modes of action. In addition, individual, social, and cultural processes not only shape modes of action and their development as a whole, but they also shape the varied action constituents that comprise wider modes of action. A great deal of research derived from a sociocultural perspective focuses on cognitive constituents of action, and more research is needed to discern how individual, social, and cultural processes shape the structuring and development of other action constituents as well.

A pointed out in Chapter 1, system constituents can be interrelated in different ways, such as weakly and strongly, directly and indirectly, and even additively at times. Conceptualizing and conducting research on how action system constituents are interrelated could lead to identifying different patterns of interrelations more specifically. Theory and research can go in a wide range of specific directions with regard to the complexities of interrelations among action system constituents. Ultimately, such efforts can illuminate the ways in which different forms of causality are played out in human action.

Psychology and the Whole Person

Clearly, the focus of this book is on the *development* of acting in relation to others. However, the notion of cultural action in relation to others is by no means exclusive to developmental psychology. A central advantage of the book's conceptualization of action is that it is applicable to all areas of psychology because it is first and foremost a conceptualization of human functioning as a whole. In other words, it is a way of conceptualizing the whole person who has been sliced up into fragmented parts by conventional practices in psychology. As such, this conceptualization of action encompasses varied processes and domains of functioning that tend to be treated separately in contemporary psychology. I personally believe that it would behoove psychology if all psychologists started by conceptualizing the functioning of a whole person in some way and by articulating how their particular research issues fit into that wider whole.

Of course, as I have repeatedly recognized, we cannot always think about or investigate all of the possible multiple and interrelated action system constituents because to do so would be utterly overwhelming and paralyzing. Indeed, I acknowledge that I myself have chosen to focus on some constituents rather than others. However, when we deal with the complexity of human functioning by focusing on one or another constituent, we do not have to lapse into the fragmentation and reductionism of treating constituent and subconstituent processes as theoretically independent or in conceptual isolation. In other words, we do not have to sacrifice the forest for the trees. Instead, as we think about or investigate any particular constituent process, we can always think about it in relation to the wider whole of action (Box 8.4). For example, say you are

---

Box 8.4 How to Use the Current Theoretical Framework to Think Systematically about Action and the Whole Person

When you are trying to understand some research in psychology,

THINK ABOUT

- The topic in terms of the wider whole of action.
- How individual, social, and cultural processes are involved.
- How multiple and interrelated action constituents are involved.
- The topic from a developmental perspective (i.e., in relation to cultural goals and in terms of differentiation and integration).

When you are trying to understand what someone is doing in the thick of daily life,

THINK ABOUT

- What he or she is doing as action that is emerging through individual, social, and cultural processes.
- How what he or she is doing involves multiple and interrelated action constituents.
- What he or she is doing from a developmental perspective (i.e., in relation to cultural goals and in terms of differentiation and integration).

interested in some aspect of thinking, or feeling, or self/identity, or social interaction, or language, or perceiving, or brain functioning. By starting with action as the wider whole of human functioning, you can think about how the action constituent of interest contributes to action in relation to others, as well as how it is linked to other action constituents. You can also think about how it emerges through interrelated individual, social, and cultural processes. You can also ponder its development.

The current theoretical approach to action is applicable to many topics in psychology because so much of what psychologists study can be understood as action in relation to others, including self-regulation, pride, prejudice, attachment, aggression, empathy, decision making in varied situations, self/identity, coping, resilience, and personality. What I am suggesting here is that almost any particular topic of inquiry in psychology can be viewed as a tree within a wider forest of cultural action in relation to others. There is, in other words, a Big Picture to consider. Thinking about such topics in terms of action involves thinking about how they emerge through individual, social, and cultural processes, as well as how they involve varied interrelated constituents of action. Moreover, these topics include modes of action that develop, thus compelling us to think about what happens during their development and how they develop.

In many ways, articulating the current theoretical framework is just the beginning, and there is still much to conceptualize and investigate about human action and its development. Indeed, I keep thinking of more issues to incorporate into this discussion, but it is not the point here to present an exhaustive account of action and development. Not only is that impossible, but I would keep reiterating the basic claims of this theoretical approach to action and development. That is, human action emerges through interrelated individual, social, and cultural processes, and also consists of multiple and interrelated domains of functioning or constituents of action. As such, much of what develops during development is cultural action in relation to others, and such action involves perceiving, moving physically, thinking, intending, valuing, feeling, interacting, perspective taking, self-regulation, language, and self/identity construction. The development of such action involves differentiation and integration in relation to cultural meanings and occurs through individual, social, and cultural processes as individuals actively participate with others in cultural practices.

As with any conceptualization of complex processes, the current version of the theoretical framework presented in this book has its constraints and limitations, and it does not address everything about human functioning and development. Nevertheless, it provides conceptual tools for thinking systematically about action, about what happens during the development of action, and about how action develops. It also opens up new directions for theory and research that can further our understanding of human action and development as people go about their lives in all corners of the world. This systems framework ultimately provides an integrative conceptualization of human functioning that can hopefully contribute to moving the field of psychology beyond the boundaries of some of its entrenched practices to enhance our ways of thinking about human complexity, variability, meaning, and dynamism.

REFERENCES

Adolph, K., & Berger, S. E. (2005). Physical and motor development. In M. H. Bornstein & M. E. Lamb (Eds.), *Developmental science: An advanced textbook* (pp. 223–281). Mahwah, NJ: Erlbaum.

Adolph, K. E., & Robinson, S. R. (2008). In defense of change processes. *Child Development, 79*, 1648–1653.

Adolph, K. E., & Tamis-LeMonda, C. S. (2014). The costs and benefits of development: The transition from crawling to walking. *Child Development Perspectives, 8*, 187–192.

Ainsworth, M. D. S., & Bell, S. M. (1970). Attachment, exploration, and separation: Illustrated by the behavior of one-year-olds in a strange situation. *Child Development, 41*, 49–67.

Anisfeld, M., Turkewitz, G., Rose, S. A., Rosenberg, F. R., Sheiber, F. J., Couturier-Fagan, D. A., Ger, J. S., & Sommer, I. (2001). No compelling evidence that newborns imitate oral gestures. *Infancy, 2*, 111–122.

Arnett, J. J. (2000). Emerging adulthood: A theory of development from the late teens through the twenties. *American Psychologist, 55*, 469–480.

Azmitia, M. (1988). Peer interaction and problem solving: When are two heads better than one? *Child Development, 59*, 87–96.

Azmitia, M., & Montgomery, R. (1993). Friendship, transactive dialogues, and the development of scientific reasoning. *Social Development, 2*, 202–221.

Bachnik, J. (1992/1995). Kejime: Defining a shifting self in multiple organizational modes. In N. R. Rosenberger (Ed.), *Japanese sense of self* (pp. 152–172). Cambridge, UK: Cambridge University Press.

Bachnik, J. M. (1994). Indexing self and society in Japanese family organization. In J. M. Bachnik & C. J. Quinn, Jr. (Eds.), *Situated meaning: Inside and outside in Japanese self, society, and language* (pp. 143–166). Princeton, NJ: Princeton University Press.

Baillargeon, R. (2004). Infants' reasoning about hidden objects: Evidence for event-general and event-specific expectations. *Developmental Science, 7*, 391–424.

Bakeman, R., & Brownlee, J. R. (1980). The strategic use of parallel play: A sequential analysis. *Child Development, 51*, 873–878.

Bamberg, M. (2011). Narrative practice and identity navigation. In J. A. Holstein & J. F. Gubrium (Eds.), *Varieties of narrative analysis* (pp. 99–124). London: SAGE Publications.

Bamberg, M. (2012). Narrative analysis. In H. Cooper (Editor-in-chief), *APA Handbook of research methods in psychology*, Vol. 2 (pp. 77–94). Washington, DC: APA Press.

Bamberg, M., & Georgakopoulou, A. (2008). Small stories as a new perspective in narrative and identity analysis. *Text & Talk, 28*, 377–396.

Bartrip, J., Morton, J., & de Schonen, S. (2001). Responses to mother's face in 3-week to 5-month-old infants. *British Journal of Developmental Psychology, 19*, 212–232.

Basseches, M., & Mascolo, M. F. (2010). *Psychotherapy as a developmental process.* New York: Routledge.

Bates, E., Camaioni, L., & Volterra, V. (1975). The acquisition of performatives prior to speech. *Merrill-Palmer Quarterly, 21,* 205–226.

Baumrind, D. (1967). Child care practices anteceding three patterns of preschool behavior. *Genetic Psychology Monographs, 75,* 43–88.

Baumrind, D. (1989). Rearing competent children. In W. Damon (Ed.), *Child development today and tomorrow* (pp. 349–378). San Francisco: Jossey-Bass.

Baumrind, D. (1996). The discipline controversy revisited. *Family Relations, 45,* 405–414.

Baumrind, D. (2005). Patterns of parental authority and adolescent autonomy. *New Directions for Child and Adolescent Development, 108,* 61–69.

Bee, H., & Boyd, D. (2010). *The developing child* (12th ed.). Boston: Allyn & Bacon.

Behne, T., Carpenter, M., Gräfenhain, M., Liebal, K., Liszkowski, U., Moll, H., . . . Wyman, E. (2008). Cultural learning and cultural creation. In U. Müller, J. I. M. Carpendale, N. Budwig, & B. Sokol (Eds.), *Social life and social knowledge: Toward a process account of development* (pp. 65–101). New York: Erlbaum.

Behrens, K. Y. (2004). A multifaceted view of the concept of *amae*: Reconsidering the indigenous Japanese concept of relatedness. *Human Development, 47,* 1–27.

Bell, N. J., Wieling, E., & Watson, W. (2005). Identity development during the first two university years: Exploring intersections between micro-ontogenetic processes. *New Ideas in Psychology, 23,* 53–73.

Bell, R. Q., & Harper, L. V. (1977). *Child effects on adults.* New York: Wiley.

Bennett, M. R., & Hacker, P. M. S. (2003). *Philosophical foundations of neuroscience.* Malden, MA: Blackwell Publishing.

Berger, K. S. (2012). *The developing person through childhood and adolescence* (9th ed.). New York: Worth Publishers.

Berk, L. E. (2013). *Child development* (9th ed.). Boston: Pearson.

Berns, G. S., Moore, S., & Capra, C. M. (2009). Adolescent engagement in dangerous behaviors is associated with increased white matter maturity of frontal cortex. *PLoS ONE 4(8): e6773,* 1–12.

Bhatia, S., & Ram, A., (2009). Theorizing identity in transnational and diaspora cultures: A critical approach to acculturation. *International Journal of Intercultural Relations, 33,* 140–149.

Bibace, R. (2005). Relating to Dr. Werner: Past and present. In J. Valsiner (Ed.), *Heinz Werner and developmental science* (pp. 235–258). New York: Kluwer Academic/Plenum Publishers.

Billig, M. (2013). *Learn to write badly: How to succeed in the social sciences.* New York: Cambridge University Press.

Bjorklund, B. R. (2015). *The journey of adulthood* (8th ed.). Boston: Pearson.

Blum-Kulka, S., Hamo, M., & Habib, T. (2010). Explanations in naturally occurring peer talk: Conversational emergence and function, thematic scope, and contribution to the development of discursive skills. *First Language, 30,* 440–460.

Boker, S. M., Molenaar, P. C. M., & Nesselroade, J. R. (2009). Issues in intraindividual variability: Individual differences in equilibria and dynamics over multiple time scales. *Psychology and Aging, 24,* 858–862.

Bornstein, M. H. (Ed.) (2010). *Handbook of cultural developmental science.* New York: Psychology Press.

Bowlby, J. (1969/1982). *Attachment and loss: Vol. 1: Attachment.* New York: Basic Books.

Bowlby, J. (1973). *Attachment and loss. Vol. 2: Separation: Anxiety and anger.* New York: Basic Books.

Brandtstädter, J. (2006). Action perspectives on human development. In W. Damon & R. M. Lerner (Eds.), *Handbook of child psychology,* Vol. 1 (pp. 516–568). Hoboken, NJ: Wiley.

Briggs, J. L. (1998). *Inuit morality play: The emotional education of a three-year-old.* New Haven: Yale University Press.

Bronfenbrenner, U. (1979). *The ecology of human development: Experiments by nature and design.* Cambridge, MA: Harvard University Press.

Bronfenbrenner, U., & Morris, P. A. (2006). The bioecological model of human development. In W. Damon & R. Lerner (Eds.), *Handbook of child psychology,* Vol. 1 (pp. 793–828). New York: Wiley.

Bronson, M. B. (2000). *Self-regulation in early childhood: Nature and nurture.* New York: Guilford Press.

Brownell, C. A., & Kopp, C. B. (Eds.) (2007). *Socioemotional development in the toddler years: Transitions and transformations.* New York: Guilford Press.

Bruner, J. (1983). *Child's talk: Learning to use language.* New York: W. W. Norton.

Bruner, J. (1990) *Acts of meaning.* Cambridge, MA: Harvard University Press.

Bruner, J. (2002). *Making stories: Law, literature, life.* Cambridge, MA: Harvard University Press.

Bruner, J., & Lucariello, J. (1989). Monologue as narrative recreation of the world. In K. Nelson (Ed.), *Narratives from the crib* (pp. 73–97). Cambridge, MA: Harvard University Press.

Budwig, N. (1989). The linguistic marking of agentivity and control in child language. *Journal of Child Language, 16,* 263–284.

Budwig, N. (2003). The role of language in human development. In J. Valsiner & K. Connolly (Eds.), *Handbook of developmental psychology* (pp. 217–237). London: SAGE Publications.

Bukowski, W. M., Motzoi, C., & Meyer, F. (2009). Friendship as process, function, and outcome. In K. H. Rubin, W. M. Bukowski, & B. Laursen (Eds.), *Handbook of peer interactions, relationships, and groups* (pp. 217–231). New York: Guilford Press.

Burman, E. (1994). *Deconstructing developmental psychology.* London: Routledge.

Butterworth, G. (1990). Self-perception in infancy. In D. Cicchetti & M. Beeghly (Eds.), *The self in transition: Infancy to childhood* (pp. 119–137). Chicago: University of Chicago Press.

Butterworth, G. (1998). Origins of joint visual attention in infancy. *Monographs of the Society for Research in Child Development, 63,* 4.

Calkins, S. D. (2007). The emergence of self-regulation: Biological and behavioral control mechanisms supporting toddler competencies. In C. A. Brownell & C. B. Kopp (Eds.). *Socioemotional development in the toddler years: Transitions and transformations* (pp. 261–284). New York: Guilford Press.

Calkins, S. D., & Bell, M. A. (2010). Introduction: Putting the domains of development into perspective. In S. D. Calkins & M. A. Bell (Eds.), *Child development at the intersection of emotion and cognition* (pp. 3–13). Washington, DC: American Psychological Association.

Campos, J. J., Anderson, D. I., Barbu-Roth, M. A., Hubbard, E. M., Hertenstein, M. J., & Witherington, D. (2000). Travel broadens the mind. *Infancy, 1,* 149–219.

Cernoch, J. M., & Porter, R. H. (1985). Recognition of maternal axillary odors by infants. *Child Development, 56,* 1593–1598.

Chao, R. K. (1994). Beyond parental control and authoritarian parenting style: Understanding Chinese parenting through the cultural notion of training. *Child Development, 65,* 1111–1119.

Chen, X., Cen, G., Li, D., & He, Y. (2005). Social functioning and adjustment in Chinese children: The imprint of historical time. *Child Development, 76,* 182–195.

Chen, X., Chung, J., & Hsiao, C. (2009). Peer interactions and relationships from a cross-cultural perspective. In K. H. Rubin, W. M. Bukowski, & B. Laursen (Eds.), *Handbook of peer interactions, relationships, and groups* (pp. 432–451). New York: Guilford Press.

Chen, X., & Wang, L. (2010). China. In M. H. Bornstein (Ed.), *Handbook of cultural developmental science* (pp. 429–444). New York: Psychology Press.

Chisholm, J. S. (1996). Learning "respect for everything": Navajo images of development. In C. P. Hwang., M. E. Lamb, & I. E. Sigel (Eds.), *Images of childhood* (pp. 167–183). Mahwah, NJ: Erlbaum.

Cho, G. E., & Miller, P. J. (2004). Personal storytelling: working-class and middle-class mothers in comparative perspective. In M. Farr (Ed.), *Ethnolinguistic Chicago: Language and literacy in the city's neighborhoods* (pp. 79–101). Mahwah, NJ: Erlbaum.

Cole, M. (1995). The supra-individual envelope of development: Activity and practice, situation and context. *New Directions for Child Development, 67,* 105–118.

Cole, M. (1996). *Cultural psychology: A once and future discipline.* Cambridge, MA: Belknap Press/ Harvard University Press.

Cook, R., Bird, G., Catmur, C., Press, C., & Heyes, C. (2014). Mirror neurons: From origin to function. *Behavioral and Brain Sciences, 37,* 177–241.

Cooley, C. H. (1902). *Human nature and the social order.* New York: Scribner's.

Coplan, R. J., & Arbeau, K. A. (2009). Peer interactions and play in early childhood. In K. H. Rubin, W. M. Bukowski, & B. Laursen (Eds.), *Handbook of peer interactions, relationships, and groups* (pp. 143–161). New York: Guilford Press.

Corsaro, W. A. (1986). Routines in peer culture. In J. Cook-Gumperz, W. A. Corsaro, & J. Streeck (Eds.), *Children's worlds and children's language* (pp. 231–251). Berlin: Mouton de Gruyter.

Corsaro, W. A. (2003). *We're friends, right"?: Inside kids' culture.* Washington, DC: Joseph Henry Press.

Corsaro, W. A., & Johannesen, B. O. (2007). The creation of new cultures in peer interaction. In J. Valsiner & A. Rosa (Eds.), *The Cambridge handbook of sociocultural psychology* (pp. 444–459). Cambridge, UK: Cambridge University Press.

Damon, W., & Hart, D. (1988). *Self-understanding in childhood and adolescence.* Cambridge, UK: Cambridge University Press.

Danziger, K. (1990/1998). *Constructing the subject: Historical origins of psychological research.* Cambridge, UK: Cambridge University Press.

Danziger, K. (1997). *Naming the mind: How psychology found its language.* London: SAGE Publications.

DeCasper, A. J., & Fifer, W. P. (1980). Of human bonding: Newborns prefer their mothers' voices. *Science, 208,* 1174–1176.

Dixon, S., Tronick, E., Keefer, C., & Brazelton, T. B. (1981). Mother-infant interaction among the Gusii of Kenya. In T. M. Field, A. M. Sostek, P. Vietze, & P. H. Leiderman (Eds.), *Culture and early interactions* (pp. 149–168). Hillsdale, NJ: Erlbaum.

Doi, T. (1973/2001). *The anatomy of dependence* (J. Bester, Trans.). Tokyo: Kodansha International.

Doi, T. (1974/1986). *Amae:* A key concept for understanding Japanese personality structure. In T. S. Lebra & W. P. Lebra (Eds.), *Japanese culture and behavior: Selected readings* (pp. 121–129). Honolulu: University of Hawaii Press.

Doi, T. (1985/1988). *The anatomy of self: The individual versus society* (M. A. Harbison, Trans.). Tokyo: Kodansha International.

Doise, W., Mugny, G., & Perret-Clermnot, A. (1975). Social interaction and the development of cognitive operations. *European Journal of Social Psychology, 5,* 367–383.

Downey, G., & Lende, D. H. (2012). Neuroanthropology and the encultured brain. In D. H. Lende & G. Downey (Eds.), *The encultured brain: An introduction to neuroanthropology* (pp. 23–65). Cambridge, MA: MIT Press.

Dunn, J. (2004). *Children's friendships: The beginnings of intimacy.* Malden, MA: Blackwell Publishing.

Dunn, J. (2008). Relationships and children's discovery of the mind. In U. Müller, J. I. M. Carpendale, N. Budwig, & B. Sokol (Eds.), *Social life and social knowledge: Toward a process account of development* (pp. 171–182). Hillsdale, NJ: Erlbaum.

Dunn, J., & Munn, P. (1985). Becoming a family member: Family conflict and the development of social understanding in the second year. *Child Development, 56,* 480–492.

Durkin, K. (1995). *Developmental social psychology from infancy to old age.* Oxford: Blackwell.

Duveen, G., & Psaltis, C. (2008). The constructive role of asymmetry in social interaction. In U. Müller, J. I. M. Carpendale, N. Budwig, & B. Sokol (Eds.), *Social life and social knowledge: Toward a process account of development* (pp. 183–204). Hillsdale, NJ: Erlbaum.

Dyson, J. (2014). *Working childhoods: Youth, agency and the environment in India.* Cambridge, UK: Cambridge University Press.

Edwards, C. P., de Guzman, M. R. T., Brown, J., & Kumru, A. (2006). Children's social behaviors and peer interactions in diverse cultures. In X. Chen, D. C. French, & B. H. Schneider (Eds.), *Peer relationships in cultural context* (pp. 23–51). Cambridge, UK: Cambridge University Press.

Ehrlich, P. R. (2000). *Human natures: Genes, cultures, and the human prospect.* New York: Penguin Books.

Erikson, E. H. (1959/1980). *Identity and the life cycle.* New York: Norton.

Feldman, C. F. (1989). Monologue as problem-solving narrative. In K. Nelson (Ed.), *Narratives from the crib* (pp. 98–119). Cambridge, MA: Harvard University Press.

Fernald, A., Marchman, V. A., & Weisleder, A. (2013). SES differences in language processing skill and vocabulary are evident at 18 months. *Developmental Science, 16,* 234–248.

Fischer, K. W. (1980). A theory of cognitive development: The control and construction of hierarchies of skills. *Psychological Review, 87,* 477–531.

Fischer, K. W., & Bidell, T. R. (2006). Dynamic development of action and thought. In W. Damon & R. Lerner (Eds.), *Handbook of child psychology,* Vol. 1 (pp. 313–399). Hoboken, NJ: Wiley.

Fischer, K., Yan, Z., & Stewart, J. (2003). Adult cognitive development: Dynamics in the developmental web. In J. Valsiner & K. Connolly (Eds.), *Handbook of developmental psychology* (pp. 491–516). London: SAGE Publications.

Fivush, R., Habermas, T., Waters, T. E. A., & Zaman, W. (2011). The making of autobiographical memory: Intersections of culture, narratives and identity. *International Journal of Psychology, 46,* 321–345.

Fivush, R., & Nelson, K. (2006). Parent-child reminiscing locates the self in the past. *British Journal of Developmental Psychology, 24,* 235–251.

Fogel, A. (1993). *Developing through relationships: Origins of communication, self, and culture.* Chicago: University of Chicago Press.

Fogel, A. (2006). Dynamic systems research on interindividual communication: The transformation of meaning-making. *Journal of Developmental Processes, 1,* 7–30.

Fogel, A. (2011). Theoretical and applied dynamic systems research in developmental science. *Child Development Perspectives, 5,* 267–272.

Ford, D. H., & Lerner, R. M. (1992). *Developmental systems theory: An integrative approach.* Newbury Park, CA: SAGE Publications.

Gaskins, S. (1999). Children's daily lives in a Mayan village: A case study of culturally constructed roles and activities. In A. Göncü (Ed.), *Children's engagement in the world: Sociocultural perspectives* (pp. 25–61). Cambridge, UK: Cambridge University Press.

Gaskins, S. (2000). Children's daily activities in a Mayan village: A culturally grounded description. *Cross-Cultural Research: The Journal of Comparative Social Science, 34,* 375–389.

Gaskins, S. (2003). From corn to cash: Change and continuity within Mayan families. *Ethos, 31,* 248–273.

Gaskins, S. (2006). The cultural organization of Yucatec Mayan children's social interactions. In X. Chen, D. C. French, & B. H. Schneider (Eds.), *Peer relationships in cultural context* (pp. 283–309). Cambridge, UK: Cambridge University Press.

Gaskins, S., Haight, W., & Lancy, D. F. (2007). The cultural construction of play. In A. Göncü & S. Gaskins (Eds.), *Play and development: Evolutionary, sociocultural, and functional perspectives* (pp. 179–202). Hillsdale, NJ: Erlbaum.

Gauvain, M. (2001). *The social context of cognitive development.* New York: Guilford Press.

Gazzaniga, M. S. (2011). *Who's in charge? Free will and the science of the brain.* New York: Harper Collins.

Gergen, K. J. (2010). The acculturated brain. *Theory and Psychology, 20,* 795–816.

Gershkoff-Stowe, L., & Thelen, E. (2004). U-shaped changes in behavior: A dynamic systems perspective. *Journal of Cognition and Development, 5,* 11–36.

Gjerde, P. F. (2004). Culture, power, and experience: Toward a person-centered cultural psychology. *Human Development, 47,* 138–157.

Glick, J. A. (1983). Piaget, Vygotsky and Werner. In S. Wapner & B. Kaplan (Eds.), *Toward a holistic developmental psychology* (pp. 35–52). Hillsdale, NJ: Erlbaum.

Glick, J. A. (1992). Werner's relevance for contemporary developmental psychology. *Developmental Psychology, 28,* 558–565.

Glick, M., & Zigler, E. (2005). Werner's developmental thought in the study of adult psychopathology. In J. Valsiner (Ed.), *Heinz Werner and developmental science* (pp. 323–344). New York: Kluwer Academic/Plenum Publishers.

Goldhaber, D. (2012). *The nature-nurture debates: Bridging the gap.* Cambridge, UK: Cambridge University Press.

Göncü, A., Mistry, J., & Mosier, C. (2000). Cultural variations in the play of toddlers. *International Journal of Behavioral Development, 24,* 321–329.

Goodnow, J. J., & Collins, W. A. (1990). *Development according to parents: The nature, sources, and consequences of parents' ideas.* Hillsdale, NJ: Erlbaum.

Gottlieb, G. (1991). Experiential canalization of behavioral development: Theory. *Developmental Psychology, 27,* 4–13.

Gottlieb, G. (2001). The relevance of developmental-psychobiological metatheory to developmental neuropsychology. *Developmental Neuropsychology, 19,* 1–9.

Gottlieb, G. (2003). On making behavioral genetics truly developmental. *Human Development, 46,* 337–355.

Gottlieb, G. (2007). Probabilistic epigenesis. *Developmental Science, 10,* 1–11.

Gottlieb, G., & Halpern, C. T. (2002). A relational view of causality in normal and abnormal development. *Development and Psychopathology, 14,* 421–435.

Gottlieb, G., Wahlsten, D., & Lickliter, R. (1998). The significance of biology for human development: A developmental psychobiological systems view. In W. Damon (Ed.), *Handbook of child psychology,* Vol. 1 (pp. 233–273). New York: Wiley.

Griffiths, P. E., & Tabery, J. (2013). Developmental systems theory: What does it explain, and how does it explain it? In R. M. Lerner & J. B. Benson (Eds.), *Advances in Child Development and Behavior,* Vol. 44 (pp. 65–94). Amsterdam: Elsevier.

Gutiérrez, K. D., & Rogoff, B. (2003). Cultural ways of learning: Individual traits or repertoires of practice. *Educational Researcher, 32,* 19–25.

Habermas, T., & deSilveira, C. (2008). The development of global coherence in life narratives across adolescence: Temporal, causal, and thematic aspects. *Developmental Psychology, 44,* 707–721.

Haith, M. M., & Benson, J. B. (1998). Infant cognition. In W. Damon (Ed.), *Handbook of child psychology,* Vol. 2 (pp. 199–254). New York: Wiley.

Harkness, S., & Super, C. M. (Eds.) (1996). *Parents' cultural belief systems: Their origins, expressions, and consequences.* New York: Guilford Press.

Harkness, S., Zylicz, P. O., Super, C. M., Welles-Nyström, B., Bermúdez, M. R., Bonichini, S., Moscardino, U., & Mavridis, C. J. (2011). Children's activities and their meanings for parents: A mixed-methods study in six western cultures. *Journal of Family Psychology, 25,* 799–813.

Harter, S. (2012). *The construction of the self: Developmental and sociocultural foundations.* New York: Guilford Press.

Harwood, R. L., Miller, J. G., & Irizarry, N. L. (1995). *Culture and attachment: Perceptions of the child in context.* New York: Guilford Press.

Hashmi, M. (2009). Dementia: An anthropological perspective. *International Journal of Geriatric Psychiatry, 24*, 207–212.

Heath, S. B. (1983/1992). *Ways with words: Language, life, and work in communities and classrooms.* Cambridge, UK: Cambridge University Press.

Heath, S. B. (1986/1992). What no bedtime story means: Narrative skills at home and school. In B. B. Schieffelin & E. Ochs (Eds.), *Language socialization across cultures* (pp. 97–124). Cambridge, UK: Cambridge University Press.

Hendry, J. (1986). *Becoming Japanese: The world of the pre-school child.* Honolulu: University of Hawaii Press.

Hermans, H. J. M. (2003). The construction and reconstruction of a dialogical self. *Journal of Constructivist Psychology, 16*, 89–130.

Herrenkohl, L. R., & Mertl, V. (2010). *How students come to be, know, and do: A case for a broad view of learning.* Cambridge, UK: Cambridge University Press.

Hickok, G. (2014). *They myth of mirror neurons: The real neuroscience of communication and cognition.* New York: W. W. Norton.

Ho, M. (2013). No genes for intelligence in the fluid genome. In R. M. Lerner & J. B. Benson (Eds.), *Advances in child development and behavior*, Vol. 45 (pp. 67–92). Amsterdam: Elsevier.

Hoff, E. (2013). Interpreting the early language trajectories of children from low-SES and language minority homes: Implications for closing achievement gaps. *Developmental Psychology, 49*, 4–14.

Hoffman, D. M. (2000). Pedagogies of self in American and Japanese early childhood education: A critical conceptual analysis. *Elementary School Journal, 101*, 193–208.

Hofstede, G. (1980/2001). *Culture's consequences: Comparing values, behaviors, institutions, and organizations across nations.* Thousand Oaks, CA: SAGE Publications.

Howe, M. L., & Lewis, M. D. (2005). The importance of dynamic systems approaches for understanding development. *Developmental Review, 25*, 247–251.

Howes, C. (1980). Peer play scale as an index of complexity of peer interaction. *Developmental Psychology, 16*, 371–372.

Howes, C., & Matheson, C. C. (1992). Sequences in the development of competent play with peers: Social and social pretend play. *Developmental Psychology, 28*, 961–974.

Howes, C., Unger, O., & Matheson, C. C. (1992). *The collaborative construction of pretend: Social pretend play functions.* Albany, NY: State University of New York Press.

Iverson, J. M. (2010). Developing language in a developing body: The relationship between motor development and language development. *Journal of Child Language, 37*, 229–261.

Jahoda, G. (2012). Critical reflections on some recent definitions of "culture." *Culture and Psychology, 18*, 289–303.

James, W. (1890/1983). *The principles of psychology.* Cambridge, MA: Harvard University Press.

Johnson, M. H. (2005). Developmental neuroscience, psychophysiology, and genetics. In M. H. Bornstein & M. E. Lamb (Eds.), *Developmental science: An advanced textbook* (pp. 187–222). Mahwah, NJ: Erlbaum.

Johnston, T. D., & Lickliter, R. (2009). A developmental systems theory perspective on psychological change. In J. P. Spencer, M. S. C. Thomas, & J. L. McClelland (Eds.), *Toward a unified theory of development: Connectionism and dynamic systems theory reconsidered* (pp. 285–296). Oxford: Oxford University Press.

Jones, S. S. (2009). The development of imitation in infancy. *Philosophical Transactions of the Royal Society B, 364*, 2325–2335.

Kagan, J. (2008a). In defense of qualitative changes in development. *Child Development, 79*, 1606–1624.

Kagan, J. (2008b). Using the proper vocabulary. *Developmental Psychobiology, 50*, 4–8.

Kagan, J. (2013). *The human spark: The science of human development.* New York: Basic Books.

Kagan, J., & Snidman, N. (2004). *The long shadow of temperament.* Cambridge, MA: Harvard University Press.

Kaplan, B. (1967). Meditations on genesis. *Human Development, 10,* 65–87.

Kaplan, B. (1983a). A trio of trials. In R. M. Lerner (Ed.), *Developmental psychology: Historical and philosophical perspectives* (pp. 185–228). Hillsdale, NJ: Erlbaum.

Kaplan, B. (1983b). Genetic-dramatism: Old wine in new bottles. In S. Wapner & B. Kaplan (Eds.), *Toward a holistic developmental psychology* (pp. 53–74). Hillsdale, NJ: Erlbaum.

Kaplan, B. (1986). Value presuppositions in theories of human development. In L. Cirillo & S. Wapner (Eds.), *Value presuppositions in theories of human development* (pp. 89–103). Hillsdale, NJ: Erlbaum.

Kaplan, B. (1994). Is a concept of development applicable to art? In M. B. Franklin & B. Kaplan (Eds.), *Development and the arts: Critical perspectives* (pp. 3–10). Hillsdale, NJ: Erlbaum.

Kaplan, B., Josephs, I. E., & Bhatia, S. (2005). Re-thinking development. In J. Valsiner (Ed.), *Heinz Werner and developmental science* (pp. 121–154). New York: Kluwer Academic/Plenum Publishers.

Karmiloff-Smith, A. (2006). The tortuous route from genes to behavior: A neuroconstructivist approach. *Cognitive, Affective, & Behavioral Neuroscience, 6,* 9–17.

Killen, M., & Wainryb, C. (2000). Independence and interdependence in diverse cultural contexts. In S. Harkness, C. Raeff, & C. M. Super (Eds.), Variability in the social construction of the child. *New Directions for Child and Adolescent Development, 87,* 5–21.

Kim, Y. S., & Merriam, S. B. (2010). Situated learning and identity development in a Korean older adults' computer classroom. *Adult Educational Quarterly, 60,* 438–455.

Kondo, D. K. (1990). *Crafting selves: Power, gender, and discourses of identity in a Japanese workplace.* Chicago: University of Chicago Press.

Kopp, C. B. (1982). Antecedents of self-regulation: A developmental perspective. *Developmental Psychology, 18,* 199–214.

Krimsky, S. (2013). Genetic causation: A cross disciplinary inquiry. In R. M. Lerner & J. B. Benson (Eds.), *Advances in child development and behavior,* Vol. 44 (pp. 307–323). Amsterdam: Elsevier.

Kumpulainen, K., & Kaartinen, S. (2003). The interpersonal dynamics of collaborative reasoning in peer interactive dyads. *Journal of Experimental Education, 7,* 333–370.

Lamiell, J. T. (2003). *Beyond individual and group differences: Human individuality, scientific psychology, and William Stern's critical personalism.* Thousand Oaks, CA: SAGE Publications.

Lancy, D. F. (1996). *Playing on the mother-ground: Cultural routines for children's development.* New York: Guilford Press.

Lancy, D. F. (2007). Accounting for variability in mother-child play. *American Anthropologist, 109,* 273–284.

Lancy, D. F. (2008/2010). *The anthropology of childhood: Cherubs, chattel, changelings.* Cambridge, UK: Cambridge University Press.

Lancy, D. F. (2010). Learning 'from nobody': The limited role of teaching in folk models of children's development. *Childhood in the Past, 3,* 79–106.

Lareau, A. (2003). *Unequal childhoods: Class, race, and family life.* Berkeley: University of California Press.

Laursen, B., & Pursell, G. (2009). Conflict in peer relationships. In K. H. Rubin, W. M. Bukowski, & B. Laursen (Eds.), *Handbook of peer interactions, relationships, and groups* (pp. 267–286). New York: Guilford Press.

Lave, J., & Wenger, E. (1991/2008). *Situated learning: Legitimate peripheral participation.* Cambridge, UK: Cambridge University Press.

Lawrence, J. A., & Valsiner, J. (2003). Making personal sense: An account of basic internalization and externalization processes. *Theory and Psychology, 13,* 723–752.

Lebra, T. S. (1992/1995). Self in Japanese culture. In N. R. Rosenberger (Ed.), *Japanese sense of self* (pp. 105–120). Cambridge, UK: Cambridge University Press.

Lerner, R. M. (1986). *Concepts and theories of human development* (2nd ed.). New York: McGraw Hill.

Lerner, R. M. (2011). Structure and process in relational, developmental systems theories: A commentary on contemporary changes in the understanding of developmental change across the life span. *Human Development, 54*, 34–43.

Lerner, R. M., & Benson, J. B. (2013). Introduction: Embodiment and epigenesis: A view of the issues. *Advances in Child Development and Behavior, 44*, 1–19.

Letendre, G. K. (2000). *Learning to be adolescent: Growing up in U.S. and Japanese middle schools.* New Haven: Yale University Press.

Levine, L. W. (1977). *Black culture and black consciousness: Afro-American folk thought from slavery to freedom.* Oxford, UK: Oxford University Press.

LeVine, R. A. (1990). Infant environments in psychoanalysis: A cross-cultural view. In J. W. Stigler, R. A. Shweder, & G. Herdt (Eds.), *Cultural psychology: Essays on comparative human development* (pp. 454–474). Cambridge, UK: Cambridge University Press.

LeVine, R. A. (2004). Challenging expert knowledge: Findings from an African study of infant care and development. In U. P. Gielen & J. Roopnarine (Eds.), *Childhood and adolescence: Cross-cultural perspectives and applications* (pp. 149–165). Westport, CT: Praeger Publishers.

LeVine, R. A., Dixon, S., LeVine, S., Richman, A., Leiderman, P. H., Keefer, C. H., & Brazelton, T. B. (1994/1998). *Child care and culture: Lessons from Africa.* Cambridge, UK: Cambridge University Press.

LeVine, R. A., Miller, P. M., & West, M. M. (Eds.) (1988). Parental behavior in diverse societies. *New Directions for Child Development, 40.*

Levitt, M. J. (2005). Social relations in childhood and adolescence: The convoy model perspective. *Human Development, 48*, 28–47.

Lewis, C. C. (1995/1999). *Educating hearts and minds: Reflections on Japanese preschool and elementary education.* Cambridge, UK: Cambridge University Press.

Lewis, M. (1997). *Altering fate: Why the past does not predict the future.* New York: Guilford Press.

Lewis, M. D. (2000). The promise of dynamic systems approaches for an integrated account of human development. *Child Development, 71*, 36–43.

Lewis, M. D. (2011). Dynamic systems approaches: Cool enough? Hot enough? *Child Development Perspectives, 5*, 279–285.

Lewontin, R. (2000). *The triple helix: Gene, organism, and environment.* Cambridge, MA: Harvard University Press.

Lightfoot, C. (1997). *The culture of adolescent risk-taking.* New York: Guilford Press.

Lourenco, O., & Machado, A. (1996). In defense of Piaget's theory: A reply to 10 common criticisms. *Psychological Review, 103*, 143–164.

Maccoby, E. E. (2007). Historical overview of socialization research and theory. In J. E. Grusec & P. D. Hastings (Eds.), *Handbook of socialization: Theory and research* (pp. 13–41). New York: The Guilford Press.

Manago, A. M. (2012). The new emerging adult in Chiapas, Mexico: Perceptions of traditional values and value change among first-generation Maya university students. *Journal of Adolescent Research, 27*, 663–713.

Manago, A. M., Graham, M. B., Greenfield, P. M., & Salimkhan, G. (2008). Self-presentation and gender on MySpace. *Journal of Applied Developmental Psychology, 29*, 446–458.

Marshall, T. C., Chuong, K., & Aikawa, A. (2011). Day-to-day experiences of *amae* in Japanese romantic relationships. *Asian Journal of Social Psychology, 14*, 26–35.

Martin, J. (2012). Coordinating with others: Outlining a pragmatic, perspectival psychology of personhood. *New Ideas in Psychology, 30*, 131–143.

Martin, J., & Gillespie, A. (2010). A neo-Meadian approach to human agency: Relating the social and the psychological in the ontogenesis of perspective-coordinating persons. *Integrative Psychology and Behavioral Science, 44*, 252–272.

Martin, J., Sugarman, J., & Thompson, J. (2003). *Psychology and the question of agency.* Albany, NY: State University of New York Press.

Martini, M., & Kirkpatrick, J. (1992/1994). Parenting in Polynesia: A view from the Marquesas. In J. L. Roopnarine & D. B. Carter (Eds.), *Parent-child socialization in diverse cultures* (pp. 199–222). Norwood, NJ: Ablex.

Mascolo, M. F. (2005). Change processes in development: The concept of coactive scaffolding. *New Ideas in Psychology, 23,* 185–196.

Mascolo, M. F. (2013). Developing through relationships: An embodied coactive systems framework. In R. M. Lerner & J. B. Benson (Eds.), *Advances in Child Development and Behavior,* Vol. 45 (pp. 185–225). Amsterdam: Elsevier.

Mascolo, M. F., & Fischer, K. W. (2007). The codevelopment of self and sociomoral emotions during the toddler years. In C. A. Brownell & C. B. Kopp (Eds.), *Socioemotional development in the toddler years: Transitions and transformations* (pp. 66–99). New York: Guilford Press.

Mascolo, M. F., & Fischer, K. W. (2010). The dynamic development of thinking, feeling, and acting over the life span. In R. M. Lerner (Editor-in-Chief) and W. Overton (Vol. Ed.), *The handbook of life-span development,* Vol. 1 (pp. 149–194). Hoboken, NJ: Wiley.

Mascolo, M. F., & Fischer, K. W. (2015). The dynamic development of thinking, feeling, and acting. In R. M. Lerner, W. Overton, & P. Molenaar (Eds.), *Handbook of child psychology and developmental science,* Vol. 1 (pp. 113–161). Hoboken, NJ: John Wiley.

Mascolo, M. F., Fischer, K. W., & Li, J. (2003). Dynamic development of component systems of emotions: Pride, shame, and guilt in China and the United States. In R. J. Davidson, K. Scherer, & H. H. Goldsmith (Eds.), *Handbook of affective sciences* (pp. 375–408). Oxford, UK: Oxford University Press.

Mathews, G. (1996). *What makes life worth living? How Japanese and Americans make sense of their worlds.* Berkeley: University of California Press.

Maynard, A. E. (2002). Cultural teaching: The development of teaching skills in Maya sibling interactions. *Child Development, 73,* 969–982.

Maynard, A. E., & Tovote, K. E. (2010/2012). Learning from other children. In D. F. Lancy, J. Bock, & S. Gaskins (Eds.), *The anthropology of learning in childhood* (pp. 181–205). Lanham, MD: AltaMira Press.

McAdams, D. P. (1993). *The stories we live by: Personal myths and the making of the self.* New York: Guilford Press.

Mead, G. H. (1934/1962). *Mind, self, & society.* Chicago: University of Chicago Press.

Meadows, D. H. (2008). *Thinking in systems: A primer.* White River Junction, VT: Chelsea Green Publishing.

Meaney, M. J. (2010). Epigenetics and the biological definition of gene × environment interactions. *Child Development, 81,* 41–79.

Meltzoff, A. N., & Moore, M. K. (1983). Newborn infants imitate adult facial gestures. *Child Development, 54,* 702–709.

Miller, J. G., & Kinsbourne, M. (2012). Culture and neuroscience in developmental psychology: Contributions and challenges. *Child Development Perspectives, 6,* 35–41.

Miller, P. J., Cho, G. E., & Bracey, J. R. (2005). Working-class children's experience through the prism of personal storytelling. *Human Development, 48,* 115–135.

Miller, P. J., Fung, H., Lin, S., Chen, E. C., & Boldt, B. R. (2012). How socialization happens on the ground: Narrative practices as alternate socializing pathways in Taiwanese and European-American families. *Monographs of the Society for Research in Child Development, 77,* 1.

Miller, P. J., & Goodnow, J. J. (1995). Cultural practices: Toward an integration of culture and development. *New Directions for Child Development, 67,* 5–16.

Miller, P., & Sperry, L. L. (1987). The socialization of anger and aggression. *Merrill-Palmer Quarterly, 33,* 1–31.

Mistry, J. (2013). Integration of culture and biology in human development. In R. M. Lerner & J. B. Benson (Eds.), *Advances in child development and behavior,* Vol. 45 (pp. 287–314). Amsterdam: Elsevier.

Molenaar, P. C. M. (2004). A manifesto on psychology as idiographic science: Bringing the person back into scientific psychology, this time forever. *Measurement, 2*, 201–218.

Molenaar, P. C. M. (2008). On the implications of the classical ergodic theorems: Analysis of developmental processes has to focus on intra-individual variation. *Developmental Psychobiology, 50*, 60–69.

Molenaar, P. C. M., & Campbell, C. G. (2009). The new person-specific paradigm in psychology. *Current Directions in Psychological Science, 18*, 112–117.

Molenaar, P. C. M., & Valsiner, J. (2008). How generalization works through the single case: A simple idiographic process analysis of an individual psychotherapy. *Yearbook of Idiographic Science, 1*, 23–38.

Moore, C., & Povinelli, D. J. (2007). Differences in how 12- and 24-month-olds interpret the gaze of adults. *Infancy, 11*, 215–231.

Moshman, D. (2013). Adolescent rationality. In R. M. Lerner & J. B. Benson (Eds.), *Advances in child development and behavior*, Vol. 45 (pp. 155–183). Amsterdam: Elsevier.

Mosier, C. E., & Rogoff, B. (2003). Privileged treatment of toddlers: Cultural aspects of individual choice and responsibility. *Developmental Psychology, 39*, 1047–1060.

Nagy, E., Pilling, K., Orvos, H., & Molnar, P. (2013). Imitation of tongue protrusion in human neonates: Specificity of the response in a large sample. *Developmental Psychology, 49*, 1628–1638.

Nelson, D. A., Hart, C. H., Keister, E. K., & Piassetskaia, K. (2010). Russia. In M. H. Bornstein (Ed.), *Handbook of cultural developmental science* (pp. 409–428). New York: Psychology Press.

Nelson, K. (Ed.) (1989). *Narratives from the crib*. Cambridge, MA: Harvard University Press.

Nelson, K. (2007). *Young minds in social worlds: Experience, meaning, and memory*. Cambridge, MA: Harvard University Press.

Nelson, K., & Fivush, R. (2004). The emergence of autobiographical memory: A social cultural developmental theory. *Psychological Review, 11*, 486–511.

Nesselroade, J. R., & Molenaar, P. C. M. (2010). Emphasizing intraindividual variability in the study of development over the life span: Concepts and issues. In R. M. Lerner (Ed.), *The handbook of life-span development*, Vol. 1 (pp. 30–54). Hoboken, NJ: Wiley.

Nicolopoulou, A. (1997). Worldmaking and identity formation in children's narrative play-acting. In B. D. Cox & C. Lightfoot (Eds.), *Sociogenetic perspectives on internalization* (pp. 157–187). Mahwah, NJ: Erlbaum.

Nisbett, R. E. (2009). *Intelligence and how to get it: Why schools and cultures count*. New York: W. W. Norton.

Nsamenang, A. B. (1992). *Human development in cultural context: A third world perspective*. Newbury Park, CA: SAGE Publications.

Nsamenang, A. B. (2006). Human ontogenesis: An indigenous African view on development and intelligence. *International Journal of Psychology, 41*, 293–297.

Nsamenang, A. B. (2011). The culturalization of developmental trajectories: A perspective on African childhoods and adolescences. In L. A. Jensen (Ed.), *Bridging cultural and developmental approaches to psychology: New syntheses in theory, research, and policy* (pp. 235–254). New York: Oxford University Press.

Nsamenang, A. B., & Lo-Oh, J. L. (2010). Afrique noire. In M. H. Bornstein (Ed.), *Handbook of cultural developmental science* (pp. 383–407). New York: Psychology Press.

Ochs, E., & Izquierdo, C. (2009). Responsibility in childhood: Three developmental trajectories. *Ethos, 37*, 391–413.

Ochs, E., & Schieffelin, B. (1984/1988). Language acquisition and socialization: Three developmental stories and their implications. In R. A. Shweder & R. A. LeVine (Eds.), *Culture theory: Essays on mind, self, and emotion* (pp. 276–320). Cambridge, UK: Cambridge University Press.

Ochs, E., & Shohet, M. (2006). The cultural structuring of mealtime socialization. *New Directions for Child and Adolescent Development, 111*, 35–49.

Odden, H., & Rochat, P. (2004). Observational learning and enculturation. *Educational and Child Psychology, 21*, 39–50.

Ohlsson, S. (2010). Questions, patterns, and explanations, not hypothesis testing is the core of psychology as of any science. In A. Toomela & J. Valsiner (Eds.), *Methodological thinking in psychology: 60 years gone astray?* (pp. 27–43). Charlotte, NC: Information Age Publishing.

Overton, W. F. (2006). Developmental psychology: Philosophy, concepts, methodology. In W. Damon & R. M. Lerner (Eds.), *Handbook of child psychology*, Vol. 1 (pp. 18–88). Hoboken, NJ: Wiley.

Overton, W. F. (2010). Life-span development: Concepts and issues. In R. M. Lerner (Ed.), *Handbook of life-span development*, Vol. 1 (pp. 1–29). Hoboken, NJ: Wiley.

Overton, W. F. (2011). Relational developmental systems and quantitative behavior genetics: Alternative or parallel methodologies? *Research in Human Development, 8*, 258–263.

Overton, W. F. (2013). Relationism and relational developmental systems: A paradigm for developmental science in the post-Cartesian era. In R. M. Lerner & J. B. Benson (Eds.), *Advances in child development and behavior*, Vol. 4, (pp. 21–64). Amsterdam: Elsevier.

Oyama, S. (2000). *Evolution's eye: A systems view of the biology-culture divide.* Durham, NC: Duke University Press.

Oyserman, D., Coon, H. M., & Kemmelmeier, M. (2002). Rethinking individualism and collectivism: Evaluation of theoretical assumptions and meta-analyses. *Psychological Bulletin, 128*, 3–72.

Paradise, R., & Rogoff, B. (2009). Side by side: Learning by observing and pitching in. *Ethos, 37*, 102–138.

Pascual-Leone, A., Amedi, A., Fregni, F., & Merabet, L. B. (2005). The plastic human brain cortex. *Annual Review of Neuroscience, 28*, 377–401.

Peak, L. (1991/1993). *Learning to go to school in Japan: The transition from home to preschool life.* Berkeley: University of California Press.

Piaget, J. (1932/1950). *The moral judgment of the child* (M. Gabain Trans.). London: Routledge & Kegan Paul.

Piaget, J. (1953). *The origin of intelligence in the child* (M. Cook, Trans.). London: Routledge & Kegan Paul.

Piaget, J. (1954/1986). *The construction of reality in the child* (M. Cook, Trans.). New York: Ballantine Books.

Piaget, J. (1955). The stages of intellectual development in childhood and adolescence. In H. E. Gruber & J. J. Vonèche (Eds.), *The essential Piaget* (pp. 814–819). New York: Basic Books.

Pipp, S. (1990). Sensorimotor and representational internal working models of self, other, and relationship: Mechanisms of connection and separation. In D. Cicchetti & M. Beeghly (Eds.), *The self in transition: Infancy to childhood* (pp. 243–264). Chicago: University of Chicago Press.

Psaltis, C., & Duveen, G. (2007). Conservation and conversation types: Forms of recognition and cognitive development. *British Journal of Developmental Psychology, 25*, 79–102.

Rabain-Jamin, J., Maynard, A. E., & Greenfield, P. (2003). Implications of sibling caregiving for sibling relations and teaching interactions in two cultures. *Ethos, 31*, 204–231.

Raeff, C. (2000). European-American parents' ideas about their toddlers' independence and interdependence. *Journal of Applied Developmental Psychology, 21*, 183–205.

Raeff, C. (2003). Patterns of cultural activity: Linking parents' ideas and parent-child interactions. In C. Raeff & J. B. Benson (Eds.), *Social and cognitive development in the context of individual, social, and cultural processes* (pp. 35–53). London: Routledge.

Raeff, C. (2006a). *Always separate, always connected: Independence and interdependence in cultural contexts of development.* Mahwah, NJ: Erlbaum.

Raeff, C. (2006b). Individuals in relation to others: Independence and interdependence in a kindergarten classroom. *Ethos, 34*, 521–557.

Raeff, C. (2006c). Multiple and inseparable: Conceptualizing the development of independence and interdependence. *Human Development, 49*, 96–121.

Raeff, C. (2010a). Independence and interdependence in children's developmental experiences. *Child Development Perspectives, 4*, 31–36.

Raeff, C. (2010b). Self constructing activities. *Theory and Psychology, 20*, 28–51.

Raeff, C. (2011). Distinguishing between development and change: Reviving organismic-developmental theory. *Human Development, 54*, 4–33.

Raeff, C. (2014). Demystifying internalization and socialization: Linking conceptions of how development happens to organismic-developmental theory. *Advances in Child Behavior and Development, 46*, 1–32.

Raghavan, C. S., Harkness, S., & Super, C. M. (2010). Parental ethnotheories in the context of immigration: Asian Indian immigrant and Euro-American mothers and daughters in an American town. *Journal of Cross-Cultural Psychology, 41*, 617–632.

Randall, W. L. (2013). Aging, irony, and wisdom: On the narrative psychology of later life. *Theory and Psychology, 23*, 164–183.

Ray, E., & Heyes, C. (2011). Imitation in infancy: The wealth of the stimulus. *Developmental Science, 14*, 92–105.

Reddy, V. (2008). *How infants know minds*. Cambridge, MA: Harvard University Press.

Reese, E., Haden, C. A., Baker-Ward, L., Bauer, P., Fivush, R., & Ornstein, P. A. (2011). Coherence of personal narratives across the lifespan: A multidimensional model and coding method. *Journal of Cognition and Development, 12*, 424–462.

Ribas, R. D. C., Jr. (2010). Central and South America. In M. H. Bornstein (Ed.), *Handbook of cultural developmental science* (pp. 323–339). New York: Psychology Press.

Richman, A. L., Miller, P. M., & Solomon, M. J. (1988). The socialization of infants in suburban Boston. *New Directions for Child Development, 40*, 65–74.

Rochat, P. (2001/2004). *The infant's world*. Cambridge, MA: Harvard University Press.

Rogoff, B. (1990). *Apprenticeship in thinking: Cognitive development in social context*. New York: Oxford University Press.

Rogoff, B. (2003). *The cultural nature of human development*. Oxford, UK: Oxford University Press.

Rogoff, B., Baker-Sennett, J., Lacasa, P., & Goldsmith, D. (1995). Development through participation in sociocultural activity. *New Directions for Child Development, 67*, 45–65.

Rogoff, B., Mistry, J., Göncü, A., & Mosier, C. (1993). Guided participation in cultural activity by toddlers and caregivers. *Monographs of the Society for Research in Child Development, 58*, 8.

Rogoff, B., Moore, L., Najafi, B., Dexter, A., Correa-Chávez, M., & Solis, J. (2007). Children's development of cultural repertoires through participation in everyday routines and practices. In J. E. Grusec & P. D. Hastings (Eds.), *Handbook of socialization: Theory and research* (pp. 490–515). New York: Guilford Press.

Rosenberger, N. (2001). *Gambling with virtue: Japanese women and the search for self in a changing nation*. Honolulu: University of Hawaii Press.

Rothbart, M. K., & Bates, J. E. (2006). Temperament. In W. Damon & R. M. Lerner, (Eds.), *Handbook of child psychology*, Vol. 3 (pp. 99–166). Hoboken, NJ: Wiley

Rubin, K. H., Bukowski, W. M., & Parker, J. G. (2006). Peer interactions, relationships, and groups. In W. Damon & R. M. Lerner (Eds.), *Handbook of child psychology*, Vol. 3 (pp. 571–645). Hoboken, NJ: Wiley.

Rutter, M. (2006). *Genes and behavior: Nature-nurture interplay explained*. Malden, MA: Blackwell Publishing.

Sacrey, L-A. R., Karl, J. M., & Whishaw, I. Q. (2012). Development of rotational movements, hand shaping, and accuracy in advance and withdrawal for the reach-to-eat movement in human infants aged 6–12 months. *Infant Behavior and Development, 35*, 543–560.

Salvatore, S., & Valsiner, J. (2010). Between the general and the unique: Overcoming the nomothetic versus idiographic opposition. *Theory and Psychology, 20*, 817–833.

Sameroff, A. (2010). A unified theory of development: A dialectic integration of nature and nurture. *Child Development, 81*, 6–22.

Sawyer, R. K. (2002). Unresolved tensions in sociocultural theory: Analogies with contemporary sociological debates. *Culture and Psychology, 8*, 283–305.

Saxe, G. B. (2012). *Cultural development of mathematical ideas: Papua New Guinea studies.* Cambridge, UK: Cambridge University Press.

Scaife, M., & Bruner, J. S. (1975). The capacity for joint visual attention in the infant. *Nature, 253*, 265–266.

Schaal, B., Soussignan, R., & Marlier, L. (2002). Olfactory cognition at the start of life: The perinatal shaping of selective odor responsiveness. In B. Schaal, C. Rouby, & A. Holley (Eds.), *Olfaction, taste, and cognition* (pp. 421–440). West Nyack, NY: Cambridge University Press.

Schaffer, H. R. (1984). *The child's entry into a social world.* London: Academic Press.

Scheper-Hughes, N. (1985). Culture, scarcity, and maternal thinking. Maternal detachment and infant survival in a Brazilian shantytown. *Ethos, 13*, 291–317.

Shantz, C. U., & Hartup, W. W. (1992). Conflict and development: An introduction. In C. U. Shantz & W. W. Hartup (Eds.), *Conflict in child and adolescent development* (pp. 1–11). Cambridge, UK: Cambridge University Press.

Shatz, M. (1994). *A toddler's life: Becoming a person.* New York: Oxford University Press.

Shotter, J. (1975). *Images of man in psychological research.* London: Methuen.

Shulman, S., Feldman, B., Blatt, S. J., Cohen, O., & Mahler, A. (2005). Emerging adulthood: Age-related tasks and underlying self processes. *Journal of Adolescent Research, 20*, 577–603.

Shwalb, D. W., Shwalb, B. J., Nakazawa, J., Hyun, J., Le, H. V., & Satiadarma, M. P. (2010). East and Southeast Asia: Japan, South Korea, Vietnam, and Indonesia. In M. H. Bornstein (Ed.), *Handbook of cultural developmental science* (pp. 445–464). New York: Psychology Press.

Shweder, R. A., Jensen, L. A., & Goldstein, W. M. (1995). Who sleeps by whom revisited: A method for extracting the moral goods implicit in practice. *New Directions for Child Development, 67*, 21–39.

Siegler, R. S., & Chen, Z. (2008). Differentiation and integration: Guiding principles for analyzing cognitive change. *Developmental Science, 1*, 433–453.

Sigel, I. E. (Ed.). (1985). *Parental belief systems: The psychological consequences for children.* Hillsdale, NJ: Erlbaum.

Sigel, I. E., McGillicuddy-DeLisi, A. V., & Goodnow, J. J. (Eds.). (1992). *Parental belief systems: The psychological consequences for children.* Hillsdale, NJ: Erlbaum.

Singer, J., Rexhaj, B., & Baddeley, J. (2007). Older, wiser, and happier? Comparing older adults' and college students' self-defining memories. *Memory, 15*, 886–898.

Smith, L. B. (2010). Action as developmental process—a commentary on Iverson's "Developing language in a developing body: the relationship between motor development and language development." *Journal of Child Language, 37*, 263–267.

Spencer, J. P., Clearfield, M., Corbetta, D., Ulrich, B., Buchanan, P., & Schöner, G. (2006). Moving toward a grand theory of development: In memory of Esther Thelen. *Child Development, 77*, 1521–1538.

Stern, D. (1977). *The first relationship: Infant and mother.* Cambridge, MA: Harvard University Press.

Stern, D. N. (1985). *The interpersonal world of the infant: A view from psychoanalysis and developmental psychology.* New York: Basic Books.

Stiles, J. (2008). *The fundamentals of brain development: Integrating nature and nurture.* Cambridge, MA: Harvard University Press.

Stiles, J. (2009). On genes, brains, and behavior: Why should developmental psychologists care about brain development? *Child Development Perspectives, 3*, 196–202.

Stipek, D., Recchia, S., & McClintic, S. (1992). Self-evaluation in young children. *Monographs of the Society for Research in Child Development, 57*, 1.

Stone, J. E., Carpendale, J. I. M., Sugarman, J., & Martin, J. (2012). A Meadian account of social understanding: Taking a non-mentalistic approach to infant and verbal false belief understanding. *New Ideas in Psychology, 30,* 166–178.

Super, C. M., Harkness, S., Barry, O., & Zeitlin, M. (2011). Think locally, act globally: Contributions of African research to child development. *Child Development Perspectives, 5,* 119–125.

Tamis-LeMonda, C. S., Way, N., Hughes, D., Yoshikawa, H., Kalman, R. K., & Niwa, E. Y. (2008). Parents' goals for children: The dynamic coexistence of individualism and collectivism in cultures and individuals. *Social Development, 17,* 183–209.

Teasley, S. D. (1995). The role of talk in children's peer collaboration. *Developmental Psychology, 31,* 207–220.

Thelen, E., & Smith, L. B. (1994/1996). *A dynamic systems approach to the development of cognition and action.* Cambridge, MA: Bradford Books/MIT Press.

Thelen, E., & Smith, L. B. (2006). Dynamic systems theories. In W. Damon & R. M. Lerner (Eds.), *Handbook of child psychology,* Vol. 1 (pp. 258–312). Hoboken, NJ: Wiley.

Thompson, R. A. (1999). Early attachment and later development. In J. Cassidy & P. R. Shaver (Eds.), *Handbook of attachment: Theory, research, and clinical applications* (pp. 265–286). New York: Guilford Press.

Tobin, J. (1992/1995). Japanese preschools and the pedagogy of selfhood. In N. R. Rosenberger (Ed.), *Japanese sense of self* (pp. 21–39). Cambridge, UK: Cambridge University Press.

Tobin, J. J, Wu, D. Y. H., & Davidson, D. H. (1989). *Preschool in three cultures: Japan, China, and the United States.* New Haven, CT: Yale University Press.

Todeschini, M. M. (2011). "Webs of engagement": Managerial responsibility in a Japanese company. *Journal of Business Ethics, 101,* 45–59.

Tomasello, M. (2003). *Constructing a language: A usage-based theory of language acquisition.* Cambridge, MA: Harvard University Press.

Tomasello, M., Carpenter, M., & Liszkowski, U. (2007). A new look at infant pointing. *Child Development, 78,* 705–722.

Toomela, A., & Valsiner, J. (2010). *Methodological thinking in psychology: 60 years gone astray?* (pp. 27–43). Charlotte, NC: Information Age Publishing.

Trevarthen, C. (1982). The primary motives for cooperative understanding. In G. Butterworth & P. Light (Eds.), *Social cognition: Studies of the development of understanding* (pp. 77–109). Chicago: University of Chicago Press.

Trevarthen, C. (1993/1996). The self born in intersubjectivity: The psychology of an infant communicating. In U. Neisser (Ed.), *The perceived self: Ecological and interpersonal sources of self-knowledge* (pp. 121–173). Cambridge, UK: Cambridge University Press.

Trevarthen, C., & Hubley, P. (1978). Secondary intersubjectivity: Confidence, confiding and acts of meaning. In A. Lock (Ed.), *Action, gesture and symbol* (pp. 183–229). London: Academic Press.

Tudge, J. R. H. (1992). Processes and consequences of peer collaboration: A Vygotskian analysis. *Child Development, 63,* 1364–1379.

Turiel, E. (1983/1985). *The development of social knowledge: Morality and convention.* Cambridge, UK: Cambridge University Press.

Turiel, E. (2003). Resistance and subversion in everyday life. *Journal of Moral Education, 32,* 115–130.

Turiel, E. (2008). Social decisions, social interactions, and the coordination of diverse judgments. In U. Müller, J. I. M. Carpendale, N. Budwig, & B. Sokol (Eds.), *Social life and social knowledge: Toward a process account of development* (pp. 255–276). New York: Erlbaum.

Turiel, E., & Perkins, S. A. (2004). Flexibilities of mind: Conflict and culture. *Human Development, 47,* 158–178.

Turiel, E., & Wainryb, C. (2000). Social life in cultures: Judgments, conflict, and subversion. *Child Development, 71,* 250–256.

Underwood, K. (2010). Interactive remembering: Insights into the communicative competence of older adults. *Journal of Aging Studies, 24,* 145–166.

Užgiris, I. Č. (1977). Plasticity and structure: The role of experience in infancy. In I. Č. Užgiris & F. Weizmann (Eds.), *The structuring of experience* (pp. 89–113). New York: Plenum Press.

Užgiris, I. Č. (1989). Infants in relation: Performers, pupils, and partners. In W. Damon (Ed.), *Child development today and tomorrow* (pp. 288–311). San Francisco: Jossey-Bass.

Užgiris, I. Č. (1991). The social context of infant imitation. In M. Lewis & S. Feinman (Eds.), *Social influences and socialization in infancy* (pp. 215–251). New York: Plenum Press.

Užgiris, I. Č. (1996). Together and apart: The enactment of values in infancy. In E. S. Reed, E. Turiel, & T. Brown (Eds.), *Values and knowledge* (pp. 17–39). Mahwah, NJ: Erlbaum.

Užgiris, I. Č. (1999). Imitation as activity: Its developmental aspects. In J. Nadel & G. Butterworth (Eds.), *Imitation in infancy* (pp. 186–206). Cambridge, UK: Cambridge University Press.

Užgiris, I. Č., Benson, J. B., Kruper, J. C., & Vasek, M. E. (1989). Contextual influences on imitative interactions between mothers and infants. In J. J. Lockman & N. L. Hazen (Eds.), *Action in social context: Perspectives on early development* (pp. 103–127). New York: Plenum Press.

Užgiris, I. Č., & Hunt, J. McV. (1975/1989). *Assessment in infancy: Ordinal scales of psychological development.* Urbana: University of Illinois Press.

Valsiner, J. (1997). *Culture and the development of children's action: A theory of human development.* New York: Wiley.

Valsiner, J. (1998). *The guided mind: A sociogenetic approach to personality.* Cambridge, MA: Harvard University Press.

Valsiner, J. (Ed.). (2005). *Heinz Werner and developmental science.* New York: Kluwer Academic/Plenum Publishers.

Valsiner, J. (2011). The development of individual purposes: Creating actuality through novelty. In L. A. Jensen (Ed.), *Bridging cultural and developmental approaches to psychology: New syntheses in theory, research, and policy* (pp. 212–232). Oxford, UK: Oxford University Press.

van Geert, P. (1998). We almost had a great future behind us: The contribution of non-linear dynamics to developmental-science-in-the-making. *Developmental Science, 1,* 143–159.

van Geert, P. (2003). Dynamic systems approaches and modeling of developmental processes. In J. Valsiner & K. Connolly (Eds.), *Handbook of developmental psychology* (pp. 640–672). London: SAGE Publications.

van Geert, P. (2011). The contribution of complex dynamic systems to development. *Child Development Perspectives, 5,* 273–278.

van Geert, P., & Fischer, K. W. (2009). Dynamic systems and the quest for individual-based models of change and development. In J. P. Spencer, M. S. C. Thomas, & J. L. McClelland (Eds.), *Toward a unified theory of development: Connectionism and dynamic systems theory reconsidered* (pp. 313–336). Oxford, UK: Oxford University Press.

van Geert, P., & Steenbeek, H. (2005). Explaining after by before: Basic aspects of a dynamic systems approach to the study of development. *Developmental Review, 25,* 408–442.

van Geert, P., & van Dijk, M. (2002). Focus on variability: New tools to study intra-individual variability in developmental data. *Infant Behavior and Development, 25,* 340–374.

von Bertalanffy, L. (1969/1998). *General system theory: Foundations, development, applications.* New York: George Braziller.

von Bertalanffy, L. (1972). The history and status of general systems theory. *The Academy of Management Journal, 15,* 407–426.

Vreeke, G. J. (2000). Nature, nurture and the future of the analysis of variance. *Human Development, 43,* 32–45.

Vygotsky, L. S. (1978). *Mind in society: The development of higher psychological processes.* Cambridge, MA: Harvard University Press.

Vygotsky, L. S. (1986/1987). *Thought and language.* Cambridge, MA: MIT Press.

Wahlsten, D. (2003). Genetics and the development of brain and behavior. In J. Valsiner & K. Connolly (Eds.), *Handbook of developmental psychology* (pp. 18–47). London: SAGE Publications.

Wahlsten, D. (2013). A contemporary view of genes and behavior: Complex systems and interactions. In R. M. Lerner & J. B. Benson (Eds.), *Advances in child development and behavior*, Vol. 44 (pp. 285–306). Amsterdam: Elsevier.

Wapner, S. (2000). Person-in-environment transitions: Developmental analysis. *Journal of Adult Development, 7,* 7–22.

Wapner, S., & Demick, J. (1998). Developmental analysis: A holistic, developmental, systems-oriented perspective. In W. Damon (Ed.), *Handbook of child psychology,* Vol. 1 (pp. 761–805). New York: Wiley.

Wapner, S., & Demick, J. (2005). Critical person-in-environment transitions across the life span. In J. Valsiner (Ed.), *Heinz Werner and developmental science* (pp. 285–305). New York: Kluwer Academic/Plenum Publishers.

Waterman, A. S. (1981). Individualism and interdependence. *American Psychologist, 36,* 762–773.

Watkins, M. (2000/2005). *Invisible guests: The development of imaginal dialogues.* Putnam, CT: Spring Publications.

Watson-Gegeo, K. A., & Gegeo, D. W. (1986/1992). Calling-out and repeating routines in Kwara'ae children's language socialization. In B. B. Schieffelin & E. Ochs (Eds.), *Language socialization across cultures* (pp. 17–50). Cambridge, UK: Cambridge University Press.

Weisner, T. S., & Gallimore, R. (1977). My brother's keeper: Child and sibling caretaking. *Current Anthropology, 18,* 169–190.

Wentzel, K. R. (2009). Peers and academic functioning at school. In K. H. Rubin, W. M. Bukowski, & B. Laursen (Eds.), *Handbook of peer interactions, relationships, and groups* (pp. 531–547). New York: Guilford Press.

Werner, H. (1940/1980). *Comparative psychology of mental development.* New York: International Universities Press.

Werner, H. (1957). The concept of development from a comparative and organismic point of view. In D. B. Harris (Ed.), *The concept of development: An issue in the study of human behavior* (pp. 125–148). Minneapolis: University of Minnesota Press.

Werner, H., & Kaplan, B. (1956/1978). The developmental approach to cognition: Its relevance to the psychological interpretation of anthropological and ethnolinguistic data. Reprinted in S. S. Barten & M. B. Franklin (Eds.), *Developmental processes: Heinz Werner's selected writings,* Vol. 1 (pp. 85–106). New York: International Universities Press.

Werner, H., & Kaplan, B. (1963/1984). *Symbol formation: An organismic-developmental approach to the psychology of language.* Hillsdale, NJ: Erlbaum.

Wertsch, J. V. (1985). *Vygotsky and the social formation of mind.* Cambridge, MA: Harvard University Press.

Wertsch, J. V. (1991). *Voices of the mind: A sociocultural approach to mediated action.* Cambridge, MA: Harvard University Press.

Wertsch, J. V. (1998). *Mind as action.* New York: Oxford University Press.

West, E. (1989). *Growing up with the country: Childhood on the far Western frontier.* Albuquerque: University of New Mexico Press.

Wexler, B. E. (2006). *Brain and culture: Neurobiology, ideology, and social change.* Cambridge, MA: MIT Press.

White, M. (1987). *The Japanese educational challenge: A commitment to children.* New York: The Free Press.

Whiting, B. (2004). Women as agents of social change. In C. P. Edwards & B. B. Whiting (Eds.), *Ngecha: A Kenyan village in a time of rapid social change* (pp. 93–117). Lincoln: University of Nebraska Press.

Whiting, B., Chesaina, C., Diru, G., Ichoya, J., Kariuki, P., Kimani, V. N., ... Streeter, L. (2004). Changing concepts of the good child and good mothering. In C. P. Edwards &

B. B. Whiting (Eds.), *Ngecha: A Kenyan village in a time of rapid social change* (pp. 119–151). Lincoln: University of Nebraska Press.

Whiting, B. B., & Edwards, C. P. (1988). *Children of different worlds: The formation of social behavior.* Cambridge, MA: Harvard University Press.

Williams, A. L., & Merten, M. J. (2008). A review of online social networking profiles by adolescents: Implications for future research and intervention. *Adolescence, 43,* 253–274.

Witherington, D. C. (2007). The dynamic systems approach as metatheory for developmental psychology. *Human Development, 50,* 127–153.

Witherington, D. C. (2011). Taking emergence seriously: The centrality of circular causality for dynamic systems approaches to development. *Human Development, 54,* 66–92.

Witherington, D. C., & Heying, S. (2013). Embodiment and agency: Toward a holistic synthesis for developmental science. In R. M. Lerner & J. B. Benson (Eds.), *Advances in child development and behavior,* Vol. 44 (pp. 161–192). Amsterdam: Elsevier.

Wood, D., Bruner, J. S., & Ross, G. (1976). The role of tutoring in problem-solving. *Journal of Child Psychology and Psychiatry, 17,* 89–100.

Xu, Y., & Farver, J. A. M. (2009). "What makes you shy?": Understanding situational elicitors of shyness in Chinese children. *International Journal of Behavioral Development, 33,* 97–104.

Yamaguchi, S., & Ariizumi, Y. (2006). Close interpersonal relationships among Japanese: Amae as distinguished from attachment and dependence. In U. Kim, K. Yang, & K. Hwang (Eds.), *Indigenous and cultural psychology: Understanding people in context* (pp. 163–174). New York: Springer.

Yan, Z., & Fischer, K. (2002). Always under construction: Dynamic variations in adult cognitive microdevelopment. *Human Development, 45,* 141–160.

Yan, Z., & Fischer, K. (2007). Pattern emergence and pattern transition in microdevelopmental variation: Evidence of complex dynamics of developmental processes. *Journal of Developmental Processes, 2,* 39–62.

Youniss, J. (2008). Making common perspectives collaboratively: The flesh and blood of everyday social life. *Human Development, 51,* 332–335.

Zukow-Goldring, P. (2002). Sibling caregiving. In M. H. Bornstein (Ed.), *Handbook of parenting,* Vol. 3 (pp. 253–286). Mahwah, NJ: Erlbaum.

ABOUT THE AUTHOR

Catherine Raeff, PhD, is Professor of Psychology at Indiana University of Pennsylvania. Her scholarship has addressed issues of individualism and collectivism, and how both are played out during development in culturally particular ways. She is continuing to work on the issues presented in this book by articulating an integrative and widely applicable conceptualization of human functioning in terms of individual, social, and cultural processes. Her publications include articles and the book, *Always Separate, Always Connected: Independence and Interdependence in Cultural Contexts of Development.*

INDEX